Wild
ENTHUSIASM
A VERY BRITISH SAFARI

Wild

ENTHUSIASM
A VERY BRITISH SAFARI

by Steve Wright

MERLIN UNWIN BOOKS

First published in Great Britain by Merlin Unwin Books Ltd 2022

Text © Steve Wright 2022
Illustrations © Merlin Unwin 2022

Merlin Unwin Books Ltd
Palmers House
Corve Street
Ludlow
Shropshire SY8 1DB
UK

www.merlinunwin.co.uk

The author asserts his moral right to be identified with this work.
ISBN 978-1-913159-49-8
Typeset in 12pt Adobe Jenson Pro by Joanne Dovey, Merlin Unwin Books
Printed by CPI Group (UK) Ltd., Croydon

Contents

Author's Note

Being a wildlife enthusiast has genuinely made me a more altruistic person. In my twenties I was detached from nature, but since I re-engaged in my thirties, I've become more relaxed and happier. Generally, I'm a better person. Fresh air, walks in the countryside and participating in multi-sensory hobbies is scientifically proven to aid mental wellbeing – my personal experience supports the evidence.

Having a close connection to nature is a gift which gives me great comfort. I'd always choose the countryside in preference to any city. To me, waterfalls are more joyful than ornamental fountains, wildflower meadows more beautiful than manicured lawns, and the excitement of a thunder storm surpasses any firework display.

I have acquaintances I know very well, we have a close understanding, and I'm able to grasp their mood by interpreting facial expressions and body postures. These tiny signals from friends are only understood by myself and those close to them: it creates a more intimate bond and strengthens our relationships. I now have a similar connection with the natural world – I can interpret wildlife behaviour and anticipate its subsequent actions (and occasionally get it right). Just like my feelings towards friends, I now care for the wildlife around me very deeply.

If you share my enthusiasm for wildlife, then please promote it to others. We need more people to join us; we are obliged to protect our environment for future generations. It's also crucial right now for our own personal wellbeing.

If you have an adventurous spirit you too can share as much joy and excitement as I've experienced. Wildlife enthusiasm is one of the cheapest, personally rewarding and most entertaining pastimes for anyone. Go out there, respect nature and enjoy exploring. Have fun! And try not to slip down any hills, get stung, get soaked or eat anything poisonous.

Opposite page: Map showing where my wildlife safaris have taken me

To Mum & Dad

Rudd

Introduction

Imagine yourself in a busy Parisian café and the locals are chatting – but you only understand English. Then envisage the same scene if you are fluent in French and how your surroundings become more interesting. A proficiency in nature's language will also widen your senses.

Like learning languages, there are many stages to becoming a fluent wildlife watcher and my journey has novice beginnings. If you want to be more connected to nature, then I hope that by following my adventures you will learn a method that'll help you see dolphins, eagles, snakes and otters.

Some friends think I witness an abundance of wildlife because I'm lucky. It won't take you many pages to realise I'm not overly blessed with luck. Instead I rely on building experience, learning field skills and being inquisitive. I don't claim to be an expert, I'm fascinated by everything and haven't specialised in any particular field. There's great complexity and diversity in British nature, and there are considerable gaps in my knowledge. I'm able to identify 200 British bird species, but there are more than a thousand moths and that's too challenging! I like the fact there's always something new, whether it's the first sighting of a species, habitat, behaviour... or a new, to me, moth.

As a youngster I was intrigued by all manner of wildlife and occasionally enjoyed great encounters. One autumn day an exotic bird landed in a hedgerow beside me and tucked into the hawthorn berries. I stared at this colourful creature and after it flew off, consulted my battered bird-book. I incorrectly thought the bird was a hoopoe and was convinced for many years I'd seen one. When older, and with somebody wiser, we saw a waxwing and my acquaintance highlighted my mistake.

My friend Kirsty once spotted a large brown bird sitting on a country path and thought she'd discovered an exotic partridge with cascading plumes of feathers. Once closer, she realised it was a pile of horse muck. It happens to everyone. Although it does seem to happen to Kirsty more than most.

Some twitchers get agitated by misidentification – I think it's a fun part of the hobby. Spotting a new species is always great, even when initially misidentified. However, the pinnacle for me has always been watching animal behaviour, such as predators chasing prey, territorial battles and courtship.

Like most people I don't have the luxury of a full-time job in nature conservation, but in my spare time I'm a wildlife tour guide and cameraman. Whenever I go for a walk or stare out of a window, I look for wildlife – never to the detriment of other pursuits – it just embellishes my daily life.

My adventures as a wildlife enthusiast have taken me across the world and most importantly to remote locations around the British Isles. What is so special about British wildlife? I once took a Russian on a guided tour and promoted our wildlife to him and he replied dryly, 'Back home we have bears and wolves.'

True, Britain lacks the megafauna of Russia or the 'Big Five' of the Serengeti. Whale watching around Britain never guarantees a sighting and our largest land mammals are red deer – tiny in comparison to African elephants. Our largest land carnivores are foxes (small dogs) and badgers (who eat worms, not zebras). I researched Britain's most dangerous creature and the overriding consensus was... a wasp. Fair enough if you are at risk of anaphylactic shock – for everybody else it's a small insect which can be trapped in a glass of orange juice. Further down the list of 'dangerous' British beasts were seagulls (I will debate the term 'seagulls' later.) I've often feared for my lunch around gulls, but never felt in personal jeopardy. I weigh eighty kilos and a herring gull weighs about one and a half, so I fancy my chances, even against a flock. From personal experience the British creatures most likely to cause you harm are horseflies, midges and customers of late-night takeaways.

Canada has bears, India has tigers and Australia has venomous snakes. It's a big positive that Britain presents little risk of lion attack or being bitten by a deadly spider whilst on the toilet. It's always best to start with modest subjects and work your way up. If your first waterfall is the Angel Falls, subsequent waterfalls might disappoint. We Bristish start with foxes and badgers, so we can get excited if we see leopards elsewhere in the world.

The British weather is often a source of criticism. Sure, winters are dark and gloomy, summer is over in a matter of weeks and where I live, trees grow at a slant because of the prevalent wind. However, the wet climate rewards us with lush green landscapes, fast-flowing rivers and species-rich woodlands. Some people peer outside and decide not to venture into horizontal rain – I'd rather go out and get soaked than spend a day indoors.

The changing seasons mean new things are poised to happen on the British calendar. After New Year I search for snowdrops or listen for song thrushes. When I get a phenological fix, the moment brightens my day. I'll then look for the next seasonal event – wood sorrel in flower, tadpoles, and birds carrying nesting material.

Across Britain there are regional specialities – eagles above mountains, snakes in southern heathlands and abundant seabird colonies around the coast. Britain has hundreds of nature reserves, each with something special to celebrate. There are 140,000 miles of public footpaths and nearly 20,000 miles of coastline. I have explored locations all around the British Isles and this book features the highlights.

There is excitement and danger in our untamed wild. Nature can be a ruthless, dirty and unpleasant place and I'm not going to hold back on the grisly realities. My adventures include me being bitten, stung, pecked, covered in crap and even farted on. To me, wildlife watching is definitely not cute and cuddly. Creatures thrive in hostile environments; they fight each other, avoid being eaten while trying to consume enough to survive, and if they're very lucky they might procreate. I'm fascinated by the fact that while I'm sat inside my centrally heated house, clashes for survival are happening outside. Could you withstand a life in the wild? I'm not sure I could. I enjoy visiting the battlefields and returning to my creature comforts.

By learning from my experiences, you can enjoy sights you might otherwise miss, your life will become more exciting and you'll have an increasing passion for nature. You can learn from my successful tricks and tactics – and hopefully avoid my mistakes.

Kingfisher

How to Begin with Birdsong

Everyone can increase their basic knowledge significantly with only a little time and effort. Just ask yourself the question, 'What's that?' and look for the answer.

Birds are the main source of study for British wildlife watchers, because most of our large diurnal mammals have been hunted to extinction by our ancestors (I'm not criticising them – my generation has succeeded in doing much worse).

Anyone who's learned birdsongs will already know it's a valuable and rewarding skill. I genuinely think it's achievable for anyone with reasonable hearing who appreciates the countryside. If New Year resolutions are your thing, January is the perfect month to begin – in May the summer migrants arrive and make it more complicated; it's like either learning to drive in an empty car park or a ring-road during rush hour.

Start by going for a relaxing walk, preferably on a sunny day in a park or woodland. Stop and listen to the surrounding bird calls; you can use the voice recorder on your phone to capture unfamiliar songs, then check them later online, or use one of those new-fangled mobile phone apps.

Birds often heard in January include song thrushes, robins and wrens, then later in March you might also hear blackbirds. Websites can help you learn their calls (it's much easier to hear them, rather than follow written descriptions). You will undoubtedly hear lots of short chirps and tweets – I suggest you only concentrate on the longer songs at first. Also, some birds have a wide range of vocalisation and their full repertoire will only become familiar with experience.

Once the above four songbird species are mastered, you can move onto the rest. These include great tits which sing, 'Teacher teacher teacher', and dunnocks who attempt to warble but lack high-pitched notes; like me emulating Michael Jackson.

Beginners can initially group two sets of birds together and separate them later. The chirps of blue tits and coal tits are similar, so too are the repetitive calls of song thrushes and mistle thrushes, so for the moment just class them as tits and thrushes.

A British bird you often hear, but rarely see, is the goldcrest. It sings a very high-pitched song which reminds me of the cavalry bugler in cowboy movies such as *Stagecoach*. Goldcrests love conifers, because their slight weight and thin beaks allow them to catch tiny morsels hidden between pine needles. So, if you hear a tiny bugler and you are near evergreens, it's probably a goldcrest and you've just encountered Europe's smallest bird.

With all those nailed, you can add more birds which sing later in spring; such as blackcaps, chaffinches, goldfinches and greenfinches. Of these, blackcaps are my favourite; they have a jaunty ditty which is the most beautiful song in my woodlands during April and May (nightingales are sadly absent from my local patch). Other migrants arrive soon afterwards and depending where you live, these will include warblers. Warblers rarely visit bird-tables and therefore are often unseen – so it's a special gift when you begin to listen to the countryside and realise warblers are plentiful. There's the willow warbler with its cascading notes and chiffchaff calling its name: 'Chiff chaff, chiff chaff'. Experienced birders might be able to identify a warbler by its legs and plumage. For the novice birdwatcher, warblers tend to look similar, so their songs are your best guide.

After learning all the above, you should be able to recognise the majority of British bird calls you'll hear – congratulations, you've done most of the hard work! Your dawn choruses will never be the same again and most importantly you can pick out rarities. One example of how this is beneficial happened during one of my autumnal riverside walks. I identified the singular chirps of chaffinch and the loud brisk song of a wren – then I heard a single high-pitched note. It was like someone blowing down a recorder (not playing a recorder, as everyone knows that sounds bloody awful). My knowledge of common bird songs enabled me to separate this unusual noise from the familiar and I turned in its direction. If I was unable to eliminate the other calls, I would've never investigated and would have missed seeing a kingfisher.

I enjoy the fact that my hobby is challenging and even if I don't see anything new, I've had fun rambling around the countryside. I always look, listen and stop for anything curious. If I'm joined by friends, I prefer to go with fellow enthusiasts. It is difficult to see wildlife in the company of unruly dogs, noisy talkers and feral children. You'll also miss out if you racewalk, have a phone in your face or blast music into your ears.

Try and create as little disturbance as possible; you ideally want to discover wildlife before it sees you, because if it's unaware of your presence, you'll have a greater chance of seeing something special. Avoid bright clothing; try and blend into the landscape rather than be a beacon. I went through a phase of wearing a camouflage jacket until a child asked, 'Are you in the army?' On a separate occasion someone else commented, 'Oh, I didn't see you there, I thought you were a shrub.' Maybe don't wear camouflage clothing for those reasons, but I still wear a foliage patterned floppy hat to the despair of my fashion-conscious friends. The rest of my attire is usually beige or green which works just as successfully as camouflage.

There are great benefits in having membership to conservation clubs. My local Wildlife Trust has enabled me to join an eclectic range of events; wildflower identification, owl pellet dissection, bat detecting and fungi foraging. Trust reserves also provide opportunities to meet other enthusiasts and they'll usually delight in sharing their knowledge.

I watch natural history documentaries and have a wide collection of field guides which I'll carry if I'm searching for something specific. Websites can yield additional support in tandem to this book, especially if you want to hear or see any of the mentioned species. You can also use local websites for recent sightings in your area.

Small Tortoiseshells

Childhood

As an infant in the 1970s, home was in a landlocked corner of Cheshire in north-west England. Wildlife watching was the second most interesting subject in my life (after dinosaurs, of course). Basic knowledge included the call of cuckoos, starlings and house sparrows, plus insects such as ladybirds, red ants and common butterflies. However, I struggled with plant names (the pace of their lives was too slow for a child), but I knew some species including dandelions, buttercups and nettles (usually after I'd been stung).

One of my most notable childhood encounters happened after a thud on our patio window. On the ground outside there was an unconscious male bullfinch. I approached and bent down. Once gently cupped in the palm of my hands he felt warm and fluffy. I was surprised by his lack of weight and how small he was close up. A red-pinkish chest, sturdy beak and black wings with a silvery band. Beautiful. Within seconds of him being safely in my hands he awoke and blinked an eye. Although I longed to curl my fingers around him and keep this treasure, I knew he should be free. It was a difficult dilemma for a child. I opened my hands flat and after a flurry of wing beats, he disappeared over my neighbour's fence. A week later he returned to the garden, and yes, I am convinced he was the same male bullfinch. He perched for a breath and looked directly at me, before he vanished forever. He gave me a memorable connection with nature and made me want to be good to wildlife and learn more.

Spring in my youth brought the cascading song of skylarks and the dancing flight of peewits – a local name for lapwings. I revelled in the summer migrations of darting swallows and calling cuckoos. I helped at a farm, herded sheep, fed pigs and got chased by geese. I hid amongst the tall lush grass of hay meadows, climbed trees and built dens. In the autumn I would scrump apples, forage field mushrooms and harvest blackberries. I witnessed some spectacular wildlife events including murmurations of starlings above wetlands surrounding Farndon and salmon leaping the River Dee's weir at Chester.

Adults were constantly questioned by my inquisitive mind and a walk in the countryside would often provoke me shouting, 'What's that?'

My parents would humour me; often through exasperation.

I would find berries and ask, 'Can we make a pie out of these?'

'No, that's deadly nightshade,' my mother would snap (as a child I had a vivid imagination – prior to that moment I thought deadly nightshade possessed vine-like hands which would grab your throat and throttle you; probably a result of watching too much *Dr Who*).

My mother was an arachnophobe, so I used to enjoy the phrase; 'Mum, look at the size of this spider.' Another favourite question was; 'Can I take this home?'

I always got a negative response to that one too; 'Put down the dead rabbit!'

Dead things had a special fascination and I'd happily spend half an hour with a stick prodding a dead hedgehog. I was equally intrigued by the lifecycles of butterflies and frogs. Tadpoles were a reliable source of study and their collection became an annual event. One February my dad presented me with a large clear plastic tank, which I filled with pond weed and tadpoles. At first, I was hypnotised by the little creatures moving inside, but like most children I had a short attention span, so went searching for other beasts to add to my microcosm. I returned to the pond at the bottom of the field with my hunting gear; a length of bamboo stick with a plastic net. This net had been successfully deployed in Devonshire rockpools the previous summer.

It wasn't long before I ensnared a large water boatman, popped him into my bucket and headed home. He seemed to thrive in his new environment, swimming between the tadpoles before settling. Over the course of a few days the tadpoles became more difficult to spot. I assumed they were hiding amongst the algae while my water boatman swam around with energetic bursts of speed. The following day, I checked my indoor pond again and saw the water boatman eating one of the tadpoles. It wasn't a vegetarian water boatman – it was a carnivorous backswimmer! Ten minutes later I was striding down the field with my bucket – containing a well-fed backswimmer – back to the pond to quench his murderous appetite on the poor critters in there.

It is only now when I reminisce about my childhood, I realise how fortunate I was to have such experiences.

Basking Shark

Adulthood

In 1992, I was twenty and moved to the Isle of Man because I was skint and required work. At first, I was completely unaware of the island's wildlife biodiversity – I was too busy being self-absorbed and partying. Over the years, I developed a great fondness for island life and rediscovered my wildlife watching hobby. One of the main triggers was the loss of both my parents. The Manx countryside was the perfect medicine for my grief. I grasped the fact that life was short and losing what I loved gave me impetus to have a more meaningful existence.

The Isle of Man has recently become a UNESCO World Biosphere Region and we have lots of sealife with occasional dolphin, whale and basking shark sightings. A basking shark boat trip helped rekindle my love for nature at that point. Very few experiences can beat bobbing in a small leisure boat while a ten-metre-long leviathan sidles up to starboard. I was also proud of the fact it wasn't me that said, 'We're going to need a bigger boat,' because someone else beat me to it.

I started to develop my wldlife knowledge as I explored and filmed things of interest. I gathered enough footage to produce a wildlife DVD called *Wild Mann* which sold successfully to the Island's residents.

Every local patch has its limitations and mine has some which might be surprising. Many small islands are bereft of mammals – the Isle of Man is no exception. There are no squirrels or deer. No moles, badgers, foxes, weasels, snakes or toads, but we do have common lizards. There are British birds which are currently absent or rare on the Isle of Man, such as bullfinches, jays, nuthatches and red kites, although we have good populations of choughs, hen harriers and black guillemots.

It was due to the limitations of island wildlife that I decided to travel back to Britain and expand my knowledge. Over the last fourteen years I've crossed the length and breadth of the British Isles for a diversity of experiences. I will tell you where I've been, what I've seen and how it was achieved. You can learn from my mistakes (there are plenty of those) and hopefully share some of my triumphs.

Avocet

Chapter 1

Norfolk (2006)

It was late spring 2006 when I had my first holiday specifically for wildlife watching. The information online was limited back then, but I read somebody's blog featuring their trip to Norfolk and it sounded good, so decided to try it myself. Over three days I planned to visit RSPB sites at Snettisham and Titchwell, plus other venues. There were no specific creatures to search for; it was primarily a relaxing break and perhaps I'd stumble across some wildlife. In short, I was going to wing it.

It was evening when I arrived at Blakeney. I'd booked a room in a rustic pub; the bar was snug with an open fire and low ceiling. It was the hub of the community and locals heaved together at the bar in a mass of bellies and beards. Every time the door opened several of the crowd would turn. If the new arrival was from their clan their appearance would be greeted with a cheer. However, if the person was a visitor, the crowd would just turn back quietly and continue their conversations. I experienced that treatment. Another way to identify locals from strangers was if they were tall. Any visitor above 5'10" would invariably crack their foreheads on one of the numerous low beams; which the locals learned to duck beneath.

The next morning, I awoke fresh and ready. Thankfully I suffered no signs of a headache; a benefit of being 5'9". I began my adventures by driving to Snettisham RSPB. It was cold and grey on arrival, yet the fresh air was invigorating. Snettisham is well known as an excellent site for winter waders when high tides send huge flocks of knot from The Wash into the lagoons. Now in late spring, the bulk of the waders were at their Arctic breeding grounds.

Nature seemed subdued on this cold spring day with only the distant song of a chaffinch. Chaffinches blast out a short tune and to me (but possibly not everybody) it sounds like a speeded-up version of the guitar riff on the White Stripes track Seven Nation Army.

One objective of my holiday was to purchase a pair of binoculars. My previous pair of bins were cheap, fared poorly in rain and filled with water. I dried them on a radiator and this caused evaporation and thick condensation inside, which made them even worse. The budget bins were eventually chucked in the bin.

Some unfamiliar bird calls came from a thicket beyond a fence. Feathery dots were moving between distant unreachable shrubbery; indistinguishable by human eyesight alone. They might have been bearded tits – without binoculars I'd never know.

The path crossed between two large lagoons – the southerly one was Stanton's Lake – and in the middle was a cormorant. Cormorants wash salt off their feathers by beating their wings in fresh water, but this was flapping more wildly than usual. My concern grew as I studied the bird – it seemed to be struggling. Perhaps it was tangled in fishing line or had oiled feathers. I strode off to find somebody and a moment later was relieved to meet a reserve manager. I asked for his opinion and we headed back to Stanton's Lake. The cormorant was still there, although now looking perfectly happy, paddling on the water, enjoying its day out at Snettisham. As if to demonstrate my allegations were a figment of my imagination, it flew off. I apologised to the manager for wasting his time while I cursed the cormorant under my breath.

A line of prefabricated chalets blocked all obvious routes to The Wash. I contemplated climbing through somebody's back garden, but decided not to ruin the start of my holiday by being arrested for trespass. Another option could have been to ask advice from the nearby reserve manager, but he already thought I was an idiot. So I retraced my steps back through Snettisham and saw a white goose, which had presumably dodged somebody's oven. The wildlife this morning was decidedly low key. That happens, particularly if you turn up at a reserve without binoculars at the wrong time of year. Being a wildlife enthusiast rarely provides instant gratification or reward, especially for the beginner. If you have expectations of immediately seeing a dolphin or eagle, this isn't the recreational choice for you. Maybe try a zoo instead.

I preferred to try Titchwell RSPB. The coast road wove through a flat landscape, with glimpses of the sea regularly appearing on the left. Titchwell's leafy car park was reached after midday; it was surprisingly busy, there were more people here than I'd seen all morning. I never considered birdwatching as a mass participation sport. My first stop was the RSPB shop to belatedly buy binoculars. I stood beside a well-stocked shelf, before noticing people carrying telescopes and tripods. I wanted to fit in, so I bought a telescope and tripod. With the assistant's help we unpacked the telescope and fitted the new tripod. It was pricey but I deserved a treat. I proudly balanced the shiny new kit on my shoulder, walked out of the shop and clanked the telescope against the top of the door frame. I convinced myself that nobody else noticed. The cackle of laughter behind suggested otherwise.

A short distance down the path, loud birdsong came from a bush right next to me. It was different to any song I'd heard before. In fact, it would be incorrect to describe it as a song. It was more like somebody coming up and shouting in my face in a high-pitched voice, 'Oi, what are you doing!' I studied the thick undergrowth, but there was no sign of the culprit.

I asked a couple approaching, 'What caused that noise?'

'Cetti's warbler,' replied the lady.

Here for five minutes and I'd already discovered a new species – most importantly it was an experience. Never before had a warbler yelled at me. I felt as though my wildlife adventures had eventually begun. I moved further down the track and behind me the Cetti hollered at someone else. The shrubs and trees ended and I strode into an open expanse of reedbed. The feeling of emerging from shady undergrowth into light was pleasing. A noticeboard listed local species, including marsh harriers. The Isle of Man is blessed with hen harriers, but I've never witnessed a marsh harrier.

A marsh harrier would be fabulous. I suddenly possessed a holiday wish-list of one.

Down the track I approached a line of camouflage-wearing birders carrying tripods, telescopes and expensive-looking cameras. I successfully dodged a tripod-jousting competition before pondering over the weight of the new kit – binoculars would've been more comfortable resting over my shoulder.

A very large bird hide stood beside the path. This was the first time I'd enter a large edifice for the purpose of wildlife watching. All the bird hides I'd previously visited were little more than converted garden sheds. The interior was lit by natural light, cascading through wide windows spanning one side. It was full of people who were seated and noticeably quiet; like entering a church during Sunday service. The obvious etiquette was to be quiet. Therefore it was a mistake to assume the door would gently close behind me unaided. Instead it slammed shut with a BANG. The boom reverberated throughout the interior. From a nearby window, waterfowl flew away with fright. Two men turned and delivered me an unfriendly sneer – I'd scared off their birds.

I shuffled to the farthest corner to an available gap on a bench. I stretched one leg across and clumsily jostled with the tripod and telescope. It was like trying to cradle a baby giraffe; legs all over the place. I managed to avoid slapping a lady with the tripod, pulled it back and nearly knocked a guy behind with the telescope. I gave him an apologetic, 'Oops.' He nodded and inched further down the bench, giving me and the flailing telescope more room. I am a naturally clumsy person – I could create a racket in a mound of cotton wool.

I eventually felt safe from further embarrassment and pointed the telescope out of the window. I was about to peer through when I realised it was completely unnecessary. Only a few metres away on the other side of the glass was an avocet. The bird strutted down the muddy bank and stopped. A big smile grew on my face and I turned to the lady next to me and whispered, 'Wow, an avocet.'

'Yes, they are one of my favourites too,' she smiled and glanced at the tripod with concern, as though I was in possession of a dangerous weapon. She bent down, rummaged in her bag and a moment later lifted a neatly wrapped parcel and said, 'Do you want some lemon drizzle cake?'

'Yes please,' I beamed.

My first introduction to an avocet was equivalent to meeting a much-loved celebrity. An elegant bird, upturned beak, no fancy colours, just perfect black and white lines.

The man on my other side spoke to his wife in a soft whisper, 'Shall we have coffee?' She nodded enthusiastically and produced a thermos flask. The bird hide became a picnic area; I chomped cake, they shared coffee and further away a large man ate a pork pie.

I adored watching the avocet for several minutes, but it was time to unleash the telescope for its inaugural outing. I focused on the opposite bank where a dozen godwits stood. Britain has two main species of godwit, although the names bar-tailed and black-tailed have never given me much guidance, as both have black markings on their tails. I whispered to the chap beside me as he slurped his coffee, 'Which type of godwit are they?'

He shrugged, 'Probably black-tailed.'

'How can you tell?'

'In Norfolk there are more black-tailed godwits.'

Fair enough. I often identify birds quickly by assuming they are the expected species for a habitat or area. If I'm at the Manx coast and someone asks if a bird is a cormorant or a shag, before I look, I'll usually say 'shag', as they are ten times more frequent.

The lady interjected, 'Bar-tailed godwits are slightly smaller.'

I digested this nugget of information and realised it wasn't particularly helpful – unless both species were beside one another. I left them to sip their coffee and withheld my grievance. I then returned to the alleged black-tailed godwits and focused on the bum of the nearest, but couldn't notice any significant black markings. I gave up and aimed at a nearby avocet; I could see remarkable detail, the crisp lines of feathers, twirled beak and a black stripe down the nape of its neck. Further subjects were identified around the pool; redshanks, teals, coots and the ubiquitous mallards, while above the reedbed vista fly-pasts were performed by lapwings and greylag geese.

A couple of benches away a conversation could be overheard; it related to something which happened yesterday. Apparently, a marsh harrier swooped over the pool, which caused the resident birds to scatter and generate cheers from the onlooking birders. Sadly, no marsh harriers were swooping today and the hide remained quiet. Someone new entered and she gently closed the door behind herself.

After an enjoyable hour I decided to explore the rest of the reserve. I granted the avocet a nod of thanks, took control of the unruly tripod, headed outside... and closed the door tentatively and quietly. A linear track led towards the North Sea and I stopped for regular peeks into the undergrowth. Other visitors paused when they noticed things, so I joined them to see what piqued their interest. This ploy rewarded me with dunlins, shelducks and oystercatchers.

The path ended at a ridge of marram grass where birders gathered, most of them armed with telescopes and binoculars. Fifty metres of beach separated us from the turbulent waves of the North Sea and a brisk wind scattered sand across my face. A brief fight ensued with the tripod, before it was grounded without injuring bystanders. Everyone was staring at a specific point in the distance, so I turned to the nearest guy and asked what was grabbing everyone's attention.

'There's scoters out there,' he replied excitedly.

I was glad he pronounced it first as I would have said scotter, rather than scoter – the bird's name apparently rhymes with voter. Scoters are a type of seaduck and there are two principal types around the British coast; common and velvet. I peered through the telescope and scanned the horizon like a pirate seeking a treasure island. A dozen black blobs bounced on the waves. I would've never distinguished the species from this distance, so I turned to the guy beside me again for extra help.

'What type of scoter?' I asked, ensuring the correct pronunciation.

'Common,' he replied.

I was tempted to enquire if that was because common scoters were more frequent around Norfolk. The birds disappeared and emerged on each wave and, to be honest, seeing distant ducks bobbing on the North Sea did little for me. I felt detached from the far-flung common scoters – I couldn't see them clearly or watch their performance. Some of the gathering people were taking photographs with long lens cameras. Even with powerful optics, I suspect they were capturing images of black blobs on grey waves. One chap was jubilant because this sighting was a new tick on his bird list. Other birders were apparently talking in a coded language, one said something 'dipped out' while another claimed he'd seen a LBJ vanish into a bush. I didn't ask what that was.

After ten minutes I'd had enough of the North Sea and the distant ducks, so returned south while continuing my search for marsh harriers – without joy. Just before the Cetti's bush, a different bird caught my attention as it clutched a swaying reed. I clumsily grounded the telescope and focused on the small bird; it was the size of a chaffinch with a black crown. It presented a good view and once again this was something new and unknown. A lady was walking towards me so I asked the stock opening question – could she identify that bird?

She was incredibly obliging, halted and peered through her binoculars. She replied instantly, 'Reed bunting, male.' I guessed from her casual reply this was a common bird around these parts.

In all my years watching birds, this species had previously eluded me. 'It's a first for me,' I explained.

'That's the fun,' she smiled and walked off.

Indeed it was. I could see the reed bunting clearly and hear his nondescript call. His face was black and on closer inspection it featured downward pointing white lines on his cheeks, which made him seem unhappy, like he'd smelt something bad. He glanced about and chirped, before fluttering away. One strange thing I found afterwards, which not only relates to reed buntings, but other wildlife too; once you see a species for the first time you subsequently see them all over the place. During the next year I saw reed buntings on five separate occasions. It was as though they had deliberately concealed themselves for years; however, once one bird let down the team, the rest gave up and came out of hiding. I imagined the 'Reed Bunting 2006 AGM' and the president addressing his audience, 'Well, as you are all probably aware, an anonymous delegate was spotted by Steve in Norfolk, therefore Steve can see you all now. But, stay vigilant, we are still successfully hiding from Sally and Dan.'

Titchwell was a great treat and an education. There were serious birders out there with decades of experience and I was a novice amongst those experts. This wasn't a problem for me. It was a blessing because without their help I'd have struggled to identify several new species. I encourage any novice to visit Titchwell and chat with others. Don't be shy – timid wildlife enthusiasts will miss out. I learned more from other visitors than any information board. In fact, I wish I'd asked more questions – I could have benefitted from somebody's help with the next day's itinerary, as the weather forecast was awful.

The final stop of the day was Holkham Hall. Apparently, lots of deer were there. A long driveway led between a wide landscape of grassland and well-appointed trees. In front of the manor house a large herd of over a hundred fallow deer stood or lounged on the grass. The fact that they were all plonked on the garden of a stately home removed any sort of excitement for me and I left.

The sun started to fall low on the horizon and my mind drifted towards dinner and a couple of pints. However, there was one unexpected wildlife encounter to enjoy first. On the return to Blakeney a white bird drifted as light as a feather across the road before disappearing behind the hedge. I pulled over, ran to a gap in the hedgerow and peeked through. But the barn owl had already vanished. I love barn owls, they are graceful in flight, floating on gentle beats on soft thick wings, ghostlike in movement. It was a wonderful way to finish a great day in Norfolk. Well, a great *afternoon* at Titchwell, the morning had been a bit rubbish. Tomorrow was going to prove even more difficult.

The next morning I had a lie-in and went for breakfast a few minutes before service closed. The rain belted down outside and, according to the chap on the neighbouring table, it would continue all day, although he ended on a positive note: 'It'll brighten tomorrow.'

I studied the map and tried to find places which wouldn't involve exposed outdoor locations and getting soaked. The options were limited. At Cromer I wandered along the pier which was patrolled by turnstones and herring gulls. The gusts flapped poster adverts for kids to go crabbing. No children were stupid enough to go crabbing in torrential rain. Only a few adults were about and they were either hiding in shop doorways or lurking in bus shelters.

After Cromer I visited a couple of beaches – if the water falling from the sky wasn't enough, I got sprayed by a windblown wave. I licked my lips and got the full salty taste of the North Sea.

At Morston Marsh I was the only animal outdoors. The rain eased during late afternoon and as the deluge subsided, I heard a willow warbler singing, a melody which sounds like cascading notes down a flute. That was my daytime wildlife highlight and by the end, every inch of my body was wet from persistent rain, which managed to soak into my boots and add a squelch to my step. I returned to the accommodation, dripped into the room, slurped out of my walking boots and put them on the windowsill. I opened the window – typical, the rain had now ceased. Hopefully the breeze would dry my boots and I dumped the rest of my wet clothing on the radiator.

Once showered, dried and refreshed, I slipped into clean clothes and checked the time. It was the cusp of beer o'clock, so I headed downstairs to the bar. It had been a poor day in the wild, but I hoped for a better time inside the warm cosy pub. Many of the annoying trappings of modern bars were banished from this fine establishment. No music, no television screens and no fruit machines. Several people were already drinking at the bar and the only noise was the friendly murmur of conversation. Perfect.

As the evening advanced more people arrived and the barman introduced me to some of the local characters. The Norfolk accent was warm and friendly, but the locals possessed a devilish sense of humour, which lit up the room with its darkness. When I passed underneath a low beam, it gently brushed the top of my head – a lady who I'd enjoyed a friendly chat with earlier pointed at me and booed. They were indulging in their favourite sport, which I'd witnessed the previous night – watching strangers cracking their craniums on the low beams. Successful strikes were documented – a post-it-note was attached to a particularly low beam which read, 'Terry from Basildon hit here 22/05/06'.

The regional real ale was named after Norfolk-lad-done-good Admiral Horatio Nelson and I asked, 'What do they drink in Suffolk, a pint of John Constable?' This kicked off a lively debate about rivalries with neighbouring counties, culminating in derogatory comments regarding Ipswich Town FC, much to the consternation of the Ipswich man. At the end of their deliberations about outsiders, the general consensus was the worst visitors were London day-trippers.

One member of the crowd looked at me, 'You're not from London, are you?'

He seemed relieved after I clarified I was from the Isle of Man, although its location confused him as he mentioned Cowes Week, which happens on the Isle of Wight. Someone else asked about the purpose of my trip.

'I'm a wildlife watcher.'

The barman leant closer, 'Have you seen marsh harriers yet?'

I shook my head.

A big chap with a beard chortled, 'Marsh harriers were outside the pub earlier.'

Another joined in, 'Saw three on my way to work.'

The barman added, 'One was in my garden this morning.'

They all laughed at my expense.

I announced loudly, in order to be heard above all the mockery, that tomorrow I'd see my first marsh harrier. They all felt pessimistic about my chances and I was accused of being full of beer and bravado.

It turned out to be a night of revelry and before closing I went outside and embarked on a night-time stroll towards Blakeney harbour. Some fresh air was required to send Horatio Nelson sailing out of my head. Bats accompanied my walk, they were small and twirling in flight, probably pipistrelles based on their size and movement. After feeling refreshed by the coastal air, I went to my room, switched on the light, wrote up my diary and dozed off on top of the bed. An hour later I was awoken by a tapping noise above.

The central light was still on and it had become the focal point for a gathering. Small flies spectated on the fringe, while a main event moth headbutted the light bulb. My moth knowledge is limited – I can only confirm it was one of those big brown ones. The insect entourage must have entered through the open window, still ajar for the purpose of airing my boots.

I leaned over the windowsill and closed it shut. Woefully I took a breath of my boots – they stank like an old wet dog. Once my lungs were cleared, I readied myself for bed, jumped under the sheets, gave the insect congregation a 'Goodnight', and switched off the main light. Hopefully the moth would also take a rest. All fell quiet as I drifted off to dreams of marsh harriers.

I was stirred from my slumber by a scratching, flapping annoyance. This was not the nocturnal flourish of a moth, but a crane fly, better known in my household as daddy longlegs. I knew this blighter from previous periods of insomnia. It could continue this noisy parade for over an hour. There was no alternative but to switch the light back on and search for the irritant. Once the room was illuminated the insect fell silent. It was playing a game of musical statues. I stalked around without any signs of my quarry. After several minutes of frustrated hunting he was found in the fold of a curtain. A brief chase ensued, finally resulting in his capture and an unceremonious flinging out of an opened window. 'I hope a bat eats you!' Window slammed shut, lights off, under the bed covers, eyes closed and a return to dreamland.

Flutter flutter.

I sighed. The moth had kicked off again.

The following morning, I ate breakfast and read last night's diary notes – written under the influence of alcohol. They appeared be in a foreign language, scribbled by someone with a nervous condition. I decided to rewrite the lot while scoffing a full English (even though I have great respect for animals, I haven't converted to vegetarianism).

The weather was bright and sunny, and I felt the urge for fresh air. I was nurturing the classic combination of a mild hangover and a poor night's sleep. The day began east of Blakeney on a raised footpath above the lagoons. It was a circular route, which was square in shape. A reed warbler sang; sounding similar to an old car engine trying to start on a cold morning, the ignition scratching away, turning and turning, but never quite biting. Further along, a sedge warbler sang, a scratchy tone resembling a reed warbler but without rhythm; sedge warblers are jazz soloists. They remind me of the noises emitted by a mad scientist's contraption. I think of Rowland Emett's *Afternoon Tea Train* or old sci-fi movies with elaborate machines rattling with tubes, cogs and whistles. As I listened to the warblers, a small happy dog bounded up, sniffed my boots, got a full blast of the aroma and scampered off quickly. God knows how bad my footwear reeked to a creature with a sense of smell forty times greater than my own.

A short distance away was Cley Next-the-Sea Beach. I don't need to elaborate on the scenery, the name says it all. This was the starting point for an invigorating ramble across Blakeney Point, a dynamic spit of shingle washed up during storms and tides. The area was recommended as a place for terns and seals. I lifted the telescope onto my shoulder and strode across the shingle beach. After a short distance I wondered whether this was a good idea. The spit stretched off into the distance, with no obvious path and the shingle was energy-sapping, like wading through treacle. After ten minutes I looked back to check my progress. The car was clearly visible behind and the blue building I was aiming towards seemed no closer. I plodded on for another twenty minutes and stopped again. Car was still there. Somehow the telescope and tripod gained weight and ate into my shoulder. I thought to myself, in recent history this was one of my worst purchases. Why didn't I just buy some bloody binoculars? Yesterday it belted with rain – today was as bright as a celebrity's teeth. I would have welcomed cool drizzle.

It was another thirty minutes before I arrived at the strange blue building, sat down and rested my weary legs. I'd trudged a flat landscape and it felt like I'd climbed a mountain. The wildlife didn't help. I only saw a solitary Sandwich tern and they are nothing new to me. I am fortunate to live somewhere this tern species visits every year on their passage to breeding grounds in Northern Ireland. They treat the Isle of Man as a location for courtship and mating before going home, like young Brits visiting Ibiza.

I spoke to someone who survived the same journey as me and asked what I might see further ahead.

He replied, 'The nesting area is all fenced off, so you are limited.'

I once joined a warden named Louise on a tour of the Ayres along the Isle of Man's northern coast. The purpose was to produce a film for the visitors' centre and let people know how dangerous their feet were in summer. Louise took me to the beach to see the nests of oystercatchers, ringed plovers and little terns. I found the nest hunting experience terrifying because the eggs were perfectly camouflaged like pebbles, laid in small sandy depressions with little nesting material to highlight their presence. Every time we discovered a nest it was a relief rather than a pleasure. I would have been horrified if I'd stepped on any.

The idea of going near ground-nesting birds again filled me with dread, and was sufficient excuse to leave Blakeney Point and return to the car. I was knackered anyway, which was the deciding factor. I pitched the tripod on my sore shoulder and noticed that no one else was stupid enough to be carrying anything heavier than binoculars.

I eventually arrived back at the car and wiped sweat off my forehead. There was one positive; I'd perspired yesterday's pints of Horatio Nelson out of my body and rid myself of any lingering hangover. I needed provisions and drove to Cley, a charming little village of cottages, some partially constructed from large shingle stones. I came to the conclusion that shingle makes better building materials than footpaths. Once stocked with food and water, I continued around the coastal road and parked at Cley Marshes. Shortly afterwards, a large skein of fifty geese lifted from a nearby hillside, and roared above as their honking mass headed towards the sea. According to a nearby birder they were pink-footed geese. I couldn't confirm the colour of their feet. I initially labelled them as greylag geese, a species which coincidentally also has pink feet.

It does amaze me when birds have names based on the least noticeable part of their anatomy. There is a bird called a short-toed eagle.... I've never seen a bird and thought, 'Blimey, look at those tiny digits!' Another example is the red-legged partridge – if you see one of those the last thing you notice is their red legs. They resemble a glitterball that's been kicked into a rainbow, a fact ignored by the ornithologist responsible for their naming.

I stood and watched the departing geese; the leaders tried to create a v-formation but behind them was a disorganised rabble. A geese skein is special, but something more exciting appeared above the reedbed. A female marsh harrier. Her wings banked and tilted as she quartered the wetland, eyes aiming down, talons ready to snatch a vole, pipit or warbler. Preferably not a warbler. The harrier continued east and behind it a moment later a second bird. You don't see a marsh harrier all your life, then two come along at once. Through the telescope I focused on the second bird – she was a female or possibly a juvenile; adult males have greyer plumage. She was similar in size and form to a female hen harrier, a familiar bird back on the Isle of Man, with the addition of cream plumage on her head and shoulders. This next statement is going to seem out of order, considering it's coming from someone with the fashion sense of Compo from *Last of the Summer Wine*. But I thought the marsh harrier was scruffier than a hen harrier. Hen harriers look like they've slept in a hotel room, while a marsh harrier resembles a bird that's drunk too much Horatio Nelson and fallen asleep in a ditch.

I was delighted to have seen my first (and second) marsh harriers and when I walked into the pub later, I was excited about confirming my success to the naysayers. As I perused the bar's patrons, I realised none of yesterday's crowd was present. Even the barman was different. I was leaving in the morning, so gave the new barman a message to pass on the happy news. I was sure they would've all been interested – in hindsight, I'm sure they weren't.

As I left Norfolk and drove across England to Cheshire, I reflected on the short break and felt invigorated by the adventure. Granted, I'd been completely out of my depth, but I learned valuable new skills and knowledge. The mistakes included being unprepared for a rainy day and having a limited number of places to visit on my schedule – all could have been resolved with more planning and preparation. I should have booked a boat trip around Blakeney Point, instead of enduring an exhausting hike. I also needed to buy binoculars. One final thing to remember – when entering a bird hide, don't let the door slam shut. That still makes me cringe with embarrassment.

At Cheshire, I met up with family and shared the pungent aroma of my boots. Shortly afterwards my footwear was permanently banished outdoors. Norfolk had been great for birds, but I wanted to encounter mammals and sea life.

So, for the next holiday I turned my focus towards Scotland.

Otter

Chapter 2

Mull (2007)

In 2007 none of my close friends were particularly interested in nature. If I volunteered to organise a Dublin trip (drinking stout and seeing rugby), I could have filled a plane, but for wildlife watching in Mull, there were no takers so I travelled alone. Even if my friends were ambivalent about the idea, I was incredibly excited. Nature-watching taps into my deepest instincts. Our ancestors would have been fuelled by adrenaline as they hunted food. I get that same buzz seeking wildlife, even though I don't catch anything for dinner – instead I usually finish up in a pub.

I hoped to see new wildlife, explore different habitats, meet delightful people, and sample the Scottish hospitality. The destination would be more remote and rugged than anywhere I'd visited before in Britain. I previously explored the flat landscape of Norfolk – mountainous Scotland would be its antithesis.

There was a good reason for choosing Mull. The previous year a documentary was broadcast about Mull called *Eagle Island* starring

Gordon Buchanan, and golden and white-tailed eagles. I put an eagle sighting at the top of the bucket list – either species would do, I wasn't fussy. There was potential for an exciting new animal – otters. I loved the films *Tarka the Otter* and *Ring of Bright Water*, but I'd never seen an otter in the wild. Finally, I wanted to spot my first bottlenose dolphin and for this I would go north of Inverness to the Black Isle. In addition to these three, I was visiting in June which should hopefully reward me with wild flowers and birdsong.

I booked a hire car, whale watching boat trip, guided wildlife tour and found details for an observation area for a pair of nesting white-tailed eagles. I was equipped with a new pair of binoculars and a video camera. I left the tripod and telescope at home – after Norfolk they left me mentally and physically scarred.

This outing and subsequent trips to Scotland began with a flight to Glasgow airport (which unfortunately increased my low carbon footprint). This part of the holiday was always slightly unpleasant, the flying wasn't an issue for me, it was the airport. Overcrowded with grumpy people who would rather be somewhere else. The security process and all the crappy waiting around for flights. It's very tiresome. Virtually everywhere else on the planet presents an opportunity for wildlife watching, but airports, nothing. The wildest thing I saw was a stag party going to Prague. If airports included some pockets of nature, perhaps a couple of trees and small gardens, it might add a little tranquillity to an otherwise oppressive environment. This would benefit everybody, not just wildlife enthusiasts. I stared out of the departure lounge window at the parked planes. There was so much grey and I peered hard into the distance to discover a tree. Then a kestrel flew past, which blew my earlier argument to pieces.

The midday flight left on time and a couple of hours later I was driving from Glasgow airport in the direction of Loch Lomond. It was a pretty drive, although at a slow pace due to a fleet of towed caravans ahead. The lethargic journey enabled me to glance occasionally at the large loch, it was vast. The convoy caught up with some mobile homes, the speed dropped further and I decided to take an alternative route left. This diversion gifted me with clear road, but involved circumnavigating most of Loch Fyne. After I eventually looped around this long length of water, I cruised up behind another tailback of motorhomes. It was nearly sunset when I arrived at my hotel on Fort William's outskirts.

The next morning, I sat in the hotel's dining room beside a large window with impressive views over Loch Linnhe. It seemed finer than Loch Fyne. I browsed the wilderness while feasting on a full Scottish breakfast. The ordering of breakfast nearly got me in trouble as I accidentally asked for a full English. Even though I corrected myself immediately, the damage had already been done. The waitress did well to disguise any offence caused. With a mouth full of haggis, I continued to admire the scenery and thought to myself, 'I really love all this.'

The map was next to me – today's route seemed straightforward. Take the A82 alongside Loch Lochy (what a great name!), follow Loch Ness to Inverness before travelling over a huge bridge to the Black Isle (the map revealed a surprising fact that the Black Isle wasn't actually an island.... it was a peninsular).

The drive was pleasant, mercifully free of motorhomes and I stopped sporadically to gaze across the lochs. I have to admit that I prefer sea watching to gazing across anything called loch, lough or lake. The lochs rewarded me with some mallards and Canada geese. The drive was lengthier than anticipated and I began to wonder whether Scottish miles were longer than English ones. At Inverness the road crossed the Moray Firth over the enormous Kessock Bridge to the Black Isle. Fortrose was signposted and the route passed through Clootie Well, where trees were draped with strands of cloth and underwear. This was a site of supernatural beliefs and items of fabric were bestowed as offerings to the fairies. It resembled the aftermath of a mass orgy. Do fairies really have a fondness for used Y-fronts?

The road wove through the attractive town of Fortrose, then dissected a golf course, before terminating beside a lighthouse. This was Chanonry Point, a name I would struggle to pronounce later to a barman, 'Today I went to Chinriney Point.... Chewrunny.... the lighthouse near Fortrose.'

'Ahhh, you mean Chanonry Point.'

'That's the chap.'

I parked in the shadow of the lighthouse and walked towards the shingle beach. Thirty people were milling about; which at least confirmed I'd arrived at the right place. The area looked familiar, as though I'd visited before. This was because this shoreline has appeared several times in wildlife documentaries as *the* prime British location for dolphin-watching. Bottlenose dolphins who reside in the Moray Firth converge on this coastline due to the underwater topography. Depending on the tide, the marine landscape funnels fish such as salmon into a narrow area and once in a concentrated shoal they become a veritable buffet for touring dolphins. Sadly, that wasn't happening at this particular moment.

I sat on a low wall and ate my lunch; a chicken, coleslaw and salad sandwich. I got halfway through before disaster – the chicken squirted out. The filling was irretrievable after it took numerous rolls in the sand. Two seconds later a herring gull circled, landed nearby and stared at the dropped food by my foot. Gulls must have remarkably good eyesight to spy a square inch of misplaced chicken. However, the gull would need to linger for its free meal – I was still peeved and it wouldn't be relinquished easily.

A Scottish gentleman sat beside me as I ate my empty bread. We made eye contact and he uttered a phrase which no wildlife enthusiast wants to hear, 'You should have been here yesterday.' He described leaping dolphins and roaring crowds being splashed by seawater. It sounded like one of those Florida sea parks but without the animal cruelty.

Once we finished chatting, I walked to the strandline and the gull snaffled my dropped chicken. I stood on the edge of the lapping water and greeted passing people.

A bubbly lady stopped to chat, she showed me her camera and flicked through pictures taken at the exact same spot yesterday. Airborne dolphins and joyous onlookers. I smiled politely but deep inside I had serious wildlife envy.

I decided to give the dolphins another half hour. An hour later I accepted defeat and strolled back to the car, scanned the sea for a final time and commenced the long drive back to Fort William, slightly disappointed. Slightly disappointed was a big understatement. Halfway along I nursed a nagging feeling that now at Chanonry Point a large triumphant crowd were being entertained by leaping dolphins. I was tempted to turn back – but didn't.

Instead I drove to the foot of Ben Nevis, sat on the bonnet of my car and stared up at the massive mountain. I wondered how anybody could have the fitness to hike all that way up, while I sat on my car and ate a packet of crisps.

The following day I took the ferry to Mull and onwards to Tobermory, where I was booked into one of the colourful harbourfront hotels. I explored the town by wandering from one end of the promenade and back again, which took thirty minutes. I soon warmed to the place. A newsagent's contained merchandise for a children's TV programme based here called *Balamory*; the cultural references went over my head. More of relevance was a conversation between the shopkeeper and a customer. This revealed one of my scheduled items had already been scuppered. The previous week a gale had swept through the island, wreaking disaster on the white-tailed eagle nest I was going to visit. The single chick had been blown out of its treetop nest, and once the youngster passed away, the adults abandoned the area. That was wretched news for the eagles and, to a far lesser extent, me.

In the evening I accepted the challenge of a pub crawl across town, which amounted to four establishments. It was a great evening and one of the nicest things was that the guy who served my last pint appeared the next morning to deliver my breakfast. People in small communities often fulfil multiple jobs and this was a good example. He certainly provided a valuable service to me. I avoided accidentally asking for a full English by selecting the lightly smoked haddock with scrambled eggs. It was an astute choice.

Today's schedule involved driving a circular route around the north of the island (I'd save the southern area called the Ross of Mull for departure day). I had the hire car, map, binoculars, packed lunch and felt prepared for all eventualities. In retrospect it would've been wise to check the weather forecast for the afternoon – and taken a raincoat.

One of the things I adored about Mull was the driving etiquette. Most roads were single lanes with passing places. If two cars approached each other, the drivers would assess who was nearest to a layby and whoever it was, would pull in and let the other pass. The drivers would then politely wave as they crossed. It was a convivial ritual which made me feel welcome and gave me great affection for the local folk.

I arrived at Calgary Bay and instantly thought, 'Wow'. A beautiful vista with a golden crescent of sand, banked by verdant green hills. On the fringe of the bay a squadron of plunge diving gannets smacked into the sea, while on the strandline, oystercatchers paraded. Oystercatchers are handsome birds but they can make more noise than a flock of gulls on a discarded takeaway.

The agitated oystercatchers built to a crescendo of piercing chatter – like a noisy infant trying to get your attention with a penny whistle.

A young couple walked barefoot on the tideline, waves lapping against their shins. The din from the oystercatchers failed to interrupt their romantic moment.

I continued the coastal drive and parked frequently to scan the surroundings; it was impossible to soak up all the natural beauty and drive at the same time. At one stop, a redshank was in the distance, giving away its location by reaching the same decibel level as an oystercatcher. Shanks is an old English name for legs, such as lamb shanks or King Edward Longshanks (you should avoid mentioning the latter in Scotland, particularly if your audience recently watched *Braveheart*). The bird's shanks were visible through binoculars and they were definitely red. It perched on a rock and made a complete racket, blasting out repetitive 'chips'. I suspect the redshank had fledglings or a nest nearby and this was a warning call for their benefit. It certainly didn't benefit my hearing. I decided to give the redshank family some space, as my presence was obviously causing concern. While moving away I wondered which would be worse at karaoke, a redshank, an oystercatcher or my friends Brendan and Emma singing; *I Got You Babe*.

A mile further along, I parked in a long layby and walked along the shoreline. The nearby trees rang with the calls of goldfinches. Their chirping reminded me of retro space arcade games in the early 1980s, when laser shots would be accompanied by random beeping noises. The collective noun for goldfinches is 'a charm'; my presence didn't charm them, because they flew off as I walked past. Various seaweed species were present on the tide line; waves swishing purple dulse, while egg wrack floated on baked-bean-shaped air sacks. As long as the water is clean and unpolluted, all British seaweeds are edible (in moderation), because none of them is poisonous. Dulse is particularly tasty and can be turned into crisps, while laver is used in sushi. However, a warning to all wannabe foragers, just because something isn't going to kill you, it doesn't mean it's going to taste nice. If you cook some fibrous tough seaweed, you should expect an eating experience similar to munching on a trawlerman's sock.

It dawned on me that I was in a big landscape all alone. The peace was magical. No human activity and the loudest sound was the gentle lapping of waves on the shore. Each encroaching wave glistened rounded stones and they sparkled in the dim sunlight. Everyone should try to find tranquillity; it puts into perspective our busy and rowdy urban lives. The simplest pleasures are usually the most enriching – like taking a sip of cold water when you have a dry mouth. I sat down and savoured this moment of solitude and when fully replenished by calm, I departed a more relaxed person.

At the next stop I sat on the car bonnet and scanned the lapping waves. I then struck gold. What initially resembled a piece of floating driftwood revealed itself fully – a looping tail flipped out of the water like an eel on the lookout, at the other end, a small dog-shaped head. My first wild otter! A heart-racing moment. No longer would my memories relate to Maxwell's otter or *Tarka*. When the otter dived underwater, I crept along the strandline and hid behind a boulder. Less than a minute later the otter resurfaced in an identical place to where it had dived, it swam a little closer and plunged again. I estimated I had thirty seconds, so I crept adjacent to a line of seaweed, slipped on two occasions but retained my balance and hesitated behind another rock. I peered around the rock as the otter surfaced much closer. It was glorious. At no point was I spotted and it continued to behave naturally. Otters have a great sense of smell and due to luck rather than any judgement, my scent was being blown inland by the sea breeze. After several minutes of wonderful viewing I slunk back up the beach, quietly stepped into the car and sat inside. Before leaving I gave the otter a final look and resumed my journey around the coast.

It was great to have success with one wish list item after the bottlenose dolphin and eagle nest catastrophes. What was not so great was the weather after lunch. The clouds thickened, the sky turned an ominous battleship grey and it chucked it down for the rest of the afternoon. The meticulous morning planning failed to include a raincoat and I returned soggy.

****

The weather thankfully cleared the next day for a whale-watching boat trip. At Tobermory harbour I met the exuberant guide; she was remarkably cheerful and full of energy for this time in the morning. I boarded the large vessel and sat on the top deck which had good height for observing and fortunately not so tall that it swayed in the wind. I'd only recently finished eating breakfast and I didn't want to see smoked haddock and scrambled eggs making a second appearance. Twenty passengers dotted themselves across the boat and amongst the crowd was a palpable air of anticipation. Boat trips are always special, perhaps it's the unnatural feeling of balancing on waves. I needed to stop thinking about that – as breakfast started to lurch and grumble in my stomach.

The tour guide enthusiastically briefed us and throughout the tour she was always there, offering nuggets of information and answering guests' questions.

A young boy asked, 'Do dolphins eat seals?'

This received a polite shake of the head.

The same boy then asked about crocodiles and she gave a few vague answers, before subtly diverting the conversation towards creatures we might actually see, specifically today's advertised species; minke whales. I've been fortunate to see minkes around the Isle of Man, but was keen to view them again. You can never see too many whales, although a dolphin might be better. I would happily trade another minke whale for my first bottlenose dolphin – sadly that's not how this hobby works.

The boat chugged out of Tobermory harbour and westerly down the Sound of Mull. As we passed Ardmore Point a pod of harbour porpoises appeared. An excellent start. Our tour guide explained that porpoises utilise the underwater terrain to herd fish, in a similar way that bottlenose dolphins would use the topography at Chanonry Point – if they bothered to turn up. It's always good to see porpoises, but during all previous encounters their behaviour has been limited to the emergence of a stubby dorsal fin and a curved back. We watched the top ten inches of the porpoises intermittently breaking the surface, like rotating upright car tyres. The porpoises rolled through the sea and disappeared, emerged a short distance further along and continued this movement until out of sight. If cetaceans had a party, the dolphins would breakdance and the porpoises would line dance.

The boat trip was scheduled to last four hours which allowed us to travel to Coll and cruise beside its rocky shore. There were harbour seals – they used to be called common seals, but they became uncommon and someone decided they required a name change. In the future they might do the same for the poor old common gull. Our boat drifted along the coastline and more harbour seals basked on the rocks, recognised by their puppy-dog faces, rather than the Atlantic grey seals with their longer muzzles. As soon as the seals spotted us, they stared back intently. I wasn't sure who was watching who.

I took out my camera as another guest approached and he asked questions relating to the camera's specifications. This is an area of ignorance for me. He mentioned something regarding megapixels and aspect ratios, the rest seemed to be in a different language. I showed him the camera and said, 'I really don't know.... it has a good zoom.' Thankfully he moved on to the subject of Tobermory pubs – and I fully contributed to that conversation.

We disembarked at a beach on Coll and stretched our legs on the golden sands. Some of the guests returned to the boat with sea shells and coloured pebbles, while I inadvertently dragged a length of seaweed back on my shoe.

The boat cruised further offshore and a short time later the guide noticed something and she called loudly, 'Movement at 9 o'clock.' This was based on the boat's bow being 12 o'clock. It might have been easier if she shouted, 'Left,' as some guests clearly didn't understand clocks. The engine was cut and we drifted silently in the water. Eventually everyone faced the correct direction. We all looked. We all saw nothing.

The choppy conditions made it tricky to distinguish between sea and potential whales. A lady nearby blurted out excitedly, 'Oooh,' and then she sighed and apologised, 'Sorry, it was just a wave.'

Once all hope was abandoned, the skipper started the boat's engine again and we aimed towards an offshore seabird gathering. We arrived alongside a raft of bobbing birds and I was delighted to see Manx shearwaters. They paddled along the surface and made a low churring noise, before the louder kittiwakes drowned them out. You might think Manx shearwaters are a common sight around the Isle of Man; sadly this isn't the case. The breeding population on the Isle of Man is restricted to a small southern island called the Calf of Man. Over many decades their eggs and young were predated by brown rats. However, a recent project has eradicated the rats and hopefully the shearwaters and other seabirds will have more breeding success in the future.

We'd been out for three hours and only an hour of our scheduled time remained. The trip had been fun and it was great to be out with other enthusiasts, but we all craved to see a whale. With thirty minutes to go we travelled back to Mull. Suddenly the guide transformed into a character from *Moby Dick* and she shouted, 'Whale at 2 o'clock!' Most of the entourage were now familiar with clock-faces and everyone looked right of the bow. The boat engine stopped and a minke whale emerged exactly where the guide directed. There was joy and relief for all; it made me smile that the most thrilled person onboard was the guide. The minke drifted above the surface like a thick black line and at the end of its roll, a stumpy dorsal fin popped up. The whale put on a good display, it surfaced to take air, repeated this a few minutes later and then on its third appearance its head broke higher and caused a splash. The whale was probably herding fish to the surface and lunge feeding at the gathering. It disappeared for five minutes and re-emerged further away and continued a similar pattern before thrusting higher on its third surface. After it submerged again, I stood back from the railings and took a deep glorious breath, it was such a relief and pleasure to see one of these magnificent creatures.

As we returned to port, I absorbed the surroundings, a wide seascape and jagged hills beyond, with the side profile of a stegosaurus. We arrived at Tobermory still in high spirits and the boat docked on the harbour's eastern end – which was conveniently next to a pub. Most of the group made a beeline for the bar and we all sat outside in the sun, still wearing our many jumpers, coats and woolly hats. On the next table a gang of local teenagers were sunbathing in T-shirts and shorts. It was sunny but the temperature was no warmer than 15°C. Perhaps this was considered toasty in these parts. One of the lads smiled at our clothing and commented to his friends, 'I bet they're tourists.'

****

The following day I joined a land-based tour, led by a husband-and-wife team, Arthur and Pam. Arthur was the driver and doyen of local wildlife, while Pam had friendly chat, geological knowledge and home cooking. It was a winning combination. There were six guests – myself, two middle-aged couples and another person who was yet to arrive. As we waited, Pam explained the missing person was Jess; she'd started working at a hotel run by Pam's friends and Pam had volunteered to acquaint Jess with Mull. When Jess turned up, she looked like she'd either had an early morning, or more likely a late night. Her head was an explosion of long black hair – I imagine she went to the same hairdresser as Edward Scissorhands. We all jumped into an off-road vehicle and the tour got underway. Jess became animated when she saw a mallard.

The initial route repeated my solo drive two days earlier, but we soon encountered something I didn't spot previously. A pair of red deer ran across a field, scampered through tussock grass and disappeared into woodland. A little further along, Arthur caught sight of something else and he pulled over at the earliest opportunity. He excitedly ran to the coast and aimed his telescope towards the loch. Everyone piled out, but Jess spotted something different – a herd of Scottish Highland cattle. She ran in the opposite direction to Arthur and tried to coax a cow with a handful of grass. Everyone, including me, were now with Jess and the cows.

Arthur attempted to bring order, 'Hi all, there are Slavonian grebes in full breeding plumage on the loch.'

We stayed with the cows, they were great animals, thick brown curly hair and rumbling moos. Slavonian grebes could wait a minute. Arthur gave up and walked over to join us.

Jess turned to him and asked, 'How do you go about having one as a pet?'

Arthur appeared to have briefly lost the will to live, before he replied wearily, 'First, you'd need a field.'

I had a sneaking feeling that Jess was planted by the hotel owners to wind up their tour guide friends. We eventually saw the grebes. They were just as Jess described, 'Oooohh, pretty'. They resembled Mandarin ducks during a gothic phase. Jess asked what was so bad about Slavonia that it caused their grebes to leave. It was a good question – and we all turned to Arthur for an answer.

Arthur picked up his telescope, 'Right, lots more to see,' and strode back to his vehicle.

If I was scoring this as a football match, so far I'd judge it level; Arthur 1 – Jess 1, but plenty of game time remained.

As we drove further along I recognised an area of coastline from two days earlier; it was where I had seen the otter. I meticulously scanned the same length of shore and remarkably an otter was still there in the water, so I blurted out loudly, 'Otter!'

Arthur swung into the verge and everyone jumped out as the otter dived. When it returned to the surface it held a fish in its jaws and began eating. From the amount of mastication, I guess it was a leathery-skinned dogfish. It reminded me of our pet Labrador when it chewed my dad's rubber soled slippers. The otter was still chomping the fish when we left ten minutes later.

We travelled around Loch na Keal and stopped beside the shore as willow warblers sang their cascading trills. Willow warblers are aptly named as they are often found near willow trees. Sometimes bird names are not as appropriate; I've never seen a herring gull eating a herring, or an oystercatcher eating an oyster, or come to think of it a Sandwich tern eating a sandwich (because of course they are named after the Kent town where they were first recorded).

Arthur pointed out some ringed plovers which scuttled across the beach like wind-up toys, then he shouted 'Eagle!' He must have eyes of an eagle; the bird was well beyond the loch. Gradually the huge bird approached and circled above, and Arthur was able to confirm it was a white-tailed sea eagle. It was an awesome creature; they call them flying barndoors, a deserved description.

I started to become light-headed while staring up at the sea eagle and had to look down after feeling giddy. I gained my composure and overheard a conversation behind.

Arthur called out, 'Jess, are you looking at sheep?'

'No,' there was a tentative pause before she replied, 'It's a lamb.'

Arthur 2 – Jess 1

Jess tore herself away from the lamb to see the eagle depart. A couple of minutes later another large bird appeared on the horizon. Arthur's voice was even more energetic this time. 'There's a golden eagle!'

I'm no eagle expert – I thought it was another white-tailed eagle. The goldie remained distant but I managed to watch it through binoculars. A pale head and tail; appropriately with less white than the previous bird. Arthur must be blessed to see both species regularly and this familiarity enabled him to immediately recognise their differences. This eagle sadly didn't come any closer, so I was unable to view it fully before it vanished over the horizon.

Everyone had a great day out, especially Jess, who asked if she could join another tour in the future. Arthur was non-committal on that and changed the subject. With that own-goal just before full time the match finished; Arthur 2 – Jess 2. A draw seemed a fair result.

Arthur's outing was a wonderful inspiration – a year afterwards I set up my own wildlife tour operation on the Isle of Man. I have yet to have the pleasure of guiding Jess.

****

The next day I planned a quick tour of the south-west peninsular called the Ross of Mull, which held the possibility of taking a ferry trip to Iona – time permitting. During the drive there were views across a glacial valley and Mull's tallest mountain Ben More. The route dropped into a wide basin of saltmarsh which swept towards distant ridges. Vast landscapes with no signs of humanity are always a pleasure to behold and Mull invigorated my inner explorer; the boat trip, guided tour, rugged scenery and exceptional wildlife. My senses were enlivened and the Scottish air breathed new energy into me. I hadn't felt so connected to nature since my childhood.

Halfway down the road a flock of twenty godwits wandered over the mudflats, occasionally stopping to poke their beaks into the earth. I filmed them, as I still had no idea how to differentiate the two godwit species. I later showed the footage to an experienced birder, who confirmed with confidence they were of the bar-tailed variety. Apparently, he could tell because they were stumpier than the black-tailed birds. I shrugged and took his word for it. To me they looked no different to the black-tailed godwits I saw in Norfolk.

Further along the saltmarsh a flock of common gulls were squawking – judging by their rumbustious mood, they were nesting. I wished them success; it would be great if they became more common. The road ran adjacent to a sea loch and I pulled over to scan for marine life; all was quiet, apart from the common gulls who could still be heard in the distance.

During breakfast I studied the map and Iona didn't seem too far away, but while parked at the roadside, I realised there was still considerable distance to travel. Each crooked turn would reveal another long road and then in the distance another corner. Later, when I arrived home, I checked whether Scottish miles were longer than English ones – apparently since 1959 they have been made consistent. Perhaps the change hadn't yet been adopted in Argyll and Bute. After travelling an hour, I got the impression that I was making my own personal pilgrimage to Iona. I was glad I wasn't travelling by foot. Eventually, Iona came into sight but the journey had taken so long that there wasn't time to board the ferry. After a quick mooch around the Columba visitor centre, I drove to Craignure. I felt sad that I'd have to drive all the way back and even more depressed that I'd soon be leaving Mull.

I arrived at Craignure ferry terminal and joined a queue of cars. A ferry company representative wearing a fluorescent yellow tabard got shirty because I hadn't booked. I was rudely pointed in the direction of the ticket shop and once inside asked for a ticket, which appeared to be no issue whatsoever. The rude ferryman was the first and only plonker I met on Mull.

Two out of three wish-list items had been achieved; otter and a white-tailed sea eagle (plus a distant goldie). The only niggling disappointment was not seeing bottlenose dolphins, but I refuse to be defeated and vow to try again. My greatest pleasure was the feeling of freedom amongst the remote beauty of Scotland. I still fondly think of Mull like a good friend. I felt cleansed from my daily worries and returned home refreshed. I would definitely revisit Scotland in the future.

Badger

Chapter 3

Cairngorms National Park (2008)

Before going on this trip, I had three memorable wildlife experiences on the Isle of Man. The first was a very brief sighting of an orca from the Langness coast, which only lasted a few seconds, but that fleeting glimpse was incredibly special. Secondly, I saw a basking shark breach. I missed the beginning as it took its upward trajectory, but I did see it plunge back down, creating an explosion of spray – like a massive lintel of black granite being thrown into the sea. The third event happened while striding through marram grass dunes at the Ayres coast, when I trod on a dead Atlantic grey seal. Not as wonderous as the other two events – yet equally enduring.

After the success of Mull, I was keen to revisit Scotland and when the opportunity arose in September for a short three-day break, I decided to explore the Cairngorms National Park. To me it seemed a good time of year – between the summer crowds and the winter skiers – which meant I could avoid the peak times for tourists. I based myself a short amble from Aviemore's town centre and hired a small hatchback car (I always get a small car because I do lots of exploring down narrow roads, get lost and perform three-point-turns). I packed insect repellent, as midges would still be hunting humans, and extra clothing which included waterproofs after getting soaked in Mull and Norfolk.

My three-part wish list possessed a familiar name, the bottlenose dolphin, as I intended to make a return journey to Chanonry Point. The remaining two species on the wish list were ptarmigan (I was travelling up Cairngorm Mountain) and pine marten (I had an evening booked in a hide to see them).

On the first day in the Cairngorms, I visited the nearby Highland Wildlife Park. I am slightly uncomfortable with zoos and wildlife parks, because I don't think animals should be imprisoned for people's entertainment (even though as a child I wanted to be a zookeeper). However, this park contained species which had become extinct in their natural habitats, such as the European bison and Mongolian wild horse, and the park has helped reintroduce them back into the wild. It was also commended for its large enclosures, particularly the one for European grey wolves. When I arrived, I made the wolves my first stop and stood by their large sturdy fence. It reminded me of the enclosure in *Jurassic Park* for the velociraptors. I exchanged looks with an imposing grey she-wolf – her glare interrogated my soul, a wonderful moment, although slightly intimidating. The metal gates and fences gave the impression of being secure, but did this wily lupine know better? I edged away...

The next enclosure housed the smaller-than-expected Arctic foxes. On wildlife programmes they are often shown in fluffy white coats – the park's foxes looked like they'd been put on poles and used to sweep chimneys. Grey and black thick coats all puffed up, giving them a bulky appearance; presumably if you shaved one, you'd be left with something resembling a small bald beagle.

Elsewhere, the Scottish wildcat enclosure contained a couple of cats hiding high in a canopy of woven branches, lazing in the autumnal sun, half asleep and surly looking. Their grumpy expressions reminded me of my neighbour's tabby after it was stuck outside on a rainy night because its cat flap broke. Adjacent to the Scottish wildcats was a red squirrel enclosure. It seemed slightly cruel to put predators and their potential prey as neighbours – the squirrels were all hiding. Then a wild stoat scampered towards their cage, turned past the wire fencing and continued along the path – perhaps the squirrels were better off safely imprisoned.

A large open area provided the opportunity for a safari drive. Beside the road a red deer stag paraded with antlers adorned with vegetation. The autumn rut was imminent and the stag already looked impressive – his muscular loins strutting and chest pumped out like Freddie Mercury at Wembley. Another stag lifted a branch and vigorously rubbed it against his antlers to satisfy an itch. His antlers were still in velvet – once this furry coating was shed, all feeling would end. It made sense to avoid antler pain during the violence of the rut. The stag bellowed and his roar rippled through me; it would be difficult to experience that in the wild!

The safari route terminated near a meadow where a large flock of barnacle geese grazed, using their beaks to snip at the lush grass. These birds were truly wild and elected to stay at this park through choice. I felt eyes facing in our direction, the wolf pack were all staring towards us and thinking of goose for lunch.

I left the wildlife park after an entertaining visit, but wanted to see more creatures enjoying their freedom. I found a car park by a woodland glen and went for a walk in the Caledonian Forest. It would be great to see two rare bird species which inhabit this pinewood habitat; crested tits and capercaillies (sometimes I am unrealistically optimistic). All was quiet – nature was taking a break. In spring the trees would have been alive with birdsong. Seasons make a big difference. Once British birds have finished rearing their young, most of them moult and hide from predators until their feathers are replenished. Afterwards they prepare for the cold winter ahead and build up their reserves. In autumn there's rarely time for singing, unless you have a berry bush to protect. A robin sang out from the woodland; he'd presumably found a rowan tree laden with fruit which was worth defending.

I felt a scratchy gnawing sensation on my head and looked up to see a cloud of midges descend. I ran out of the woodland with arms flailing and jumped into the safety of the car. That would teach me for thinking there was no wildlife about. I'd become a reluctant part of the local food chain. Some midges followed me inside the car and flitted across the windscreen. I am normally a forgiving sort of person, but if something bites me, it should expect retaliation. I knew it would create bad karma, but I squashed the little bleeders. I said a little prayer for them, which included some swearing and wiped off the mess. I belatedly sprayed myself with insect repellent – which was about five minutes too late.

Aviemore at first impression was purpose-built for the hiking and skiing fraternity – rather than me. The high street had clothes shops for trendy ramblers, global themed restaurants and bars lacking the traditional Scottish warmth I'd previously cherished in Mull. My perfect holiday destination is a quiet countryside village or a coastal town, all within walking distance of a local pub (that's very important). I am a beast of simple pleasures. After a bit of trial and error I finally discovered a traditional pub and that cheered up my evening.

While propped up against the bar an elderly gentleman, his beard tightly woven like a warbler's nest was engaged in conversation. He complained that some tourists traded their social skills for designer labels. Then he peered deeply into my eyes and asked, 'So why are you here? You don't look like a skier.'

It is true, the only winter leisure pursuit which my body shape fits is being a model for a snowman. I explained I came here to watch wildlife.

A cheeky little glint appeared in his bloodshot eyes. 'Have you seen any wild haggis?'

I smiled and played along, 'No, not yet, do you recommend any places where I might see them?'

He kept a deadpan expression, 'Aye, there's some on the Rothiemurchus estate, we go hunting them with big nets.'

'Are they difficult to catch?'

'Aye, dangerous beasties, you have to wear thick gloves, they nip your fingers.' He pointed to a scar on the back of his hand. 'One got me right there, it was awfully painful.'

The following day I took a second visit to the Black Isle in search of bottlenose dolphins, but this time I had a contingency plan. I would try Chanonry Point and if that failed for a second time, I would go to Cromarty where I could join a dolphin-watching boat trip. The drive across the Black Isle was cheered by the sight of the trees adorned by underwear at Clootie Well. Something new was hanging from the branches – a bra – which must have been owned by a very large-chested lady. The twigs sagged under its weight. It had potential to be a nesting site for a capercaillie.

Chanonry Point once again had a good crowd of visitors, most of them milling about on the beach, their footsteps crunching as they crossed the shingle. I plonked myself on a low wall and gazed across the Moray Forth. The water was smooth, ideal for seeing dolphins; if any bothered to turn up.

After looking at the rippling waves for a few minutes I checked the folk around the shoreline. There were some serious birders about, easily identified by their camouflage clothing, long lens cameras and unkempt hair. I am careful to use the term birder instead of twitcher. I've created my own personal criteria for people being one or the other, based on the small number of twitchers I've met. To me, a birder is someone who enjoys watching birds, spotting new species and appreciating the hobby as a relaxed pastime (similar to me). Twitchers are comparable to birders but they're the extremists. They'd travel hundreds of miles for the rare sight in Britain of a Siberian thrush, even though those thrushes are as common as house sparrows in Siberia. Twitchers take little interest in any other wildlife outside their target species and don't support conservation projects, while some create disturbance to deliberately flush out birds. Others will go online and have heated arguments with fellow twitchers about subspecies. Every hobby has irritating obnoxious fringe elements. Football has hooligans, social media has trolls and birdwatching has twitchers.

The birders moved *en masse*, until one lady froze after glimpsing an approaching seabird. She showed interest and pointed her binoculars in the bird's direction. The others joined in unison – and so did I. It was a black-headed gull. No one was impressed by the lady and she received several 'looks' – she'd let down the team.

The lady glanced back at them and said, 'Sorry.'

One of the gentlemen nudged her in the ribs and said, 'It's just a seagull.'

He immediately got a slap on the arm and was scolded, 'I've told you before, there's no such thing as a seagull!'

He laughed – it must have been their in-joke.

It's true, if you open any bird book, you'll not discover any species called 'seagull'. The birds which people often refer to as seagulls are herring gulls. I now find myself correcting friends when they say seagull and it appears to have become our in-joke too. Some of my more creative friends have branched out and now call our local Atlantic grey seals; sealions. They are a funny bunch.

I started to eat my lunch and a herring gull landed nearby. Maybe word had spread amongst the local gull community that some bloke sits on this wall and drops chicken from his sandwich. I studiously ate the entirety of my lunch without any spillage and the gull tried to hide its disappointment.

Chanonry's atmosphere was friendly, something often recognisable at places of natural beauty; they are magnets for lovely people. The only disappointment was no one had yet pointed at the water and shouted, 'Dolphins!'

I really wanted to be that person.

Among the other visitors, there was a smattering of ordinary tourists, including different nationalities based on the overheard conversations. It was great to see families here too, with kids skimming stones over the water in the absence of dolphin entertainment. I imagined it would be bad timing if a dolphin unexpectedly poked its head up and got hit in the face with a skimming rock.

A little time later a lady joined me and she commented that it was a poor time to visit – as the tide was going out. I felt stupid for not checking the tide tables beforehand, I knew it was important. Research claims the best chance for dolphins is when the tide (and the accompanying fish) come in, which she confirmed wouldn't occur for another three hours. We talked about the local wildlife and she mentioned she saw a pomarine skua here recently, which was a new addition to her bird list.

Many birders have a list of British species they've seen. I've no list and perhaps I'm missing out on an important aspect of the wildlife watching hobby. However, there are reasons why I've never started. I'm not a naturally competitive person and the possession of a list seems a way of ranking yourself above others, 'Oh, you only have two hundred, I have three hundred.' I want to share my knowledge and help people see wildlife, I don't aspire to beat their score. I also struggle to understand the difference between spotting a bird in the UK or elsewhere in the world. Seeing a new bird is exciting – to me its location is of lesser importance, particularly when the boundaries are dictated by political divides. A mistle thrush doesn't care whether it is in France or England, so why should I? I'd choose to see an American robin in America, rather than a poor bedraggled bird that finds itself hounded by twitchers after being accidentally blown across the Atlantic.

In 2010 a cattle egret made a rare stopover on the Isle of Man and many people were excited about its appearance. My friend June is from Africa and she said cattle egrets were as common as pigeons out there, so she didn't bother. I decided to make the effort, viewed the bird which resembled a little egret (apart from the beak, which was yellow, not black) and unsurprisingly it was amongst cattle. The egret would've been more interesting to me if it was on the back of a water buffalo in Tanzania.

Admittedly, if I'd discovered a griffon vulture on my allotment, I'd be thrilled. Obviously it'd be more remarkable than seeing a griffon vulture in the Pyrenees. In fact, it would be downright weird. Ultimately in both circumstances I would've seen a griffon vulture. I may even feel sorry for a vulture on my allotment, as the only available carrion would be the flattened rabbits on the nearby road.

I prefer to rank my sightings on the quality of the experience, with a strong emphasis on behaviour and proximity. A griffon vulture circling in the sky half a mile above isn't going to be as good as seeing one nearby on a carcass. I would happily travel miles to hear a nightingale sing, watch grebes performing their courtship dance or see stag beetles fight, but wouldn't go further than the next town for my first tawny pipit. I would go further to relive the experience of being yelled at by a Cetti's warbler. The beauty of being a wildlife enthusiast is that witnessing unusual behaviour in common species can be just as rewarding as finding new species. There is great pleasure in seeing starling murmurations, trout leaping and hares boxing. Those experiences have given me more joy than my first cattle egret. Therefore, you'll not see me crossing Britain to chase down some poor bird that's been shat out of a hurricane.

The lady went off for a ciggie while I deployed my binoculars and checked the shoreline for pomarine skuas: there were none. A gang of turnstones were doing as their name suggests, turning stones to reveal hidden critters. A little further away, a herring gull delved into a rockpool and plucked out a shore crab the size of a small skinny hand. The crab was dropped on its back and the gull began to tear off its legs. When the poor crab was down to just three twitching appendages, I was tempted to shout, 'Oh, just put the bloody crab out of its misery!' The gull then began hammering its beak into the crab's chest. I couldn't endure watching the carnage any longer and turned away.

Half an hour later there was a sudden rush of enthusiastic pointing by the people on the shore. My heart raised for a second, until I saw the source of their excitement. Myself and some old wiser observers knew the score. This was pure Scotch mist. I didn't want to be the one to pour cold water on their moment, but the approaching dorsal fins were not those of bottlenose dolphins.

The lady returned from her ciggie break, stood next to me and sighed, 'Those won't put on a performance.'

Six harbour porpoises approached in a spinning rotating row before disappearing under the surface. Thirty seconds later, they reappeared and advanced. This movement continued as they headed down the middle of the Moray Firth towards the people on the shore who had their cameras primed and ready to capture some acrobatics. The porpoises continued past and departed without fuss. The crowd were underwhelmed.

A small girl moaned to her Dad, 'Was that it?'

I felt her pain.

I waited another hour with only a guillemot in winter plumage to keep my boredom at bay. It paddled on top of the water, took a breath and submerged on an underwater hunt. After twenty minutes viewing the guillemot's progress, I started to wonder whether this wasn't an adult in winter plumage, but a juvenile – because it was rubbish at fishing. I trudged back to the car and stopped as a large flock of starlings swirled around the lighthouse. I gave the flat undisturbed seascape a final glance before once again leaving Chanonry Point unfulfilled.

Fortunately, there was a Plan B. I went to Cromarty, booked myself on the next dolphin-watching outing and an hour later I was bouncing over the waves on a rib speedboat. The tour leader spoke in a beautiful soft Scottish accent. She highlighted all the safety features and I found myself listening more to the melody of her charming voice than the content. In the end I only picked up on the fact that the sea was very cold, so it'd be a mistake to fall in. I took heed.

The sky was pale grey and the sea a darker grey. I turned on my camera and started to film, just in case a dolphin crept up from nowhere. The rib bounced and rocked, which caused the camera to lurch, so when I reviewed the footage later it made me feel seasick. We continued in a lunging movement, I filmed the bounding grey sky and waves, while the man beside me took several photographs. We both had a lot of deleting to do later.

Less than thirty minutes into the tour, the guide called out, 'There's one!' Everyone's heads shot upwards and peered around like meerkats on high-alert. Within seconds everybody faced the same direction. After so many years, I eventually saw my very first bottlenose dolphin and shortly afterwards my second. I was tempted to jump out of my seat and cheer, but managed to restrain my exhilaration.

The two robust dolphins swam side by side, while our rib moved a safe distance adjacent to their flanks. The guide recognised one of the pair due to its dorsal fin markings; a similar process is used to identify basking sharks in Manx waters. Sadly, I had difficulty hearing the guide when she said the dolphin's name, I think it may have been Hoolie and he and his partner, were a dark shade of grey, similar to the scenery, but they gave me a fuzzy warm glow inside. The most striking thing about the pair was their size – they were big. I was brought up watching *Flipper*, a much smaller warm water variant of this species. The Moray Firth ecotypes protect themselves against the cold North Sea with insulating blubber, which gives them considerable bulk. We viewed the dolphins for fifteen minutes as they roamed through the choppy waters. They progressed without acrobatics; but they didn't need to put on a show, it was simply a privilege to witness these animals behaving naturally. The other travellers displayed a mass of smiles; that was the dolphin effect. You never get the same reaction when people see pigeons.

The boat returned to shore and I drove back to Aviemore a very happy man. I contemplated revisiting Chanonry Point on the journey back. The tide would be coming in now, but I decided to save my third disappointing visit for another holiday.

That evening in the pub I chatted with a local and mentioned, 'I saw dolphins today.'

'Oh, where was that?'

'First I went to Charrony….. Chuninry Point?'

'Chanonry Point.'

'Yes, but none were there, so I went to Cromarty and saw them from a boat.'

'You don't have problems saying Cromarty.'
'I only struggle saying Chardonorory.'
He corrected me again; 'Chanonry.'
I shrugged dismissively.

****

The day after, I drove to Cairngorm Mountain and travelled to the summit using the funicular railway. There was an option to climb up by foot, but Cairngorm is one of Scotland's highest mountains and I'm out of shape and lazy. The sights during the ascent were incredible and I spent most of the time with my face pressed up against the window – not least because the carriage was full. Once at the top I wanted to go out and explore; sadly the external options on the summit were restricted to a small platform area. I looked at all the fencing and felt trapped, like the wolves in the wildlife park. An information board explained the boundary fence was there to protect the mountain habitat from being damaged by tourist footfall. I can appreciate that, but still felt disgruntled. If I was the energetic sort, I could have hiked up and examined the mountain at leisure without any barriers; my lack of fitness deprived me of that experience. There were guided tours outside the perimeter, but I hadn't booked, so I jumped onto the next train down with the sad realisation I would never scout Cairngorm Mountain for ptarmigan.

I'd expected to spend longer on Cairngorm and now needed something else to fill the void. I went for a ramble, but a word of caution to walkers in Aviemore – some paths are for pedestrians, while others are for mountain bikers. I was nearly mown down by a peloton.

The moment I heard them coming I plunged into the undergrowth. The cyclists were all very cordial and greeted me as I skulked in the shrubbery.

'Thank you!'
'Afternoon.'
'Cheers.'

It was nice to know that if I had been flattened, it would've been by friendly people.

A short distance down the road there was a picnic area, I sat down, ate lunch and was soon joined by a robin. I have to concede that I'm guilty of labelling assumed genders to some species when there is little difference between the sexes. For some reason I've always given robins a male name. The resident robin in my garden is called Frank. Even though I fail to recognise sexes, I can distinguish individual personality traits. I know for a fact that Frank replaced my pal Bob two years ago (I suspect Bob was devoured by next door's cat). Frank is a timid character and not a people person, whereas Bob was chirpy and would happily come within centimetres for a juicy worm.

I miss Bob.

This Scottish robin reminded me of Bob, and he (or she!) hopped onto the table and jigged across like a spring lamb. I tempted him closer with a piece of ham from my sandwich, but he flew off before taking the offering.

A magpie immediately appeared in a nearby tree and summoned her partner with a cackling call. He joined her and they swayed together on a flimsy branch, before she glided onto the ground while he stayed above as lookout. Mountain bikers rattled past and the magpies screeched and both flew away. I've always considered magpies' wings to be inefficient during take-off, they seem to do a lot more flapping than other birds their size. I suspect any extra energy they expend is compensated by their intelligence and sneakiness.

I finished lunch and was ready to leave when out of the corner of my eye I spotted some fast movement. It was a female sparrowhawk; I was certain of her sex because females are much larger than males. The disparity in size allows them to tackle different prey and avoids direct competition between partners. She streaked beside the hedgerow, lifted on tilted wings and carved through a gap in the vegetation. A well-practised manoeuvre. After she vanished there was a warning call, a high-pitched sorrowful sound like an old gate hinge in need of oiling, 'Tsssseeeee,' then a four second pause, 'Tssseeeeeee.' I searched and eventually saw my robin in the shadow of a blackthorn bush, safely out of danger of any passing hawks. He emitted another, 'Tssseeeeeee.'

I turned to him and said, 'It's a bit late now Bob.'

He ignored me and responded with a further, 'Tssseeeeeee.'

An area of farmland was my next stop and a murder of crows crossed at speed into a neighbouring field. I paused by a gap and looked across the expanse of stubble. There is a country phrase about how to distinguish a solitary carrion crow from gregarious rooks, which goes something like,

'A crow in a crowd is a rook, and a rook on its own is a crow'. The saying was well illustrated here; the most numerous birds foraging amongst the stubble were rooks, while in a tree there was a billy-no-mates carrion crow. I have occasionally observed aggregations of carrion crows during autumn but within minutes they have a noisy bust up and go their separate ways. It's as though they decide to give communal life a try each year, but soon realise they don't enjoy one another's company. My dad used to say something similar after family gatherings at Christmas.

At the far end of the field some objects were also reminiscent of my dad. When I was a young boy we passed a field of stubble containing several large black plastic cylindrical objects, each the size of my mum's mini car. I'd never seen them before and asked what they were. Instead of telling me the truth, that they were baleage and filled with damp hay, my dad with a deadpan expression said, 'They are cow eggs.'

Months later we passed the same field, the baleage had been removed and the field was full of cows.

I shouted with excitement, 'The cows have hatched!'

My dad belatedly confessed the truth. It was an important lesson to learn, that adults are prone to telling children a load of tosh. However, in my adult life, I have taken on the responsibility of continuing my dad's fine tradition.

I scanned the field of stubble and baleage, and noticed amongst the rooks there were also jackdaws, both species teaming up together during a time of plenty. A few jackdaws were acrobatically spiralling in the breeze. One particularly agile bird performed a barrel roll stunt and another flipped backwards. Was this evidence of birds having fun or simply learning new flight skills?

The crows helped denote the wind direction. At one time, I thought birds faced the oncoming wind to avert a blustery bum, but the true reason relates to their take-off. Airport runways aim towards the prevalent wind because it gives the plane wings extra lift. Birds have similar aerodynamics, so if a rook is targeted by a predator, such as a fox, it can take off quicker if it's facing the wind, rather than a bird facing the other way. This could mean the difference between escaping or being fox food. Virtually all the rooks were pointing south-westerly which indicated the wind direction.

A group of rooks were nearby and they prodded the ground with their beaks. Closer inspection using binoculars rewarded me with a new revelation about their behaviour. I'd always assumed that rooks just poked the dirt with closed beaks in a random attempt to dig up worms and insects. The beaks of all these foraging rooks were slightly ajar and this suggested something more was going on. A gaping mouth could unleash senses from the tongue and mouth (such as taste, smell and touch), plus if something tasty was uncovered, the beak was poised to snap shut quickly on its prey. It's always hugely satisfying to discover new behaviours of common species.

Later that evening I'd a booked wildlife outing with the possibility of seeing pine martens. I arrived at the meeting point before dusk and mingled with ten other guests. The guide gathered everyone together and led us through a woodland trail towards a large cabin nestled in a glade. The crowd wafted along with the strong scent of insect repellent, which reminded me that I'd forgotten to spray myself (again). The guide, as with all the Scottish guides I've ever met, was enthusiastic and knowledgeable. Amongst his general chat he recalled a spooky story from a place nearby, when one night a large black cat, the size of a leopard, crossed his path. With his deep Scottish accent, fading light and eerie rustling of the leaves, it seemed as though he was reading a horror movie script.

We entered the hide which was perfectly designed for wildlife viewing – big glass windows with lights outside illuminating the surrounding undergrowth. Night soon enveloped the glade and beyond the cabin there was only darkness. The guide explained that the nearby tree stumps and patches of grass had been liberally scattered with peanuts, to entice the local wildlife towards the lit areas. It wasn't long before a badger bounded out of the darkness and into the dining area. He immediately snuffled for peanuts; presumably he was a regular visitor and knew the score. Another badger arrived soon afterwards and sidled up to the first, they both worked in tandem across the grass. A roe deer briefly made an appearance before it was spooked by the onset of more badgers.

The badgers gradually came closer as they finished hoovering up the food on the outskirts. From inside the cabin we could see them from almost every window – I counted six. One fed so closely that when I placed my ear to the glass, I could hear the sound of peanuts being chomped. Each individual rough hair of his coat was visible and while he chewed I could see his teeth (they were big enough to tackle more challenging prey than legumes). The guide sat next to me and we talked about the badger's anatomy – large paws for digging, poor eyesight, yet good hearing and smell. He confirmed the nearest badger was a boar due to his large head and we compared his size to a nearby sow who was smaller.

From the moment we stepped into the cabin, everyone talked quietly to avoid disturbing the wildlife.

A lady whispered to the guide, 'Do the badgers know we are watching them?'

'Yes,' replied the guide, 'They know we are here.'

BANG!

The loud noise gave me a terrible fright. I turned towards the source and saw another guest; he was as clumsy as me and he'd dropped his heavy camera. The badgers didn't flinch. They were too busy tucking into their peanuts – like drunks in a pub with free nibbles.

Outside the window a field mouse peeked out of its entrance hole; it jumped out, snatched a nut and bounded back as though it was attached to elastic. I beckoned a lady nearby to join me and we both watched as the mouse repeated the action.

The evening was coming to an end, it had been a fun experience, albeit with absentee pine martens. I guess they don't share their meals with badgers. However, I thoroughly enjoyed seeing badgers at close proximity, particularly as they are absent on the Isle of Man.

Once we exited the cabin the badgers scattered into the darkness. Tomorrow I would head home too (along with my unused waterproofs, as it never rained once, plus a can of rarely-used insect repellent).

The holiday had not been dull – Dull was a village I passed through in Perthshire (twinned with Boring, Oregon – true!) but it could have been easily improved. All the problems were self-inflicted. The biggest mistake was going in September; it would have undoubtedly been better in spring or early summer. My cunning plan to dodge the crowds also meant I probably missed wildlife experiences. With more preparation I could have booked a guided tour on the top of Cairngorm or timed my arrival at Chanonry Point to coincide with the incoming tide.

I didn't see pine martens or ptarmigans, but on reflection, this trip was special for other reasons – it helped increase my understanding of common species. Wish lists and target species add interest and challenges, but the true joy of wildlife watching is achieved by engaging and appreciating **all** of nature.

Fulmars

Chapter 4

Lake District and Isle of Man (2009)

During the summer of 2009 I attended several local wildlife events. Fortunately, I live somewhere with lots of conservation charities and members willing to share their interests. One memorable event happened in August, when the Isle of Man hosted a basking shark conservation conference. Multi-national delegates attended and I had the privilege to guide them on an excursion. I was joined by Laura Hanley (a marine biologist) and our purpose was to provide local knowledge. We dropped the visitors off at Peel for a boat trip with Malcolm Kelly, but there wasn't enough space for everyone, so I stayed at the harbour and bought a crab bap from the kiosk. I chomped lunch as Malcolm's little boat headed offshore.

Through binoculars I scanned the sea and a gentleman sidled up to me and said, 'Looking for basking sharks?'

'Yep, I haven't spotted any yet.'

He smiled, 'I've just been to Niarbyl, there's lots in the bay.'

'Lots?'

'At least twenty.'

If you were counting red ants – twenty would be insignificant, but when it comes to basking sharks it was a colossal number. A big smile grew on my face – we would be driving past Niarbyl on our way back. I thanked him and waited impatiently for the boat to return.

An hour later all the delegates cheerfully disembarked and they chatted about seeing four sharks, particularly one which came close to their boat. This was all good news, because if the tip-off failed, the day was already a success. We all got into the minibus and I announced to the crowd, 'On the way back we'll visit Niarbyl.' I didn't explain why – I wanted to surprise them. It was a quick drive, we parked at the top of the headland, only a short distance away from a flat area with views across the entire bay.

Basking sharks appear at the sea's surface for food; small marine animals called zooplankton. If zooplankton gathers at greater density in deeper water, the sharks will stay submerged, because unlike dolphins they don't need to come to the surface to breathe. They are enormous beasts but can still be discreet, as witnessed by my kayaking friend Craig. While near Niarbyl, a basking shark approached him and swam nearby. He held his waterproof camera under his kayak and filmed the leviathan as it passed. Once home he reviewed the footage and realised in addition to the passing shark, unbeknown to him, two other huge sharks were lurking directly beneath his kayak. So, one shark at the surface could mean more hidden below.

Fortunately for us today the zooplankton had risen, otherwise there wouldn't have been lots of black triangular dorsal fins slicing a metre-high above the sea. You rarely see more of a basking shark from a distance, but during calm conditions at close range, you might spot their tail fin and nose breaking the surface.

I waited a moment to build suspense before shouting to the delegates, 'Sharks!'

They all ran excitedly to the promontory like a group of school children on a day out. With one sweep across the bay we counted twenty-five sharks, a remarkable and privileged vision to behold, and witnessed by the ideal audience. They were so blown away that one conservationist joked, 'Why are we so worried about protecting these sharks? There are loads here.'

We both knew that wasn't true.

The fun didn't stop there. One delegate turned to me and asked, 'Okay, we've seen lots of sharks, but I haven't spotted a single chough. I thought they were common here?'

With perfect timing, two black crows flew overhead and one made the distinctive 'Cheow!' call of a chough. It couldn't have been a better day out, with amazing wildlife and people.

Afterwards I had the opportunity to take a short break in the Lake District and combine the visit with meeting two friends. The Lake District was a place I'd visited twice before, the first occasion was in my childhood and my memories were of it constantly raining. I recall dad complaining, 'That's why there's so many bloody lakes.' We stayed in a log cabin amongst majestic conifer trees which emitted the fresh scent of pine. In the evenings I was mesmerised by the 'kewick' and 'hoohoo', of tawny owls. At the time I assumed the call was made by one owl, rather than the female doing the 'kewick' and a male replying with a 'hoohoo'. The hotel grounds included a viewing hide for a badger sett, and my dad treated me to an evening out. Sadly I was a child with a short attention span and after an hour sitting inside a cold shed staring at an empty mound of earth, boredom won the day. In the morning we met the hotel owner and he told us, 'With patience you'd have seen five badgers'. He seemed slightly smug and even at such a tender age, I was astute enough to conclude he was a git. Fortunately, I exorcised the badger hide demon last year in Aviemore.

My second visit to the Lake District was in my late teens with my friend Dylan. My Ford Cortina got a flat tyre on the M6 and we were fleeced by a motorway recovery van outside Kirkby Lonsdale. When we eventually arrived at Windemere we only had enough money to cross on the ferry. I suggested we hike around the remainder. For some reason, I thought rambling halfway round the largest lake in England would be a short stroll. The exuberance and stupidity of youth. It took three hours and because we were cleaned out by Dick Turpin's Car Recovery, we couldn't afford to shorten our journey by using one of the mockingly frequent buses.

For my tour this year, I wanted to avoid trudging around the circumference of an enormous lake or hiking up a mountain. A few relaxing rambles would be splendid. The first day I planned to explore the countryside and coast. The second day I would pick up two friends, Ian and David, and we'd go for a walk – to a pub. I had no expectations of spotting any particular wildlife, although I would visit Leighton Moss RSPB which had the possibility of bearded tits.

I drove from Liverpool docks to the Lake District, and was pleased to get off the M6 and become surrounded by magnificent green hills. The narrow roads were shrouded by overhanging trees – I would disappear under their dark canopy and emerge again in the low autumnal sun. The pleasant drive ended abruptly on a sharp corner, when an oncoming coach swept onto my side of the road. I managed to brake and swerve from its path, a frightening and unexpected shock. The second time it happened was less surprising. When it happened a third time, I became acclimatised to the possibility of being squashed by coaches on every corner.

It was evening when I arrived at Hawkshead and I immediately fell in love with the village. A beautiful location with old buildings and a friendly atmosphere. The nearby pub beer garden was dog friendly, and I sat beside a sociable chocolate Labrador. She was great company, in fact, she would rate higher than some of my friends if she got the round in occasionally and didn't eat all the crisps.

The next morning Hawkshead transformed from a peaceful idyllic village to my idea of hell. Outside the lodgings, hordes of boisterous tourists milled around souvenir shops and took photographs of obscure objects such as lampposts and front doors. I got into my car to escape, but the car park was crammed with coaches, forcing me to edge out of a narrow gap before joining a queue.

I eventually found quiet refuge beside Coniston Water. The vast scenery was incredibly pleasing; however I was unhappy that I needed to pay, particularly in an empty parking plot in the middle of nowhere.

I walked off my annoyance along a lakeside path and stopped by a large rock, which was the perfect height for sitting. The background was dominated by mountains worthy of a landscape painting, the only sound was of fresh clear water gently lapping the shoreline. Above me, people wandered over the crests of the summits, from my viewpoint they appeared like ants on a molehill. I'm sure the sights up there would've been even more impressive than mine, but I preferred my less strenuous option. It was thoroughly relaxing and tranquil, so much nicer than the daytime bedlam offered at Hawkshead. After becoming at peace with nature, I returned to the car and headed for the coast. The views en route were superb, although lacking any unfamiliar wildlife – I'd seen rabbits, starlings, house sparrows and a chaffinch.

The biggest negative so far during the journey was that all the car parks charged, which prohibited stopping at several places. I guess it was a deliberate plan by Cumbria County Council to reduce congestion and enable wannabe Lewis Hamiltons to drive their coaches over both lanes.

It was midday when I parked beneath St Bees Head – and once again paid for the pleasure. A weaving footpath climbed the red sandstone headland and halfway up, I was rewarded with views across the Irish Sea towards the Isle of Man. I've always found it satisfying to see my home from different perspectives.

Near the top of the headland a small elderly gentleman approached with a huge dog on a lead. I think it was a dog. Perhaps one of its parents was a bear. The beast was intimidating as it lumbered down the grassy path, but thankfully at close range the overgrown Alsatian was quite friendly. The owner tried to gain control, which was difficult as he was fighting both gravity and the pull of the giant creature.

I greeted the man with a 'Good morning,' while stroking the fur mound.

'Sit Roger!' said the old man in a commanding voice.

Roger didn't sit – I suspect he didn't take orders from someone half his size.

After giving up on his disobedient dog, the exasperated old man looked at me, 'Are you with the dolphin watchers?'

I was intrigued, 'No, is an event going on?'

'Yes,' he sighed, 'It's like Piccadilly Circus up there.'

After a quick chat I said farewell and trekked to the top, gazed over the wide panorama and progressed a little further to meet nine people. Piccadilly Circus from memory was busier – I suspect the old dog walker never normally encountered anyone. I had a quick chat with the dolphin watchers and asked if they'd seen anything; they replied in the negative so I continued along the clifftop path.

Fulmars glided past but all the other seabirds had departed the summer nest sites after their young fledged in July and August, so I didn't see any guillemots, razorbills or kittiwakes. Fulmar chicks take a little longer to fledge and one adult flew close enough so I could see the tube on its beak. This tube enables fulmars to drink seawater and sneeze out the salt, and this adaptation provides their seabird order name: tubenoses. This group of birds includes albatrosses which have facial similarities to fulmars, but are significantly larger.

Then there was a brief glimpse of an LBJ. When I first heard this birding phrase, I thought it might have been an acronym for something rude or an American president, although I was baffled why Lyndon B. Johnson would be hiding in a bush in Norfolk. I later found out that LBJ referred to 'little brown jobs'. This describes a small brown bird which disappears before identification. I guessed my LBJ was a pipit of either the rock or meadow variety. These two species can be identified by their legs – rocks are grey and meadows are pinkish. Pipits are nonconformists; I've observed rock pipits in meadows and meadow pipits on rocks. They have no respect for their ornithological names.

I walked for half an hour before stopping to evaluate my options. The lighthouse, which was my original intended target, was still in the distance and I considered whether I really wanted to see it close up. Further inland, people were probably struggling up the side of England's tallest mountain, Scafell Pike, but that was their choice. I decided to turn round and return along the headland.

The dolphin watchers were still about, they'd swelled to ten people, enough to surround Eros; yet still insufficient numbers to spot a dolphin. One lady was excited because she'd seen a black guillemot and pointed me in its direction. I looked through binoculars towards a little black blob nearly a mile out, but it may have been a lobster pot buoy. I chose not to be negative, kept my opinion to myself and said, 'Oh yeah, I see it.'

A further scan of the surrounding sea only rewarded me with a few gulls and more buoys. I enquired with the group about any noteworthy local insect or plant life. A lady was called closer; she was apparently the oracle for smaller things. She talked about common butterflies and beetles, before saying, 'And we have bloody crane's-bill.'

My ignorance was undoubtedly written on my face, as I was wondering whether it was a particularly unpopular plant.

Thankfully the lady presented more facts; bloody crane's-bill was a wild geranium with pinkish petals and blood-coloured veins, hence the name. She explained more about St Bees Head in her deep Lancastrian accent, 'Most of the interesting wildlife is either on the wane, finished its summer lifecycle or buggered off for winter.' I thanked her for the information, said farewell and descended the cliffside path. Halfway down I paused to glance across the sea. Then something moved in the waves. Identification is always difficult during a first brief glimpse, so further viewing was required. A minute later a harbour porpoise popped up and submerged; it was swimming north towards the dolphin-spotters. I had a dilemma. Continue my journey downwards or hike back up the cliff and tell the group about the porpoise. Ten minutes later I was in my car and driving to Whitehaven. The spotters could spot things for themselves.

At Whitehaven I strolled around the harbour and immersed myself in the refreshing sea air – which was sullied when I passed a trawler stinking of old fish. A curious moment in history happened here in 1778 during the American Revolution when a gang led by John Paul Jones attacked the British naval vessels and battlements. Apparently, some of the party decided to forego their duties and sample the harbourfront pubs, which caused the raid to be mostly unsuccessful. I checked the time and estimated that in a few hours I'd return to Hawkshead and could visit some pubs myself.

The drive back took me through Keswick and the roads beyond provided parking places without cost. The greatest pleasure was seeing farmland sympathetic to nature, unlike other places in England, which are dominated by large swathes of industrial-style agriculture. The Lake District has hedges, trees and ponds, with long lengths of stone walls from which stoats can nip out and reduce the numerous rabbits. I found a suitable layby near a footpath marker and rambled into the hills. The track followed a stone wall and I searched for stoats and whinchat; I've seen lots of stonechats back home, but whinchats have always remained elusive. Predictably, I saw a stonechat. The stonechat's name derives from its call, which sounds like two pebbles being chinked together. This particular stonechat was silent but it perfectly represented its Manx Gaelic name 'Point of the Gorse', as it balanced proudly on a gorse bush, like a small cherry on a very large Bakewell tart.

It was late afternoon and rabbits of varying sizes came out of their warrens in the fading light. Some bobbed over the hillside while others rested and chewed grass. My arrival caused a few nervous looks, twitching ears and occasionally a fleeting white fluffy bum. On my left there was a valley and above this a buzzard circled. It suddenly swooped downwards from height at a sharp angle of descent. I stopped in my tracks as the bird picked up speed, falling below my level into the valley, then its wings angled and it swept back upwards in my direction. Raptors on a hunt are often single-minded. I've had many memorable sparrowhawk experiences when they've targeted prey and ignored my presence. Likewise, nothing was going to halt this buzzard on its mission – it would be as futile as trying to block my ex-girlfriend from entering a shoe shop.

The buzzard raced up the side of the valley, over my hillside path, the climb reduced its speed and it dropped out of sight beyond the hill's ridge. A split second later a sound pierced the air, the high-pitched squeal of something being murdered. The buzzard soon reappeared; its wings beating heavily and talons grasping a small rabbit. The buzzard gave me a nonchalant glance and glided away with its meal.

I began to assess this buzzard's hunt. It must have spotted the rabbit while flying above, then used the valley to both gain speed and disguise its approach. The buzzard gambled on the fact that the rabbit wouldn't move while out of sight, and the rabbit was still there when the buzzard popped up from nowhere and pounced.

All across the hillside, rabbits scattered into their burrows – alerted by the squeal of death. This left only grazing sheep, mostly the local breed, Herdwicks. They are fine beasts; much more handsome than the scraggly mountain sheep back home on the Isle of Man. I pondered whether they tasted different.

At Grasmere the tourists were out in good numbers – this was definitely more reminiscent of Piccadilly Circus. Dozens of people queued for gingerbread while I walked to the back of the churchyard to see William Wordsworth's burial place. The rear boundary was marked by a stone wall, beyond which was the River Rothay. The sparkling river was home for a skilled hunter – a goosander. The goosander was a chestnut-headed female – adult males have black heads. She paddled and ducked her head beneath the river's surface, while people on the opposite side of the river supped tea in a café, totally oblivious to this special bird. The goosander detected a snack below and dived into the pristine waters and chased a minnow. I watched her subaquatic progress as she darted and twisted energetically in pursuit, before she bobbed back to the surface with a small fish in her serrated beak. The goosander flicked the minnow into a head-first position, her beak opened and the snack slinked down her elegant throat.

The crowds around the churchyard began to depart and this afforded some relief – until it dawned on me that their next destination could be Hawkshead. The thought caused me to sigh.

To make sure Hawkshead would be clear, I made a couple more stops and was delighted when I returned to a vision of tranquillity. In the evening I quaffed pints in the beer garden, joined by border collies and a golden retriever. Yesterday's chocolate Labrador was flirting with another man who was offering her pork scratchings. The hussy.

****

The next morning, I called into Leighton Moss RSPB, a wetland reserve dominated by acres of tall reeds. I hoped to spot bearded tits; maybe I missed them by a whisker. I did however step in some deer poo – which wasn't on the wish list. After studying the muck in my shoe grips, based on its wide coverage it probably came from the backside of a red deer.

The wall of reeds blocked most views from the path for anyone less than eight feet tall or wearing stilts (I couldn't fit stilts into my luggage). A raised platform has since been constructed, allowing average-height people such as myself to view the sights above the reeds.

I visited Morecambe but left shortly afterwards as the tide was out, leaving a featureless expanse of mud. Coastal mud contains lots of food for waders, but none were in sight today, they were probably a mile away on the distant shoreline.

My friends Ian and David were then collected from the Heysham ferry, they checked in at Hawkshead while I avoided the tourists by hiding in my room. An hour later we rambled over fields towards a pub at Barngates. The well-worn route led through glorious countryside between mature oaks and sycamores. My friends were not wildlife experts, but they took a keen interest in the local nature. They regularly asked for help to identify certain plants or passing birds in flight. With an inquisitive audience a wildlife enthusiast can become a magician, conjuring up a mysterious world unseen by others.

A jay called; it can't be described as a song; it sounds more like a cat bringing up a nasty furball. Jays are absent from the Isle of Man so none of us had sighted one for ages. Sadly, we didn't see much of this one either; shortly after coughing up, it flew off.

After an invigorating uphill trek, we arrived at the pub and soaked up the afternoon sunshine in the beer garden. At dusk we retraced our steps through the fields in fading light, as several large bats quartered the deep hedgerows. Without the aid of a bat detector I wasn't able to accurately confirm the species, but I guessed they were noctule bats based on their size and movement.

On the Isle of Man, bat watching nights are regularly organised by the Manx Bat Group. These events are great opportunities to have nocturnal adventures, armed with bat detectors and joined by knowledgeable friendly company. They have helped me identify pipistrelle, brown long-eared and Daubenton's bats. I'm fond of bats – their frenetic flight, clacking echo-locations and particularly their appetite for midges.

Before the trip to the Lake District, I attended a bat and owl event which turned out to be quite farcical. At sunset I arrived at the rendezvous point near Ballaugh and joined thirty other enthusiasts. As a guy in my mid-thirties I was considerably younger than the other attendees; this was a familiar scenario, I rarely encountered people my own age at these events.

Our guide for the evening was a local expert and he explained that a farmer had kindly given us permission to explore one of his fields. The area was special because barn owls roosted nearby, and several bat species hunted along the hedgerows. The guide had emphasised that to improve our chances we needed to be quiet and not use lights after we parked. After the briefing we drove in a convoy for a mile before bouncing up a bumpy track into a field. Once there, we were directed to park our cars in a circular formation in the centre of the field, like cowboy wagons preparing for an attack by Apaches.

Engines stopped, lights off, and we were ready for a night of wildlife spotting. The overcast sky blanketed out the moonlight and the field became pitch black. My eyes gradually acclimatised to the dark, but I still couldn't see most of the other attendees, let alone any owls. Bat detectors were handed out and once switched on, they emitted eerie crackles and clicks.

The first half an hour was quiet, without a sniff of bat or owl, and some people began to get restless and go wandering. Car doors were opened and automatic lights were cursed, folding chairs were unpacked, blankets unfurled and flasks of tea unscrewed. Behind me a male voice called, 'Did you pack the biscuits?'

From the front of the same car there was a thud and a faint groan, then a hesitant female voice said, 'Kenneth, I've tripped over.'

'Where are you?'

'At the front of the car.'

Some shuffling and wheezing. 'Ahh, there you are. You are wet.'

'I spilt tea down my leg.'

Suddenly, excitement rippled through the crowd as we all heard mechanical rasping and clicking. Somebody has detected a bat!

'Common pipistrelle,' said a lady in a hushed voice.

'They heard a pipistrelle,' whispered a guy behind.

Another lady's voice said, 'That's lovely dear,' in a tone that lacked any sort of pleasantry. 'Can you find something to dry my leg?'

Then a 'domestic' kicked off as the lady tore a strip off poor Kenneth. It may have been too dark for them to be seen, but thirty people could clearly hear their bickering.

I decided to give them space and moved towards the dark silhouette of a hedgerow. The volume dial on my bat detector was turned up in an attempt to drown out their argument with echo-locations. Ten minutes passed before I picked up a strange pattering noise further away, unlike any bat I'd heard before; my investigation revealed someone behind a tree having a pee. I returned to the cars and nearly came a cropper on several occasions. The ground was uneven because cows had recently inhabited the field and left deep holes with their muddy hooves. I stretched out my arms in preparation for tumbling forwards and managed to arrive safely back at the wagon fort.

Two gentlemen greeted me, I recognised their dark figures from previous bat-watching events, but couldn't remember their names. I have a great talent for forgetting names, usually within seconds of being introduced.

One gentleman hailed me, 'Evening, Steve.'

'Evening,' I replied. I didn't commit to a name – he might have been Tony, or Peter, or possibly Robert.

He offered me his hipflask, 'Sloe gin.'

I was driving, so politely declined and continued to search for my car.

A commotion then started at the opposite side of the wagon circle. It was difficult to understand the cause of the hubbub before the sound of a loud rumbling, 'Moooooo!'

Some cattle had infiltrated the field, perhaps they'd been hiding in a corner, or maybe a gate had been accidentally left open. The cows gradually surrounded the circle of cars. I suspect they were lured by the smell of hot malty drinks and homemade cakes. The posh voice of a gentleman spoke out in the dark, 'Penelope, we appear to have a cow.'

I returned to my car which had become a meeting point for three Friesians. Torches were switched on and people tried to ward off the bovine insurgents with waving arms and shouts. The cows seemed unfazed and instead the humans retreated, some biscuits were dropped and folding chairs knocked over. Behind me a cow rubbed herself against a Range Rover and set off its car alarm, which was one of those obnoxious inventions combining whistles, honks and flashing lights. The cow was startled and this set off a mini stampede.

'Kenneth, where are you?' called a lady's voice.

'Where did he go?' asked another voice.

'I'm worried he may have been taken by the cows.'

To assist the search, headlights were turned on and the field was lit so brightly, it hurt my eyes. They successfully illuminated Kenneth as he walked back from the trees. I suspect he was the person having a pee. After the stampede settled, our guide gathered everybody together and suggested we call it a night. Apparently, a floodlit field, booming car alarms and a cattle stampede weren't conducive for bats nor owls. I may have not seen any wildlife, but I smiled all the way home.

The bat-watching evening in the Lake District was not as eventful, although I did see some bats. We downed a couple of beers in Hawkshead, I introduced Ian and David to some of my favourite dogs, and we fed them pork scratchings before retiring merry.

****

The next morning David didn't rise: apparently the previous day's drinking pace was more than he could stomach. I said farewell to Ian before departing and then immediately ran into traffic coming in the opposite direction.

Just outside Hawkshead a red squirrel scampered across the road and this caused a coach laden with tourists to judder to a halt. If a Lake District coach driver flattens a Beatrix Potter character, they fail to get five-star reviews. The squirrel stopped in the middle of the road and the coach's windows filled with cameras, the occupants taking photos of Squirrel Nutkin. Nutkin got bored of being a celebrity and pegged into a nearby tree.

On the motorway I trailed behind a slow-moving coach (based on it sticking to a single lane, it wasn't from the Lake District), then I passed Kirkby Lonsdale without needing the 'help' of roadside recovery. I glanced at my watch; there was plenty of time before the ferry departed Liverpool so I visited Martin Mere, a Wildfowl and Wetlands Trust reserve, part wild and part enclosure for endangered wildfowl. I was surprised to see a male eider duck in one of the ponds, as they are seabirds rather than a freshwater species; perhaps it was a rescue animal. Areas named 'marsh harrier' and 'kingfisher' provided neither species. In another hide I sat beside a family and helped them identify the difference between a coot (white beak) and a moorhen (red beak).

The boy retorted, 'Which would win in a fight?'

I replied diplomatically based on the young audience, 'I think they would try and avoid fighting; they could hurt each other.'

His father joined the conversation, 'What if they'd both been drinking and were up for a scrap?'

That was the sort of question my dad would have asked and it made me smile.

Even though I discovered no new wildlife at Martin Mere, I enjoyed the reserve and appreciated seeing families having a fun day out. Anything which helps future generations enjoy nature has got to be good.

****

As my ferry departed for home, I reflected on the break. You can go to the countryside for wildlife and also beautiful scenery – for me the Lake District is a great example of the latter. Cumbria celebrates traditional agriculture, mountains, lakes and mature woodlands. Alas, some areas are commercialised, but still at its core is a rural idyll among natural surroundings.

I didn't experience the same sense of wilderness which pleased me so greatly in Scotland. My personal preference is to see nature in the raw, but lots of my friends love Cumbria and are regular visitors – so it works for them. They get kicks out of the long hikes and scaling mountains for the reward of spectacular views.

Lots of interesting wildlife behaviour was seen; the hunting buzzard, fishing goosander and a fleeting red squirrel were all special. Plus a porpoise and the noctule bats. I only scraped the surface of a large region during a short stay – so I really shouldn't expect more. I had failed to learn my lessons from Cairngorms and repeated the same mistake of travelling in September, and once again I was guilty of insufficient planning. I would make amends on my next holiday.

Over the subsequent twelve months I investigated more nature than at any other time in my life. I embarked on the production of a wildlife film covering all seasons on the Isle of Man and spent most days within twenty miles of my house seeking nature. The wildlife filming process was deeply rewarding, although the meagre budget prevented a production to the standards of a David Attenborough documentary. I was fortunate to film some exceptional wildlife – my favourites were eighty bottlenose dolphins passing Douglas (doing the acrobatic things which they should have been doing at Chanonry Point) and an Arctic skua chasing a Sandwich tern at the Ayres. The most intriguing thing was much smaller – a colony of andrena, a species of mining bee. It was only with the help of a local expert that I was able to understand their remarkable life cycle. The andrena burrow into the side of a bank of earth, and try to avoid predatory green tiger beetles on the ground and spiders lurking in some chambers. They also fend off cuckoo bees which, like their feathered namesakes, try and lay their eggs in the nests of others. If a cuckoo bee is successful in its endeavours, their young will hatch and devour the andrena larvae. I spent a lot of time in the company of these bees, fully aware that in previous years I'd walked straight past this patch of earth, oblivious to the life and death struggles around my feet. It was another reminder of how a knowledge of nature can make your world a more stimulating place.

Gannet

Chapter 5

Shetland –
Lerwick and Brae (2010)

This holiday would be an adventure in the furthest and wildest region of the British Isles I'd ever visited – an exciting prospect. I received a helpful pack of information from the Shetland tourist board, which included a map of recommended walks. I circled places with potential for wildlife spotting and there were lots. The research also involved watching a documentary about Shetland featuring Gordon Buchanan, and before you start to wonder, I'm not stalking him. He encountered otters, minke whales and lots of seabirds; I hoped to see some of those.

Based on earlier experience, Scotland was in its prime during late spring and early summer, so I booked the first week of June. It was a six-night vacation, spread across Shetland's mainland. I'd have two nights in a cheap guesthouse in Lerwick, two in a posh hotel up in Brae and finally a couple of nights down south in Sumburgh. I had three items on my wish list – to see my first great skua, observe a large nesting colony of gannets and have a close encounter with a puffin. On the Isle of Man, I've seen many gannets and the occasional puffin, but they've always been offshore and relatively distant; I yearned for close intimate experiences. Great skuas, or bonxies as they're also known, are a species that excite me; they are depicted as aggressive bolshy creatures and I'm fond of birds with attitude. Apparently, they dive-bomb anyone approaching their nests and by luck it was the start of their nesting season. I didn't want to disturb them, but if I happened to be strolling along a path, minding my own business and got attacked by a large skua, then that would be great. I told friends about this and they thought I was bonkers.

A small plane took me into Sumburgh, the security process was quickly passed and I jumped into a taxi. The driver was a friendly elderly gent, he welcomed me to Shetland and asked what I planned to see. I replied, 'I'm wildlife watching, hopefully I might spot some whales and puffins.'

He smiled and immediately took the next left, 'Puffins are easily achieved.' The taxi climbed a steep hill towards a lighthouse signposted 'Sumburgh Head' and we parked at the top. The driver got out and encouraged me towards a stone wall. I peered over the wall and just on the other side, only two metres away; a puffin! We exchanged looks – I think I was the most surprised out of the two of us. I'd been on Shetland for twenty minutes and it was already awesome. I explained to the driver I was staying at Sumburgh at the end of my trip, so I'd revisit here later, and we continued north to Lerwick.

As we travelled, the side-window presented views of barren moorland and weather-beaten livestock. The driver pointed out places of interest on the route, his accent distinctly different to other folks I'd met in Scotland – he sounded slightly Scandinavian. This was due to the island's strong Viking heritage, which they celebrate each January during their Up Helly Ya festival (a good excuse to dress up as Vikings, carry flaming torches and drink heavily).

We passed a signpost for St Ninians Isle and the driver gushed about its beauty, so I made a mental note to include that in my future itinerary. Every area he mentioned was given a glowing review but when I named my Lerwick guesthouse a series of deep ridges appeared on his brow which was slightly ominous. He changed the conversation to Lerwick's pubs, as he correctly deduced I'd require that information.

I deliberately wanted to avoid making a trite comment about the lack of trees on Shetland; I'm sure holidaymakers say that all the time and it must get annoying. I get the same from strangers when I say my name is Steve Wright (identical to a famous BBC radio DJ), which always prompts the catchphrase reply, 'Steve Wright in the afternoon!'

I quickly came up with something relating to Shetland which steered well clear of the absent trees. It was only after it was blurted out, I realised my alternative was equally daft, 'There's lots of Shetland ponies...'

The driver politely declined to comment and nodded. Perhaps he was impressed that this particular visitor didn't ask about trees. I clung to that hope.

In short time we arrived on the outskirts of Lerwick and parked beside my guesthouse. I gave the driver the fare and offered him a richly deserved tip; he refused to accept it, instead he wished me a pleasant holiday and bid me farewell. He was a very special gentleman.

I checked into the guesthouse and was immediately escorted next door. I wouldn't be in the main building, the annex was probably for trouble makers; fair enough. I trudged up a flight of stairs and met a couple of big hairy guys wearing yellow raincoats coming in the opposite direction. I squeezed past and found my room, forced the key into the lock and the door shuddered open. It was very pokey – I've entered bigger wardrobes. That's what you get for choosing 'budget'.

I showered, changed and hit the town. A fish and chip shop was soon discovered, dinner bought and I decided to eat outside as it was a pleasant evening. Benches on the quayside provided views of the ferry heading towards Bressay Island. An audience of herring gulls gradually amassed, inspecting my every move as I devoured my fish supper. Suddenly the crowd kicked off as two gulls interlocked their beaks and fought, screeching and howling. It was a brutal contest, both participants seemingly intent on murdering each other. I stood up and strode towards the fighters in order to break them up.

Then the other spectating gulls turned and stared at my dinner, left unprotected on the bench. Were the brawling gulls just a clever decoy to lure me from my chips? Are the local gulls that devious? I quickly scampered back, wrapped up the food, put it under my arm and once again approached the duelists. They'd been going at it for nearly a minute and the lower bill of one was yanked and it shrieked. They were completely oblivious to me as I towered above them but eventually they looked up and with startled expressions, relinquished their grip, split up in an angry feathery flourish and flew off. If this was how violent the gulls were, what were the great skuas going to be like? I began to wonder whether I still fancied being attacked by one.

I finished my meal and left a disappointed crowd of remaining gulls, who naively anticipated leftovers: I was brought up to clean my plate.

The harbour road narrowed into an alleyway which funnelled the wind, before an opening appeared for a small sheltered harbour. Above the docked boats, an Arctic tern circled. They are delicate and pretty, but feisty birds… similar to Tinkerbell after eight gins. The tern completed a couple of laps around the harbour before it swooped down onto the sea's surface. The dive was fast, it pushed its head underwater up to its shoulders, recoiled and rapidly lifted into the air. The movement was swift, like somebody dipping their toe into a bath to test the temperature. The tern flew off with a sand eel wagging in its beak. The catch wasn't scoffed immediately, so it must have been returning to a nest to feed a chick. It was a pleasing and special encounter – in most towns you only see crusty-toed pigeons.

A large old hotel dominated one street corner and I went in for a pint. A couple of elderly men propped up the bar while putting the world to rights. After eavesdropping for a few minutes, I reckoned their perfect utopian society would lack certain neighbours, the borough council and a selection of family members. I didn't feel the urge to join in their conversation, so finished my pint and returned to the B&B.

Once back in the room I turned on the TV, the volume wasn't loud but immediately there was a thundering bang as somebody hit the dividing wall to my room. The partition between neighbours appeared to be the thickness of a couple of sheets of plasterboard. I turned off the TV straightaway. Nobody wants to antagonise a sleep-deprived fisherman. I decided to have an early night and after a busy day was soon asleep.

My consideration towards my neighbours was not reciprocated. At 5.30am I was awoken by everybody else in the block. Slamming doors, raised voices, people searching for lost shoes, then loud stomps down the stairway as they each left. I returned to sleep just before the alarm went off at 8am. I stirred slowly, sat on the end of the bed and noticed something on the back of the door which I'd previously missed. I was surprised I'd overlooked anything in such a confined space. The item of interest was a 'No Smoking' sign which depicted a local auk with a cigarette in its mouth and the message, 'No Puffin'.

****

This morning's scheduled event was a seabird-watching boat trip around the coast of the islands Bressay and Noss. In preparation for a rough sea, I ate a tactically light breakfast. After a leisurely walk to the harbour I met the tour guide. We chatted briefly about the boat trip and he assured me I'd have an excellent voyage and see amazing wildlife. I provide wildlife tours on the Isle of Man and during my welcome talks I underplay everyone's chances of seeing anything. The last thing I want is to have guests with high expectations which subsequently become quashed.

The Shetland tour guide's confidence proved to be well founded.

I boarded the boat and positioned myself on the top deck with two other tourists, while the remaining six passengers stayed below on the comfy seats. We embarked over choppy waters, the swell lifted and dropped the boat and I felt my digestive system objecting. I took a deep breath of sea air and looked over the side – if something did come up, I wanted it to have a clear point of exit. Thankfully the swell lessened once we reached Bressay's southern coast.

The first wildlife seen were lined along a low steep headland – over a hundred nesting guillemots. Their shrill calls always evoke for me a feeling of early summer, and it's saddening at the end of July when the guillemots depart their nests, swim offshore with their young, and the cliffs fall silent. Shelves of rocks jutted from the base of the headland and we drifted past harbour seals lazing in the morning sun, who glared intently at us as we passed. So far so good.

Suddenly it got even better. I saw my very first great skua. It drifted up behind and was only spotted once it was above my head. It lacked the graceful shape of an Arctic skua, in fact, I thought it looked a bit dumpy (I realise me saying that is like a hippopotamus calling a pig 'Fatty'). Great skuas have brown plumage with white patches on their wings, and these flapped gently as it glided. I was so excited at seeing my first great skua I announced it to couple beside me – they were both blasé. I suspect it wasn't their first encounter. The guy sneered in the bird's direction – perhaps he'd recently been beaten up by one and was still resentful.

The boat pursued the great skua around the headland and as we turned, we accessed a huge cove resembling the inside of an enormous amphitheatre. It was like entering the Colosseum packed to the rafters with birds in countless number. Sight was the first overwhelming sense, then the warmth of the sun's heat captured within the cove, then came the smell. The temperature and odour were comparable to sticking your nose into an oven filled with fish and camembert. I managed to hold onto my breakfast and after a couple of minutes, I acclimatised to the aroma.

Thousands of gannets greeted us, mostly on the cliffs with others spiralling above. The boat's skipper maintained a running commentary on his speaker system, explaining that Bressay and Noss were home to as many as 25,000 gannets. I think most of them were there in front of me. Some of the cliffs resembled white marble, but it was sandstone rock and the whiteness was caused by gannet poo. The towering cliffs were stratified with smelly white bands and crowded with birds; it was like being beneath a block of flats with dodgy plumbing. The headland echoed with the reverberating sound of 'Carrr carrr carrr carrrr'. In amongst the cacophony of gannets came the occasional outburst from kittiwakes. The surging noise bombarded my ears. The squawking of all the birds wasn't as melodic as a dawn chorus, but it held greater power (like comparing a symphony orchestra to a heavy metal band).

We passed alongside a vertical cliff and overlooked a low ledge of gannets, where the birds could be viewed at close range. I was impressed, they were stunners, forward-facing blue eyes, sturdy bills, golden heads and their remaining plumage was mostly white. One bird stretched its long neck upwards and resembled a feathered llama. A crowd of gannets sat on poorly constructed nests of twigs and seaweed. No eggs were visible – we were probably a week too early. Pairs mutually preened; necks as slender as snakes, curving together and beaks tickling conjointly at their partner's collars; as though they were delivering little kisses. Other gannets pointed their heads to the sky and bill tapped like sword-fighting musketeers. All was not affection; some birds squabbled with their neighbours, thrusting their bills forwards in an attempt to stab their rivals.

The noise of 'Carr, carr, carr, carrrr,' became louder as we floated closer to the cliffs. Hundreds of gannets swirled on their long wings, like an airshow of manned gliders. The gannets with nests on the higher shelves peered down from their penthouse pads. The value of the prime real estate was illustrated when one bird backed-up and fired a stream of poop down onto the unfortunate gannets beneath. Something white then fell in my direction, I quickly ducked from its path and was mightily relieved when I saw it was a passing feather.

A flock of juvenile gannets bobbed on the water, their grey plumage scruffier than their flashy parents. As our boat approached, they gradually took to the air, long wings clattering over the water, feet and wingtips breaking the surface. Around the next corner there were more gannets! How many tons of fish do they collectively consume each day, and how much poop does this generate? That's a statistic I could probably live without knowing.

The boat aimed north and we left the gannets behind, gradually drifting away from the energy, noise and smell. I'd never experienced such a multi-sensory wildlife event and was still buzzing when we disembarked at Lerwick, an incredible place which I'd recommend to anyone visiting Shetland during summer. If you turn up in October you'll possibly only get a faint lingering smell.

During the afternoon I explored the local museum but had a sudden urge to get back outdoors again and see more of the coast. My free map promoted several footpaths nearby. I picked one place, left the museum and was soon in a taxi heading west to Hamnavoe. Hamnavoe was reached by crossing the Burra Bridge but if I'd visited before 1971, a boat would have been required. Hamnavoe was a place of peaceful seclusion with pretty beaches and grassy low headlands where I could sit and admire the coast (and eat a chocolate bar). The hour-long circular walk was in solitude, with no people, but sadly no otters or cetaceans either. Afterwards I started back towards Lerwick, a route of approximately ten miles. It was manageable – there wasn't any rush and it wouldn't get dark until after midnight.

But all thoughts of an energetic hike back were dismissed when I found a bus shelter and decided public transport might be a nicer way to travel. No timetable was available inside but hopefully a bus would come past soon. A short time later I was delighted to see one approach. As it neared,

I read the banner on the front – 'NOT IN SERVICE'. I stood outside the shelter and forlornly watched it go by. A short distance further the bus slowed and stopped. I ran to the doors and the driver pressed a button and the doors hissed as they opened, 'Where are you going?' he asked.

'Lerwick.'

'Hop in then.' I went for my wallet. He shook his head, 'You don't need to pay, I'm returning to the depot.'

'Thank you very much!' I chirped gratefully.

The world's best bus and taxi drivers are employed in Shetland.

That evening, after a Chinese dinner (admittedly not traditional Scottish fare), I had a couple of pints in a pub while participating in a quiz. I did okay as a one-man team called 'Billy no mates at the bar' and finished one point behind a group of six sat behind; they appeared to be more intent on heckling the quiz master than posting a competitive score. Afterwards I joined them for a couple more drinks. They were all locals and a blonde lady in the group was intrigued by my choice of Shetland as a holiday destination. She lent closer, 'Why on earth would you choose to spend a week on Shetland?'

'The fresh air, wildlife, beautiful coastlines, miles of footpaths,' I took a glug of drink, 'And the beer isn't bad.'

She wasn't convinced, 'Don't you crave a warm country, where you can drink cheap booze, go nightclubbing and swim in the sea without getting hypothermia?'

'I'm not a fan of places with lots of people. Plus, hot weather makes me feel uncomfortable and sweaty.'

She sat back proudly, 'We're going to Majorca next month. I'm going to lie by a swimming pool and get some colour on my skin which isn't windburn.'

They were a friendly bunch and it turned out to be a late one. I left before them, wandered back to the guesthouse and absorbed the atmosphere of the Shetland midsummer evening; known locally as the 'simmer dim'. The 11pm gloom was similar to an overcast day. The narrow lanes felt eerie, reminiscent of when nature fell silent during the partial solar eclipse in 1999.

Once back in the confines of my room, I crept quietly inside and slipped into bed without touching the TV (to avoid disturbing my cantankerous neighbour). It was a while before I settled as I was fully aware it was still light outside, before finally managing a good night's sleep. That was until everybody else woke me again at 5:30am. I comforted myself that it'd be the last time they'd do this and after the final person thundered down the stairs, I drifted back to sleep until 9am.

****

I was collecting a hire-car at midday, which allowed time for a walk around Lerwick. 'Wick' in a Shetland place name means 'bay', the 'Ler' means mud. It didn't seem particularly muddy along the southern coast footpath. I followed a low stone wall which terminated at a viewing point. Last night one of the quiz team recommended this as a place to see orca, but I'm not sure why I listened to his advice, he'd drunk a lot of whiskey. After seeing several gulls (and no orcas), I took a leisurely stroll back to the harbour, collected the hire car, returned to the guesthouse and checked-out. I went upstairs to collect my luggage and just before entering the room, I noticed the door to my neighbour's was open.

A petite girl with a round smiley face bobbed out of her doorway and greeted me in a soft Scottish accent, 'Good morning.'

I replied with a friendly, 'Morning.'

She grinned before she closed her door. She wasn't who I expected as my wall-thumping neighbour, I'd always imagined a huge hairy fisherman with anger issues.

From Lerwick I headed north to spend two days at Brae. Halfway along the main road – which was practically the only route north – I passed a sloping field with a loch below. In my peripheral vision, a splash was followed by something dark moving under the water. I decided to investigate further, parked and walked to the shore. Perhaps it was an otter, a red-throated diver or maybe a sea-monster. I waited and watched the loch. As a wildlife enthusiast it is important to examine anything which has potential interest. It does pay off sometimes. But not on this occasion.

I passed through Brae without stopping; I would check-in at the end of the day. There were three sites to visit beforehand: Esha Ness, Hillswick and North Roe. I pulled into a layby along the superb coastline at Mavis Grind. On the right the North Sea gently lapped the shore, while on the left the pulsating Atlantic smashed against the rocks. If I was going to be on a boat today, I'd prefer to sail the North Sea. It was a beautiful venue and I scanned the whole area – it was recommended in my tourist literature as a place to see otters, but I think they 'must have lied' about the 'mustelids'. I usually try to refrain from mustelid puns; they are stoately unnecessary and weasely avoided.

The next destination was a steep headland on the western point of the mainland called Esha Ness. When I stepped out of the car, I noticed one significant thing – it was unbelievably windy. I faced into the teeth of the storm, it slapped my jowls, hurt my eyes and caused tears to run down my cheeks. I hadn't considered the day windy until arriving here, there was only a stiff breeze at Mavis Grind. The beating wind and crashing waves soon became invigorating. This was raw Shetland and I loved this untamed bleak environment much more than any manicured landscape. In the same way I also find women with expensive clothing and sports cars less attractive than those with unkempt hair who drive old bangers.

Esha Ness's only signs of humanity were a rust-stained lighthouse, a tarmacked track and some people in the distance being bullied by the wind. One of the guys lost his hat and it took a dash for freedom with him in pursuit. On two opportunities he got close, bent down and was centimetres from retrieving his headwear, before it blew from his grasp. Eventually he trapped it under a stamping foot and placed the squashed hat firmly back on his head.

I felt released from the modern world and at peace with nature in this extreme location. I stood on the precipice of a cliff as gusts whipped off the Atlantic into my chest and made me gasp for breath. I followed the cliff and strolled across the rugged edge as the sea pounded beneath. The dark rocks were the colour of oxidised blood, a foreboding barrier at the end of the civilised world. During previous storms, the sea had torn chunks from the cliffs and hurled gnarly boulders the size of telephone boxes inland. It was like a giant's rockery. Wind battered my face and I stared into the tumultuous waves as they crashed through caverns and arches. I am okay with heights, but if the wind had been on my back shoving me closer to the brink, it would have been uncomfortable. Mercifully it pushed me away from danger.

The only wildlife to be seen on the low-grazed turf was a pipit being buffered by the wind; it scampered diagonally, its final destination apparently outside of its control. Along the cliff edge the gusts intermittently propelled fulmars past at high-speed, while inland a lone red-throated diver sought refuge in a sheltered pool. Back at the car, I fought with the wind to close the door, sat down inside and gasped. No longer did the wind force itself down my throat or pound my chest; it was the first time in half an hour that I'd managed to breathe without impediment. I felt charged with adrenalin, then I sensed hunger. I checked the time. My stomach was right, I'd missed lunch!

I drove to Hillswick and found a secluded coastal pub, the exterior resembling *Psycho's* Bates Motel, but inside it was friendly and welcoming. I had a substantial late lunch and enjoyed the traditional interior – far too many pubs have been transformed into blandness due to modernisation. I chatted with the two barmaids and mentioned I was about to hike around the Hillswick peninsular and they sang its praises.

One of the ladies added, 'You cannot accompany the tour guide today, because the sheep are out.'

I was bemused, 'Why would sheep hinder a tour guide?'

She explained, 'A border collie guides people along the route, but she's not allowed out until after the lambing season.'

The other barmaid chipped in, 'She's got a badge on her collar to say she's our official guide.'

I bid them farewell, headed out and immediately saw a border collie waiting at the roadside. I approached her to give her a pat, but she was wary of strangers and kept a metre away. The dog trailed in my shadow as we walked down the road before I stopped beside a signpost for the footpath. The dog nestled herself into the corner of the gate, urging me to open it and let her through. I climbed over the stile, looked down and gave her an apologetic, 'Sorry,' and left her trapped outside. The expression on her face was one of umbrage.

I ambled across the fields and followed the path as it hugged the coast. I was surprised it wasn't particularly windy, Esha Ness must have its own microclimate, which is a hurricane. Some people admire cityscapes and the architectural achievements of men; in my eyes they are always surpassed by natural terrain. Hillswick was manufactured over millennia, a result of colliding continents, glaciers and pounding waves, colonised by a living community of plants and creatures. You can keep your Gherkin, Cheesegrater and Shard, I prefer Shetland's offshore rocky towers, standing proudly against the raging Atlantic.

The Hillswick Ness circular was wonderful, I could understand why it was such a popular choice for the collie. All the lambs were now a good size so perhaps she could return soon and scamper the paths. Shetland seemed blessed with miles of accessible coastline and well-defined footpaths although on this occasion I found myself travelling down a gully and nearly lost my shoe in a sticky marsh. I suspect the official tour guide would have led me along a better path.

On the way back to the car there were no signs of the dog, although something else was visible on the horizon – the sky was filled with dark clouds the colour of charcoal. Hopefully time remained before the clouds unleashed their contents. It took thirty minutes to get up to North Roe. I abandoned the car in a small parking area and trudged up a gravel track. The weather turned gloomy and drizzle began to fall, I pressed on but the rain thickened and showed no signs of abating so I was forced to turn around and jog back (I don't have the physique to run far) and managed to get into the car before getting completely soaked. The day's explorations had undoubtedly concluded.

On the drive back to Brae, a pedestrian on the roadside saw me and stuck out his thumb. The weather was awful and I remembered I'd benefitted from the kindness of other Shetland drivers during my visit, so decided to pass on their generosity to this hitchhiker. I parked and waited for him to catch up. Even though it was raining heavily he appeared to be in no hurry. When he belatedly reached the car, he yanked the door open and sat inside with a plonk. He shuffled in his seat and covered me with water then complained about the weather. It took a while for his moaning to cease before I could ask, 'Where are you headed?'

'Brae,' he stated in his antipodean accent.

I never tried guessing which country – I've speculated in the past, got it wrong and suffered the consequences.

His conversation revolved around several themes, each concerning his many irks and grievances. People in power, the dollar to pound exchange rate, his breakfast, bus times and the holes in his walking boots were all sources of complaint. People have warned me that hitchhikers are dangerous but this guy was deadly: deadly boring. I tried to change the subject and asked if he'd seen much wildlife and was bombarded by locations in the world where the wildlife was better. I asked about puffins and got, 'Puffins, puffins? I've seen albatross – that's what you call a proper seabird.'

I started to wonder how long before Brae…

He then banged on about how frigatebirds were superior to skuas. From the varied species he listed off, he was definitely a globetrotter. I suspect if he stayed in one place too long, he'd be dragged by locals to a Wicker Man. I needed to divert him from animal one-upmanship so I asked where he planned to explore tomorrow (as I intended to avoid those places).

'I'm going to Esha Ness and Mavis Grind,' he replied.

First, I was relieved that he wasn't travelling to my planned destination in Unst, and then I conjured up a ruse which would've made my dad proud. I said, 'Mavis Grind, they named that after a woman who lived there, she was a prostitute.'

This halted him in his tracks and he gasped, 'Really, a prossie, you are jokin?'

'I read it in my guidebook.'

'Mavis Grind?'

'Yep, it was some time ago; Mavis isn't there anymore,' I confidently confirmed, while managing to retain a straight face.

'Well, I never knew that.'

The respite was brief – he started bitching about modern pop music.

I decided to blank him out for the rest of the journey and concentrate on driving. I put my foot on the accelerator in an urge to reach Brae quicker and deliver this problem package. When we entered the town outskirts I asked where he was staying while sidestepping naming my accommodation. I didn't want him popping in for a one-sided whiney chat later. He pointed me to a housing estate and stated, 'I'm just getting my bag, then drop me off at the café in town.'

I have friends who complain about their teenage children treating them as a taxi service. I had that same feeling, but at least my friends have parental obligations. We reached the house where his bag was located and he walked slowly to the front door; as though my time wasn't precious. For a moment I contemplated driving off without him. In the end I decided to wait. When he returned he threw his bag onto the back seat and knocked some of my belongings into the footwell. I sighed, yet didn't comment and rushed him over to the café. He got out and gave me no thanks or acknowledgement for the lift. I watched him go indoors, presumably to share his special form of conversation with the café patrons. God bless each and every one. I felt guilty for dumping him on them, but their loss was my gain.

My hotel was a bit posh: chocolates were on the pillow (briefly) and the towels were as soft as a pile of ducklings. In the evening I finely dined in the restaurant and sat near a pair of oil industry executives. They talked loudly about money and sales, which caused me to wonder which of the boorish conversations I heard today was the most banal. Gratefully I now had a glass of red wine in my hand and that made their tedious chat more tolerable.

The whole day reminded me why I enjoy my own company so much.

Puffin

Chapter 6

Shetland – Unst and Sumburgh *(2010)*

I had a good night's sleep which was vastly improved by the absence of a 5:30am stampede. There was also a spring in my step because I was excited about the day's itinerary. I was going from one far-flung place to somewhere even more remote. Today had potential for otters, great skuas, puffins, gannets and if I was very lucky a red-necked phalarope. I would travel on two ferries, the first to Yell, the second to Unst, and apparently both ports were regular haunts for otters. I would then head to the most northerly destination in the UK; Hermaness Nature Reserve – which was renowned for seabirds and the occasional phalarope, those small elegant waders.

The drive north covered open stretches of moorland, sporadically dotted by fresh water pools and glimpses of the sea. No trees, very few houses and lots of sheep. The locals seemed vastly outnumbered by their livestock. Once high on the upland, the panorama consisted mostly of sky – it was like gazing into outer space. The first ferry trip was calm and I scanned the surroundings, sadly through no lack of trying I failed to see an otter. Yell was crossed relatively quickly before embarking on the second ferry to Unst.

After ten minutes on Unst, I came to the opinion that it was very similar to Yell, apart from Baltasound village, which contained two housing estates (there was no such equivalent of mass urbanisation on Yell). The houses were tightly packed together on a hillside – maybe huddling together for warmth in the winter, like Antarctic colonies of emperor penguins. As the road led further north it narrowed and twisted, elevated into hills, undulated and just as it petered out, some parking. I'd arrived at Hermaness. I stepped outside and was invigorated by the isolation.

A footpath led up a hill, towards a piping call; sorrowful and lonesome like a children's swing in the breeze. It took a while before the source of the noise was spotted, a small wader, standing proudly on the moorland. I edged closer and wondered whether it was a red-necked phalarope. Shetland is on the southern limit of their range and only a small number of these birds' nest here each year. The most fascinating phalarope fact is the normal gender roles are reversed: the males brood the eggs and look after the chicks, while the females have colourful plumage and have it away with other guys. Good on them, about time birds got with the times. Once within sight of the lonesome wader, I was disappointed to discover it was only a golden plover. Nothing against golden plovers personally, but they are regular winter visitors back home and I'd travelled six hundred miles for something new.

My discontent vanished when I saw a pair of great skuas flying in my direction. My protective headwear was firmly donned and I waited for the inevitable avian assault. They passed me by as though I didn't exist. I kept to the track and continued up the hill where more great skuas roamed. I stopped to keep an eye on them: if they decided to attack, I wanted to see them coming. They flew over the moor and dispersed. Further along another great skua stood in the heather. I waited for it to pounce. It had a mean stare and reminded me of Joe Pesci when he played thugs in gangster movies – briefly relaxed before an explosion of violence. However, there was no lunge, terrifying screech or frenzy of feathers. It glanced at me and did a bit of preening.

One of the fundamental rules of being a wildlife enthusiast is to respect nature and avoid unnecessary disturbance. I was convinced that if I took one step off the path in the great skua's direction I'd be skewered, but rules are rules and I remained on the path unmolested.

The walk was longer than expected and quite bracing, but the reveal at the coast was awesome. Here I was alone on a remote peninsula with the most northerly point of the United Kingdom ahead of me – a lump of rock called Out Stack. In the foreground was Muckle Flugga lighthouse surrounded by islets resembling icebergs. It was too warm for ice; they were painted white by gannet poop. One rounded skerry appeared to be a giant fairy cake; gannet droppings providing the smelly white icing, with the birds themselves sprinkled on top like hundreds and thousands.

A steep grassy slope presented a relaxing place to sit, and I reclined in the soft sward. Puffins zipped about in the air; one came straight at me, banked and aborted his landing. He swirled around and did another lap. I was clearly too close to his burrow entrance, so I got up, moved higher and sat down again on the grass. The puffin circled back, came into land and within two seconds of touchdown, he scurried on his little orange feet and dived into a rabbit hole. He had a beakful of sand eels for his brooding partner, or possibly a recently hatched puffling. Puffling; what a great name for a young puffin.

It was a superb place to sit and watch nature. The puffins kept on whizzing above, gannets soared offshore and great skuas lurked ominously. One landed nearby and gave me a glare which implied, 'What are you looking at?'

I avoided eye contact; I didn't want any trouble.

I walked further west and gazed across the coast to an archway of rock as an elegant skua passed below. I've seen dark phase Arctic skuas, but this bird possessed white banding around its neck. Subsequent research confirmed it was a pale phase Arctic skua and not a new species (some humans have black hair and others are blonde – some Arctic skuas have dark feathers while others are pale).

I found another viewpoint to rest, laid on the slope and soaked up the atmosphere. It was very relaxing; I spent an hour at peace and nearly nodded off. I woke myself with a vigorous face rub. It was time to depart: there was a long drive back including two ferry journeys.

On the path back to the car park, a skylark flew above, fluttering high in the heavens and singing its heart out. When I lowered my gaze, two people approached, holding hands, faces beaming with smiles. We exchanged pleasantries on Hermaness's loveliness and went our separate ways. During all my time on the reserve, they were the only two people I saw – and now Hermaness was all theirs. I returned to the car and drove a short distance before I observed something interesting and stopped to investigate. A body of freshwater called the Loch of Cliff was a magnet for dozens of great skuas. They stood on the shore and washing their feathers (probably to clean out sea salt and the remnants of recent murders) and I listened to their honking calls, watched their behaviour, and started to wonder whether I'd misjudged them. Throughout my time in their company they'd never harassed me once. If I wandered off the path and entered their nesting area, in my opinion, they would be justified in attacking me. It's only natural to try to protect your children. I was hoping to encounter a bit of danger during this Shetland adventure – man versus beast – but on this occasion, I discovered tranquillity and beauty. I couldn't complain.

During the long drive back to Brae, I took regular breaks to sea watch, but saw only seawater. The ferry trips once again eluded otters and the waves became choppy which prevented cetacean spotting. I eventually returned to Brae during early evening, which on Shetland looked very similar to how it looked at midday. I procured a bag of goodies from a local shop and picnicked in my room, I didn't want to risk going downstairs and overhearing boorish salesmen again.

****

The following morning, I went for breakfast and was delighted to be sat next to a couple who were visiting Shetland for the wildlife. They regaled me with an exciting tale from two days earlier when they inadvertently entered a great skua nesting area. The gentleman waved his hands like flapping wings as he described being chased under a bombardment of screeching and pecking beaks. The lady rubbed her scalp as though the pain of a great skua's beak was still resonating. I felt envious at missing out, but most of all, my faith in the species was restored. The badass 'bonxie' was back.

As I checked out of the hotel, one of the local receptionists enthused about a little inlet near Gunnister. I decided to make that my first destination of the morning. After going down the wrong track and visiting someone's driveway, I finally arrived at the beautiful cove. The leg stretch on the shore was wonderful – it's always great to start the morning with a stroll, particularly at a gorgeous location. The grass had been shorn low by grazing sheep; it was as smooth as a golf club fairway with intermittent lumps of sheep poo. Once suitably refreshed by the morning amble, I progressed south in the direction of my evening accommodation in Sumburgh.

I took a diversion towards Culswick, compelled to find another place en route. I used the map to drive into the target area and arrived in a small hamlet of scattered houses. However, I was saddened by the absence of road signs naming the destination. I had promised my friend Joe that I'd have my photo taken beside the place name; but I suspect they'd all been claimed by passing students. I left Twatt disappointed.

On Shetland the closer you get to the coast, the narrower and more undulating the road becomes. The track degenerated into nothing before it reached a parking place. On the horizon the hills met in a 'v' shape and the sea peeked between the gap. Lunch was stuffed into a rucksack and I rambled up a footpath. In the basin of a green meadow a lone Arctic skua mithered some Arctic terns (there seemed to be some animosity between Arctic species, like an intense local derby). The terns put up an unyielding defence – they were probably nesting in the lower wetland area. Arctic skuas regularly chase terns and steal their fish, and I guess they wouldn't miss the opportunity to take a chick. The tern parents kept up their harrying and through combined team effort, eventually chased off the interloper.

The footpath led onto a gravel track which bisected the end of a loch and led on to the hill. Once at the summit of the large grassy dome I stood among the ruins of a large historic construction, presumably a broch. Some brochs are over 2000 years old; but to me they resemble small cooling towers of power stations. This broch looked like a cooling tower after it'd been blown up by Fred Dibnah.

The scenery was stunning; expansive blue seas to the west and green undulating pastures to the east. The elevation gave 360° views and seemed a perfect settlement site. You could go fishing in the sea, keep livestock in the surrounding grasslands and fetch fresh water from the loch below. If attackers came over the landward side they could easily be seen approaching, allowing the settlers precious time to prepare defences. The other side was protected by the sea. However, all that probably changed when the Vikings rocked up in their longships. Perhaps the residents relocated to Lerwick for its modern comforts (or they were massacred a millennium earlier by Vikings).

The hill was an idyllic spot for a picnic and I sat on a comfortable flat rock on the rubble's fringe. As I gazed over the sea a large black line moved offshore; it wasn't a wave because it travelled in the opposite direction to the sea's current. Through binoculars I studied the area and fifteen minutes later I spotted a minke whale. It glided through the water and its wet flank glistened with reflected sun. I munched my sandwiches while the minke swallowed its fish. This was a truly amazing location, enhanced by marine megafauna, pleasant weather and high-quality ham sandwiches. I finished my lunch before the whale finished his, and I looked around for other people within sight. One of the most joyful parts of this hobby is sharing wildlife events. Nobody else was around. I could have shouted to the sheep below, although I doubt they'd have cared. I spent an hour walking the coastline, regularly stopping to glance out to sea, wait, wait, wait, then the minke would rise again. When I departed it was still in the vicinity, along with the Arctic skua who'd returned to pester the terns. Unlike the skua, my time at Culswick seemed to have gone completely unnoticed by the local wildlife and that made me feel happy.

The next destination was a bit of a drive but every mile along the road to St Ninian's Isle was worth it. It had come recommended by the first person I met on Shetland; the taxi driver. St Ninian's was a small green island connected to the mainland by a causeway of bright white sand. The car park already contained six vehicles, which seemed a mighty large gathering for Shetland. I looked for the mass of humanity, yet only saw one family on the beach. A child flew a kite, another explored the rockpools and the smallest was being taken for a walk by a large dog which dragged him along the sand. I strode onto the tombolo and headed towards the island; the tide was out and hopefully it'd stay that way for the duration of my visit. Once on St Ninian's Isle I turned to look back – the reverse view was equally impressive, as the causeway led away and met the beach in a T-shape.

A wheatear called out in chirps and clicks. At home these birds are mostly seen on their passage north and rarely emit more than a solitary tweet.

Male wheatears are striking birds, pale orange chest with a black band on their faces like Zorro. He flew off and revealed his white tail feathers, and this noticeable feature supplies the wheatear's name. The first part has nothing to do with wheat; it's an old Norse name for white. The second part is similar to the French word *arrière*, which is bum. So, wheatears are white bums and this bird's white bum vanished behind the heather.

The route was reminiscent of the paths on Hillswick. I stopped regularly to admire the seascape and it took an hour to circumnavigate at leisure – at the conclusion I was glad to see the causeway hadn't been submerged by an incoming tide.

Once back inside the car I relaxed in the seat. It had been a beautiful day, but my legs were now shot. I drove to the hotel in Sumburgh and later found the energy to go to the bar. The locals seemed intent on drinking doubles but I called it a day at 10pm because today's activities had sapped all my energy. It was only after returning to my room that I realised it was Friday night. I'd completely lost track of the days of the week and I was delighted to have escaped one of the shackles of modern life.

****

In the morning I gave my stiff legs a good rub. One final day of action was required. Several interesting places were within walking distance around Sumburgh. The car was returned to the nearby airport and the savings in hire rental would be invested wisely in the hotel bar later. I began to dwell on the fact that I'd soon be departing Shetland and that caused my morning to be veiled with some sadness; I often get melancholic on the last day of a wonderful holiday.

The coastal footpath led upwards to Sumburgh Head; the incline didn't appear to be this steep when I journeyed up by taxi. I paused several times to catch my breath, before eventually arriving at the top. I peeped over the stone wall and the puffins were still there, although I guessed they'd moved at some point during the week. I began to study their behaviour. They are an intriguing species with thoughtful expressions, maybe pondering the meaning of life and their part in the universe… or just thinking about eating fish.

One puffin appeared with a short twig in its beak, which reminded me of the 'no smoking' sign in the Lerwick guesthouse. A puffin would welcome the company of one other puffin, but they dislike a threesome. When a single bird tried to mingle with a couple it caused a kerfuffle. Once the unwanted guest was turfed out, the remaining pair relaxed and faced in opposite directions. They peered over each other's shoulders and shared lookout duties for any approaching falcons or great skuas. A solitary puffin was further away and he seemed uncomfortable, having to undertake the burden of being lone sentry, continually checking for danger creeping up behind.

Much lower down the headland, a hooded crow strutted over the grassy slope – she was up to something. I'm of the opinion that crows spend most of their day involved in mischief or scheming future devilment. This crow had a sprat in her beak, which was presumably dropped by a puffin on its way back from the 'shop'. The crow decided not to eat her free treat, so the fish sagged lifelessly in her beak.

The crow was ten metres beneath me when she stopped and inspected the entrance of an old rabbit warren. She laid the fish invitingly outside the hole and stood by the side, out of sight of anything within. The crow glared intently at the dark opening, while I watched the crow. I could only deduce the dropped fish was bait to lure out a subterranean occupant. I witnessed the situation with excitement and trepidation. It's always thrilling to see wildlife participate in cunning behaviour, but I wondered whether I might spot my first puffling – then seconds later observe it being devoured. After five minutes of tension the crow decided her trap would not be sprung, she picked up her fish and flew off.

A lady joined me – she was wearing a uniform which indicated she was a local wildlife warden. As we chatted, I remembered her from Gordon Buchanan's documentary about Shetland. I recollected Gordon interviewing her at this very same spot and they saw minke whales.

'Any chance of a minke whale today?' I asked.

'We've not seen any here for weeks.'

I tried to not to sound boastful as I replied. 'I saw one yesterday.'

She was impressed and took details of the time and place of my sighting at Culswick. We chatted about puffins, whales, skuas and Gordon, until more visitors arrived and she helped them with their questions. None of them asked her about Gordon – which was surprising.

I moved a short distance away, before hearing a piercing screech from behind the stone wall – I dashed over to see the cause of the commotion.

Below me a hooded crow flew off with something sizeable in her beak, not a puffling but a young starling – because pursuing her were two angry adult starlings.

The sand eel trick had clearly paid dividends.

I stopped at various points around the lighthouse and watched the abundant wildlife: Arctic skuas, fulmars and plenty more puffins. A confident puffin came within a metre of me and we exchanged looks. I could see all the detail of his plumage, the coloured bands on his beak, white cheeks and a dark flash behind his eye. He entered a burrow and was immediately ejected by the occupier.

I accept the charge that I'm guilty of anthropomorphism, as well as of guessing genders of species, but when I stared into the eyes of this solitary puffin, he seemed sorrowful (even though his facial structure was no different to any other puffin I've met). The expression on a puffin is the exact opposite of a bottlenose dolphin; the upturned mouth of a dolphin provides them with a permanent smile, which would remain fixed even if they were eaten alive by a shark. It is a great advantage of being human, if one day I have the misfortune of being devoured by a shark, I'd be able to display a suitable grimace.

I sat down and the puffin paused by my outstretched leg and inspected me. Perhaps this was a bachelor who was unlucky in love; I could empathise. In early spring when there's a tree full of jackdaws, they usually gather in pairs, but there's always one bird perched on his own. He probably sits there viewing his rivals and wishing one of them would be visited by a goshawk. Wild bachelors don't get the same rewards as their human counterparts; I dodge shopping trips, choose what I watch on TV and I'm never asked my opinions on fashion. Those advantages give me great comfort.

The puffin occasionally emitted a quizzical, 'Urrrrmmmmmm'. When you look this good you probably don't need to sing. The lonesome puffin then waddled past my foot, had a stretch and a yawn. His little wings flapped furiously. These stumpy limbs limit his flying skills, but they enable him to dart through the water like a penguin.

Sometimes to truly appreciate wildlife you have to immerse yourself in their environment, keep silent and try to see the world from their perspective. It was a relaxing intimate experience as the puffin grew content with my company. Maybe he expected me to help him keep lookout. Thankfully at no point did I have to shout, 'Watch out – Bonxie!!!'

I wasn't keeping track of time; I'd probably sat for over an hour in 'Puffinworld'. I stayed until my mate flew off to sea, which was my signal to gather lunch for myself. I completed the circular walk around the coast and returned to the hotel.

After lunch there was a prehistoric settlement called Jarlshof to explore; conveniently located at the back of the hotel. Jarlshof was no longer a home for humans, instead it had become a residence for dozens of starlings. Parent birds commuted back and forth to the gaps in the stone walls, squeezing inside and feeding their hidden nestlings. If I knew starling language, I would have spoken to the young chirping occupants and warned them, 'If you see a sprat lying outside – leave it alone.'

Beside Jarlshof, a small paddock held a troop of Shetland ponies. These little horses have evolved a physique perfectly adapted to the local weather with barrel-shaped bodies on stumpy legs to keep them upright during the furious winter storms. Amongst the adults were foals and one tentatively approached me. I stopped on the other side of the pen's wire fence, lowered myself down and sat on the grass. I hoped that once at eye level, I would appear less intimidating. I gathered a handful of fresh grass and wafted it invitingly towards her. The foal became curious and edged closer. This enabled me to have a good view; she was an attractive chestnut and white colour, with deep dark eyes and a long face. The handful of grass failed to tempt her any closer; she remained out of range and nervously sniffed at the offering.

Her mother gently guided her youngster away from the strange grass-waving beast. She reversed in my direction, swished her tail and farted. This was not a small pop of air; it was a rumbling package of warm guff which bounced off my head. Think of someone blowing up a large balloon and releasing the reverberating gas in your face. That's what it was like – particularly if the air smelt like half-digested hay. I blinked and held my breath, stood up and gasped for fresh air. That was a new experience and an animal interaction I'd choose to skip in the future.

Back at the hotel bar, the TV had World Cup football between England and the USA. I sat down and hoped I didn't smell of horse flatulence.

The audience was partisan – two England supporters were sat right in front of the TV, bravely wearing their national team shirts. Behind them was a large group of rowdy locals, one with a large star-spangled banner (no idea where he found that flag on Shetland).

I decided to sit in a neutral zone between the two factions. England scored, liberating a cheer from the English pair, before a goalkeeping howler gave USA the equaliser and the place went ballistic. Some locals directed mockery at me, but in such circumstances I have a useful get-out clause; 'I'm from the Isle of Man.' This safely saw me through the rest of the football match unscathed.

After full-time I sat with the subdued English couple for a chat on any subject but sport. They were visiting Shetland for coastal hikes and the local wildlife. They enthused about a tour they joined the previous evening to Mousa – a small island off the eastern coast. It's a place well-known for seabirds called storm petrels which resemble swallows in flight. Petrels catch marine creatures near the sea's surface by scampering across the water on their webbed feet (they're named petrel after St Peter who was famed for walking on water). The first part of their name relates to them taking refuge onboard ships during storms. Storm petrels spend daytime offshore but need to travel onto land for procreation. The narrow crevices within the walls of the Broch of Mousa offer safe nesting, but due to the bird's diminutive size, they are at danger of being ambushed by avian predators while travelling inland. Therefore petrels use the cover of the darkness to return, reducing the risk of being snaffled by a gull or bird of prey (Manx shearwaters use the same tactic). In addition, petrels and shearwaters prefer to nest on islands containing no land predators, such as stoats or rats.

The English couple described standing beside the broch in the dusky evening light with swirling small birds making noises like tropical frogs. It sounded wonderful and I wished I'd arranged to do that myself, but it was too late now. If I revisit Shetland in the future it will definitely be on my next wish list.

Shortly afterwards, I saw something much more saddening than England's footballing performance. Behind the TV screen a large window faced seawards and who should go past but the hitchhiker from Brae. I quickly lent forwards, picked up a newspaper and lifted it towards my face. I was too slow; I'd been spotted. The hitchhiker walked through the doorway and aimed right for me. I threw the newspaper back down onto the table in disdain.

'Alright mate,' he chirped, as though we were long-lost buddies. He seemed more chipper than when I picked him up in the rain.

'Fancy seeing you here,' I replied.

'I'm on a guided tour with a bunch of pensioners to Jarlshof. I escaped for a wander.'

'Did you enjoy Jarlshof?'

'It's hardly Machu Picchu.'

He was at least predictable. He then listed some of his new complaints, which featured his Lerwick accommodation (perhaps we both stayed in the same B&B), the cost of his lunch, the old folk on his tour and the benefits of euthanasia. He then taunted the English couple about the football before he paused. His eyebrows raised and eyes widened as he recalled something. He pointed at me with an accusing finger and barked, 'Oh! Mavis Grind!'

My blood pressure started to rise and beads of sweat formed on my brow.

He continued to point at me and ranted, 'I told a local what you said about the place name... he thought I was a bleedin idiot.'

I suspect the local had already gathered that fact.

He snapped, 'It's named after the geology, not some prossie!'

Next to me, the Englishman choked on his drink.

'Really?' I said, pretending that this was news to me. 'My source must have been incorrect.'

This is why you should never tell lies. Telling lies is like disturbing a horsefly, it will probably return later and bite you on the backside.

Fortunately, the hitchhiker got distracted by something happening outside, he walked to the window, peered through and turned back sharply, 'The coffin dodgers are getting back onto my coach. I had an argument with the tour guide, I bet she would love to drive off without me.'

I can't think of anyone who would consider doing that to him.

He made one final remark, 'You never know, we might bump into each other again.'

I was confident there was little risk of that – I was departing on a plane tomorrow. 'Yes, maybe we will.' I smiled.

After he disappeared, I sighed with relief, finished my pint and went to my room to freshen up. I returned later as the warden from Sumburgh Head appeared and she began serving behind the bar. We chatted about the local wildlife and Gordon Buchanan. Later while propping up the bar, I was joined by an elderly local man whose Shetland accent grew more Norwegian with every pint he sank. By the end of the evening his speech degenerated into an unfathomable slurred language. I'm a fan of Nordic noir dramas and this chap's conversation would have benefitted from subtitles.

It was a great final night of a magnificent trip, but when I woke in the morning my head felt battered as if it'd been set upon by great skuas. I had no recollection of that happening.

This had been one of the best holidays I could remember. Shetland was different to visiting Scotland, and not just because there were no mountains and thankfully no midges. The beauty and peace provided an incredibly relaxing and calming atmosphere. It reminded me of my childhood when I would go out exploring alone in local woodlands and forget about my worries.

A lack of trees didn't mean a lack of wildlife – I had experienced amazing spectacles. I had researched well and set realistic targets for my wish list and they all featured in my most memorable moments; great skuas, puffins and gannets. Spending a week wildlife watching clearly provides more sightings than a weekend, but the season and region also makes a big difference.

I never saw otters, although I may have been more successful if I'd visited the recommended places at dusk or dawn, rather than during the middle of the day. The only major thing I missed out on was being dive-bombed by great skuas and that wasn't such a bad thing.

Upon arriving home, I enthusiastically told my friends about Shetland and for some reason, out of all my stories, they were mostly interested in hearing about me being gassed by a pony. Later in the year, I went with some of those 'friends' for a short break to London for David Wiseman's stag weekend. We stayed in Richmond to see rugby at Twickenham, and I had no expectations of any wildlife spotting. Remarkably I was treated to a couple of great moments. The first was seeing a squadron of screeching ring-necked parakeets flying outside the hotel. The second happened at night outside a surprising venue – a kebab house.

I'm sure many Londoners would baulk at this being either special or a wildlife event, yet for me and other Isle of Man residents it was a delight to see a fox (as we don't get them back home). It was probably made even more memorable because we were slightly tipsy.

The encounter happened after we collected our takeaways, walked outside and I saw something rustling in the alleyway. I signalled to my friends and we all stood eating our kebabs as a fox rummaged in the bins. Based on my blurred recollection of the events, our conversation went something like;

'Give it some of your kebab.'

'I'm not giving it any of my kebab, you give it some of yours.'

'I have too much chilli sauce on mine.'

'Shhh, you are disturbing it.'

A door opened in the alleyway and a loud Turkish voice shouted, 'What are all you guys doing out here!?!'

The fox ran out of the bins with a chicken carcass in its mouth, we watched it scamper past us before we skulked off sheepishly. It was one of my best wildlife experiences ever.

Atlantic Grey Seals

Chapter 7

Galloway, Northumbria and Yorkshire (2012)

Previous experience indicated June was the ideal time for wildlife watching, so I repeated that winning formula. An eight-day holiday would take me from Glasgow down to Galloway, across the Borders to Northumbria, finishing in Yorkshire. The primary purpose was to study historic sites for a part-time degree course; and the route also offered plenty of opportunities for nature; principally at the Farne Islands, Lindisfarne and Bempton Cliffs RSPB.

From Glasgow airport I drove south to my first destination, Newton Stewart. Twenty minutes later I was back alongside the runway at Glasgow airport – contradicting my belief that I possessed a good sense of direction. I performed a quick U-turn and headed south before anyone else noticed. After Kilmarnock the A77 touched the coast and a chunk of rock appeared in the Firth of Clyde; the plug of an extinct volcano called Ailsa Craig. It's quarried for the manufacture of curling stones and I've seen this granite before, as riebeckite shingle washes up on the Isle of

Man's northern beaches. It was nice to see the source of some of my pretty pebble collection.

Newton Stewart was a charming place to stay, and a short distance north was the Wood of Cree RSPB. It was a damp day and the woodland air was filled with invigorating freshness, moist as the fine spray from a pounding waterfall. The forest seemed primeval and untarnished by mankind, deep and dark with old gnarly oaks and lanky birches. Many of the tree trunks were fitted with bird and bat boxes (bat boxes have a hole on the base, rather than at the front).

The Wood of Cree was the exact opposite of conifer plantations, which feel arid and starved of life; this was fresh and wholesome. I immediately fell in love with this dappled green glen.

I'd only been here a minute before I heard my first-ever wood warbler. The sound was distinctly different to any other British bird calls; in fact it seemed out of place and more reminiscent of something you'd hear in the tropics. The call resounded like a penny being spun on a varnished surface, the noise accelerating as the coin descended. The bird itself remained out of sight, but the song of several wood warblers accompanied me throughout my visit.

A squirrel scurried up a tree, its tail wriggling behind. Moments later a buzzard followed the squirrel's route through the canopy; chasing its shadow.

Dor beetles, which lay their eggs in buried herbivore poo, marched between the leaf litter. One of these large beetles crossed a twig and managed to flip itself over, revealing its iridescent underside; purples and blues. The beetle's black sturdy legs waved in the air before it righted itself and continued unperturbed.

An undulating path wove between verdant vegetation and gushing streams. The route reached Knockman Wood, a Neolithic burial site surrounded by a perimeter of tall deer fences. They were high enough to repel moose and successfully kept big grazers off the Wood of Cree's lush flora.

The next destination was reached by car, the Galloway coast, where the land became as wet as the sea. The heavy rain was particularly grim at the Mull of Galloway. I stood above the cliff and stared across the seascape; apparently the Isle of Man was somewhere behind this torrential downpour. It became wetter at the Isle of Whithorn and I was saturated beside the Neolithic stones at Cairnholy. As water dripped off my nose, I decided that was enough for the day and drove back behind a forestry truck laden with timber. After five minutes of my car being sprayed by water and pine bark, I was presented with an opportunity to overtake. I pulled out at the beginning of a long straight and accelerated while being pelted by tree detritus. It was only once I drew level with the truck's cabin, that I realised the lowest point of the road was flooded. Both vehicles hit the temporary pond at the same time and my car became submerged, like James Bond's Lotus in *The Spy Who Loved Me*. The windscreen wipers failed to cope with the aquatic conditions. Eventually my car resurfaced and managed to complete the overtaking manoeuvre, then at the first opportunity I swung into a layby. I needed to stop and regain my composure. I felt as though I'd just escaped death. The truck thundered past and scattered my car with more bark. It was five minutes before I resumed my journey back to Newton Stewart.

****

The day after I drove across the Borders and passed through Dumfries, Hawick, Jedburgh and Berwick-upon-Tweed. They were all interesting towns and contained plenty of history, but little wildlife, apart from half-a-dozen goosanders on the River Nith at Dumfries.

My evening's accommodation was south of Berwick-upon-Tweed and the following day I'd have two nights on Lindisfarne. It seemed sensible to take a reconnaissance mission to view Lindisfarne's causeway and research the tide times. During daytime there's approximately a seven-hour window of opportunity to cross, followed by five hours of closure during high tide.

When I arrived, a queue of drivers were waiting patiently for the tidal markers to become exposed, which would signal safe passage. Unlike most of the Northumbrian coast, this area wasn't bright and sandy, it was brown and muddy. In the middle of the causeway a white shed was held aloft by tall posts. The purpose of this raised shelter was to provide refuge for anyone who got their tide times wrong. I didn't want to end up in that shed, so using the information board I noted that tomorrow the causeway would magically appear from the North Sea at 6pm. I looked up as a gigantic 4x4 overtook the queue and charged onto the causeway with a splash. It pushed through the waves, engine steaming and water crashing over the bonnet. It reached the other side safely, while everyone else continued to wait.

****

The next day there was plenty of time to explore the Northumbrian coast before going to Lindisfarne in the evening. The morning was spent at three castles: Bamburgh, Dunstanburgh and Warkworth. Northumbria has more castles than any other English county because throughout history this coast was a battleground, from early Viking raiders, border wars with Scotland and internal wars with other Englishmen (it got a bit heated around these parts during the War of the Roses). The castles along this beautiful coastline currently held a calm magnificence.

In the afternoon I explored Seahouses, a charming seaside village with a busy harbour. Boats departed from here to the Farne Islands, famous for its seals and nesting seabirds. I booked a two-and-a-half-hour cruise which included disembarking at Inner Farne.

The boat was full and most of the forty passengers donned headwear, a sensible precaution for what was to come. I put on my trusty camouflage hat, which surprisingly failed to raise admiring glances from the other passengers. However, it did attract the attention of a black-headed gull. It had no fear of people; presumably as a result of living somewhere visited annually by thousands of bird lovers. Black-headed gulls are smaller than herring gulls; in the summer their heads are a dark chocolate colour; during winter their head feathers moult, leaving dark smudges where you might expect the ears. Throughout the year they retain their red legs and I watched these appendages as the bird stopped a few centimetres away. The gull assessed whether any of me was edible, then swaggered off to check out an elderly couple. Gulls strut around with an air of self-importance, like traffic wardens; and both have the capacity to leave something unpleasant on your windscreen.

Most of the tour party went for the available seating inside; I stood on the deck at the stern. It was only after we set off that I realised I was above the boat's engine; so in addition to fresh sea air, I received the occasional lung of diesel smoke. The passengers spoke in a variety of accents and foreign languages, emphasising that the Farnes attracted more than local interest.

The boat chugged across the calm sea and Farne's low-lying islands were soon in sight. Fulmars were gliding on the updrafts, jinking their stiff wings and reeling away. As we approached the rocks, the chatter of seabirds became louder, especially the screech of kittiwakes. We sidled up to a shelf of bare rock holding more than a thousand guillemots, parading smartly in their black and white plumage. When a gull passed above, the guillemots pointed their beaks upwards like medieval pikemen. They needed to protect their snack-sized youngsters from opportunistic pirates. Amongst the deep chatter of seabirds, I could hear the high-pitched chirping of the guillemot chicks, but had to wait before I eventually saw a little ball of black fluff peeking out from the crowd of adults. The chick was considerably shorter than its parents, but curiously had similar sized feet. Reminiscent of my childhood when I'd clop about in my dad's size ten boots.

Further along, Atlantic grey seals rested on the rocks, relaxing after a fishy lunch and digesting the nutrients. If they didn't lounge about after feeding, they would get indigestion: would you go for a swim immediately after eating a Sunday roast? Seals squabbled over the prime basking spots and a female raised her head towards one antagonist, mouth agape and emitted a sound resembling an aggrieved coyote. More seals were beyond the next corner, probably in excess of a hundred and this caused the man beside me to exclaim, 'Jeepers.' They were mostly Atlantic greys with intermittent harbour seals – all of them lying over the rocks like giant scatter cushions.

Our boat approached Inner Farne and we docked at the end of a concrete jetty. On the right of the island there was a sturdy stone building, home to the resident wardens. The wardens arrive in March each year and spend six months without regular hot showers and take-away meals. I heard a story about a pair of wardens based on the Calf of Man (a small island at the south of the Isle of Man). The wardens arrived in spring and immediately had an argument. Imagine being trapped on an isolated island with only one other person, and you detest each other. They avoided talking for six months and communicated instead using post-it-notes:

'Did you drink all the milk?'

'It's your turn to put out the bins.'

'I've lost one sock, is it in your laundry?'

'Those biscuits were mine!'

I was at the rear of the boat which meant I'd be last to disembark. The first passengers walked up the concrete jetty and stepped onto a stone path which wove upwards. When they reached a patch of green, a flock of white seabirds lifted into the air like angry bees from a hive. The Arctic terns hovered for a few seconds before starting their attack, swooping and castigating their foreign invaders. This was a place where birds ruled the roost. There were two audible sounds; the clattering bird calls and howls of pain from pecked people. Some folk held brollies and canes aloft, which deterred the descending sharp beaks, but couldn't save them from being strafed by poo bombs. One lady gained a nice white stripe down her shoulder. My fertile imagination compared this scene to the Normandy beach landings. Not as harrowing, but equally dramatic.

I stepped off the boat and glanced at the bespectacled gentleman beside me; he raised his eyebrows. We both knew what was in store for us. I checked my hat was securely fastened and we strode up the jetty. The terns were so confident of their place, they nested beside the paths and chastised anyone who strayed close. Fortunately, as we reached the higher section, some of the terns had already resettled on the ground after their earlier exertions. They'd emptied their bowels and had little else to give. Just as I felt safe, a piercing screech was followed by a painful sensation. It was identical to being stabbed in the back of the head by a sharp pencil, an injury I'm familiar with as I went to secondary school in Cheshire. My flimsy camouflage hat was ill-equipped to deflect the peck. I winced and gave my skull a rub.

A voice behind said, 'Oooh, that got you too!' I turned and nodded in agreement with the bespectacled gentleman, his glasses dripping with bird poo. He removed his spectacles and used his handkerchief to smear the mess over a wider area. We both ducked in unison as another tern swooped at our faces.

On Shetland I had anticipated, but never experienced being attacked by a far larger bird; a great skua. The smaller tern reached my pain threshold sufficiently and I was thankful I was never on the receiving end of a great skua's beak. I was pecked again and I looked up at the culprit as it hovered above. It was graceful, yet feisty, with a pointed crimson beak (natural colouration rather than anything to do with drawing my blood).

As the visitors strolled deeper into the island's interior, the skirmishes diminished and we were able to observe Inner Farne without fear of attack. There were other resident bird species; an open area of scurvy-grass was dotted with the entrances to subterranean puffin nests. Puffins darted in from all directions with black-headed gulls in pursuit – the puffins outnumbered the gulls, so the majority successfully ran the gauntlet. However, the gulls were more accomplished fliers and a team of four ganged up on one returning puffin. The poor puffin landed, became surrounded and was grabbed by the beak, lifted and spun upwards. During an inelegant flip, it released its hard-earned catch and the sprayed fish were devoured in a gull feeding frenzy. It seemed unfair and a nearby gentleman commented, 'Bleedin gulls.'

Further along, a large flock of Arctic terns were in the air and thankfully not in attack mode. They swirled in a tight formation around the lighthouse, a beautiful and pain-free sight. The rocky coastline beyond was deep with nesting seabirds who were accustomed to people, allowing visitors to sit within arm's reach. I perched on a rock and gradually edged closer to a shag's nest which contained an adult and two youngsters. I was expecting my presence to create signs of unease, but they didn't care a jot about me. The adult was a meticulous preener, she bowed her head and gave it a vigorous scrub with her foot. The bird's shimmering black and green wing plumage resembled reptilian scales, her youngsters like little fluffy black crocodiles making soft squealing noises. The easiest way to distinguish between shags and cormorants is their size – cormorants are twice as big. In addition, shags are mostly found at the coast, while cormorants occasionally travel inland to exploit freshwater opportunities, such as the ponds of posh people and eat their koi carp.

On a nearby column of rock there was a kittiwake nest. Adult kittiwakes are stylish and more appealing than herring gulls (and they don't have the same devious stare). Kittiwakes feed near the sea's surface by poking their heads underwater to pluck out small fish and shrimps. They have pale yellow beaks and dark legs. The kittiwake stood up and revealed a pair of fluffy chicks on her nest. They had piercing black eyes set against their cotton-white faces.

As I relaxed amongst the birds I felt at peace with nature. This area contained a feeling of serenity, particularly in comparison to the initial combat zone; although it retained a stronger smell of bird poo. All of Farne's seabird species can be seen at home around the Isle of Man but I felt privileged to have this more intimate experience. I could have spent a day in their company, but fellow tour members began to roam back down the jetty – it was time for us to return to our boat.

On the way back I passed the wardens' accommodation. Outside the front gate was a female eider duck, motionless on her nest. She was probably hungry as she needed to wait for her chicks to hatch before they'd all go together and feed in the sea. Male eider ducks take little participation in parental duties, instead loitering about in gangs of absent fathers. The males' flashy plumage is conspicuous; if one stayed at a nesting site, he could betray his location to a predator. Human males have a similar adaptation to get out of domestic duties – when we mess up the ironing to avoid being asked again in the future.

The female eider gave me a stare which said, 'Move along, there's nothing to see here.'

I moved along.

As I approached the jetty, the Arctic terns had replenished their bowels, recharged their batteries and unleashed their fury with an encore performance. One tern perched on a post and I foolishly decided to approach, leaning in for a closer look at this delightful bird. It went for my face like a striking python. I was surrounded by a cacophony of clicks and screeches – vision blurred by flapping white feathers. Thankfully it only pecked me once before it flew off to attack some elderly ladies. The ladies howled in pain before one of them shrieked, 'Arggh, you varmint!' Birds apparently have no respect for age or gender.

All the passengers eventually returned to the boat and we chugged away. Travellers compared pecks and poo stains. One lady was struck so sharply on the head that it drew blood, but instead of being concerned, she carried it as a badge of honour. I applauded her attitude. The wind direction was now behind as we returned to port, which meant more diesel fumes in my face than during the outbound journey.

I drove back to Lindisfarne and joined the back of the queue approaching the tidal causeway. Once again a mammoth 4x4 overtook those waiting, charged into the water and sent a two-metre-high spray cascading into the sky. I had contrasting opinions; my first thought was from my inner-child,

'That looks fun', the second my darker side, 'I hope he gets stuck and has to take refuge in the elevated white shed'. The driver clearly knew the tide and terrain, as his steaming vehicle safely emerged on the opposite side of the causeway. He quickly disappeared down the road towards the village on the right; possibly to wash the corrosive salt off his car. It was another hour before we other mortals in ordinary cars ventured safely onto the wet causeway.

Lindisfarne village was cheerfully old-fashioned; narrow alleyways, stone cottages prettied by hanging baskets and very little traffic. I soon found my accommodation, approached the reception desk and greeted the smiling lady behind, 'Hello, I have a booking in the name of Wright.'

She studied her book and said, 'Ah, yes,' then she paused and smiled at me, 'Have you just been to the Farne Islands?'

I assumed I mentioned it when I phoned with the booking and replied. 'Yes, it was wonderful.'

Having checked in, I went to my room which was bright, cosy and clean, with a large bed and modern facilities. Potpourri made the room smell like a floral meadow, but in the background an unpleasant aroma lurked, as if the floral meadow had recently been manured. I sniffed around and soon concluded – with personal disappointment – that the odour was coming from me. I investigated my front, the soles of my boots, but nothing was apparent. The source of the smell was eventually unearthed when I turned my back to a full-length mirror. Unbeknown to me, during my Farne adventure, I had taken several hits of guano from Arctic terns, causing the back of my coat to be painted like a Jackson Pollock. While out and about I must have acclimatised to the reek, although inside a delicately perfumed room my new fragrance was highly noticeable. I reflected on my chat with the receptionist and realised she must have smelt me when I entered. I sighed with embarrassment at that thought.

I took a shower; joined by my coat.

****

Early next morning, I explored the Holy Island, first by visiting the priory and church, before crossing by foot over rocks to the diminutive St Cuthbert's Isle. The population on St Cuthbert's Isle consisted of me, two Dutch tourists and a herring gull.

When I returned to the village, the lanes steadily filled with tourists. The tide must have let them in. It gradually became swamped and reminded me of daytime Hawkshead – that wasn't a good memory, so I left the crowded village and headed for the outer regions. Above the next bay, upturned fishing boats had been creatively converted into makeshift sheds. Beyond was a tall steep sided mound of dolerite rock, with Lindisfarne Castle sat on top. It looked the sort of place where Dracula might live, but I wasn't able to check for vampires, as it was closed to the public. Behind the castle, cavernous lime kilns were dug into the rock and something moved in a dark gloomy corner. Initially I thought I'd disturbed a bat, but it was a wren which fluttered closer. The wren's Latin name is appropriately *troglodytes troglodytes* and the little cave-dweller departed. I followed behind and commenced an anti-clockwise coastal walk around the island.

My latest film project had been a slight departure from my previous wildlife documentaries. I was making an environmental movie called *Seasons*, and the basic synopsis was the negative impact of human activity on nature. I always film anything unusual, including the macabre. While on the strandline I stumbled across a dead Atlantic grey seal and I took out my camera to film the gory scene – deceased wildlife met the film's brief. I panned down the body and I was surprised by its bulk and length; over two metres long. The teeth were bigger than a Rottweiler's, the smell worse than my coat yesterday.

My friend Louise, a wildlife warden, one day found a dead seal and wanted the skeleton for educational purposes. She buried the animal's body in her back garden and left it for the little subterranean organisms to clean the bones. Five years later she remembered about the seal; although in the meantime she'd moved house. In the intervening period the new home owners must have made an unexpected revelation, while digging a flower bed...

A short distance from Lindisfarne Castle was a bird hide beside a small body of water, which rewarded me with three mallards. I continued my journey underwhelmed. After wandering along the rocky coastline in the refreshing sea air, the path met a man-made circular building the size of an igloo, known locally as 'The Seal Hut'. The walls of the hut must have been constructed by somebody with a talent for stonewalling. I squeezed through the narrow doorway, sat down and relaxed. Bric-a-brac scattered the shelves and a visitors' book contained people's memories and drawings – an interesting read. I decided to make my own entry, took the book and a pencil, and went outside to find something to draw. A short distance away I found the perfect subject; an early marsh orchid. With the pencil I intricately captured its beauty. I savoured a final admiring glance of my artwork before returning the book to the hut. Once again I sat inside and gazed out of the little window to view the waves and passing seabirds. The seclusion was pleasant; however it was a nice surprise when ten minutes later a jolly middle-aged couple peered around the doorway. They both wore matching red jackets and identical glasses – although she seemed to have a greater allocation of teeth.

'Oh, snug!' chirped the lady with a toothy grin.

We squeezed together inside the hut; three was a good number, four may have been a crowd. The lady began to examine the bits-n-pieces on the shelves, which included single shoes. How does anyone lose one shoe and not a pair? I lifted a rounded red stone, which in a former life was a square brick, before it had been rolled in the surf a thousand times or more. The lady twirled a length of warped wood, while the gentleman picked through piles of plastic, much of it from the fishing industry. If this was the plastic washed up on the shore, how much was still out at sea?

The lady located the visitors' book and immediately flicked past my orchid drawing. She gushed over the pictorial endeavours of Amy aged nine, who'd optimistically titled her effort 'Seal'. I'm not an admirer of children's artwork and usually keep my critiques to myself, so, I didn't mention that Amy's seal resembled a drowning pig. I decided to continue my stroll and bid them farewell as they marvelled at seven-year-old Maxwell's picture of a boat, which I mistook for a hat in a puddle. Some numpty torched the Seal Hut two years later and presumably my orchid masterpiece went up in flames, along with abstract depictions of drowning pigs and wet hats.

I crossed the dunes and roamed across a long wide stretch of beach. A bracing wind fired off the North Sea and blew away my cobwebs. I treasured the beach's desolation and became mesmerised by the undulating sea. The sea state was energetic, waves churning and rumbling like my mum's old top-loading washing machine. On the shoreline a yellow foam danced in the wind – spume. When I was younger I thought spume was pollution; I later learned it's a by-product of decaying algae and seaweed.

In the distance a group of four people approached – at first I had mistaken them for thick fence posts. I decided to avoid bumping into them and cut inland through the dunes. Here lived an invasive New Zealand plant called pirri-pirri bur. The seed buds are similar shaped to teasels mixed with dandelion seed heads. The barbed pods are spread by attaching themselves to clothing, so I checked I wasn't escalating the problem. As I examined my shoes, a fox moth caterpillar crossed my path, hairy little critters, resembling a string of liquorish that's been rolled over a barbershop floor. The caterpillar had a decent pace and quickly disappeared into the marram grass.

I soon met the main road – to my left were dunes, on my right a wide mudflat stretching towards the Northumbrian mainland. Ducks flew past, while oystercatchers and curlews used their long beaks to probe the mud. At the side of the road was a sad sight; a female red fox had been hit by a car. It seemed a strange place to find a dead fox, but perhaps there were enough nesting birds and the occasional rabbit to keep one sustained. I held the camera, panned across the dead animal and a passing driver blasted his horn at me. I turned and saw an angry-faced man castigate me as he drove past, who knows why? I'd enjoyed the last two hours detached from the modern world and upon my return to civilisation, the first person I interact with is a pillock. As I walked back along the road, the traffic flow lessened which cheered me up – it signalled the imminent closure of the causeway – and I would have the island to myself once again. Bliss.

A day walking in fresh sea air always results in a glorious night's sleep. After breakfast I prepared the hire car for driving south to York. On the dashboard a sign said, 'No Smoking', but no notices prohibited the smearing of bird poo on the upholstery. Nevertheless, I washed the driver's seat, as my jacket had indeed transferred some excrement from Farne's birdlife.

During the planning of the journey, Lindisfarne to York didn't look like a four-hour jaunt. By the time I eventually arrived at York's outskirts, I had added to the travel time with two bonus laps of the ring road.

The city centre reminded me of my childhood hometown of Chester; Tudor houses, sturdy defensive walls and narrow passageways. I resumed my sightseeing the following morning: first the Jorvik centre, then York minster where I climbed to the top and searched for peregrine falcons –

they are known to nest on cathedrals. Sadly, there were no falcons about, but plenty of pigeons. With this abundance of food, I suspect it wouldn't be long before a pair took up residence.

By mid-afternoon I'd enjoyed the highlights of the city and decided to drive south to Blacktoft Sands RSPB. I followed the course of the River Ouse along a flat landscape which reminded me of Norfolk. One benefit of choosing an RSPB site is they are normally well signposted and this was no exception (it also stood out as an oasis of wild amongst a desert of industrial farming).

The first bird hide was empty, so I took my pick of the available benches, and sat near the door. Within seconds of taking out my binoculars I spotted a marsh harrier, prowling above the deep reed bed, quartering the swaying vegetation. It spun on angled wings and dipped down in an attempt to catch prey; without success.

A few minutes later a young couple entered the hide, they saw me, giggled to themselves and scuttled off into the furthest corner. The marsh harrier flew away but shortly afterwards a second one arrived. I glanced at the couple to mention the bird's appearance, but kept quiet after realising they were busy snogging. I felt uncomfortable playing gooseberry, so left to go to the neighbouring hide. The second hide was busier but thankfully nobody was canoodling. The female harrier remained in sight and for a moment she pointed directly towards me and her wings formed a perfect 'v' shape. After the harrier departed, I listened to the birds outside. Sedge warbler, great tit and reed bunting, and thankfully no loving noises coming from the neighbouring hide.

At times during my holiday safari adventures, my energy wanes. I'd reached the point of exhaustion while sitting in a bird hide watching a great tit, so it was time to drive back to York and do another unwanted lap of the ring road.

****

I had an early night, and woke refreshed for more exploring. First I drove east to Bridlington, then onwards to Flamborough Head. The north-east coast was a popular place for kittiwakes and they nested in their hundreds along the chalk cliffs (prior to this, I naively thought chalk only occurred in southern England). Flamborough Head was lower than Beachy Head, but no less spectacular. An archway gushed with frothing waves, while seabirds clung to the cliffs like rock-climbers.

Today's primary destination was a short distance north of Flamborough: Bempton Cliffs RSPB. Parking charges at Bempton help support the RSPB, but some visitors chose to park further away to avoid donating to the charity.... they were probably twitchers. Inside the reserve entrance a feeding station was busy with sparrows and a bit of wildlife knowledge allowed me to establish these weren't your average sparrow. They had copper-coloured heads, indicating they were a rarer species; tree sparrows. I'd hate to be disparaging to my friends the good old house sparrow, but tree sparrows look more dapper.

Flamborough's chalk cliffs continued into Bempton and the main pathway led above the cliff tops. The reserve bustled with visitors and I followed behind the herd. A group of seven people were in front who clearly knew each other as they chatted amongst themselves. I loved the fact that six had gone to the trouble to wear camouflage patterned clothing and their seventh member sported a bright orange fluorescent jacket. Maybe she didn't get the memo about the day's dress code or she deliberately did it to annoy her mates. I hoped it was the latter. It would be the sort of thing I would do to my friends, or more likely, they'd do to me.

Wooden platforms jutted out above the steep cliffs, allowing visitors to peer down at thousands of seabirds. Gannets nested along a wide stretch and it was a pleasing new perspective to see them from above, in comparison to from below during the Shetland boat trip. The distinctive smell of a seabird nesting colony filled the air and I hoped none of it would end up on me that day, as I had the distinct feeling that my coat retained some of Farne's odour.

Gannets soared past at eye level and some landed amongst flowering red campion (the flowers deep pink rather than red). A pair of gannets reunited at their nest and began mutual preening and bill tapping. A chancer then attempted to land beside them, only to be loudly rebuked. Jabbing beaks finally sent him flapping off. The gannets took the cliff's open sites, while razorbills, kittiwakes and fulmars tucked themselves into the available nooks and crannies.

It was three people deep at the best viewpoints and I stood amongst the crowd and hoped those at the front would be courteous and rotate. Sadly, consideration for others was not forthcoming from those with big cameras dominating the front row.

Among the scrummage a lady asked someone beside me, 'Where's the best place to see puffins?'

I was tempted to reply on her behalf and say, 'The Farnes.'

The other visitor was more helpful and pointed the lady further along the headland. I decided to go too, because the front row showed no signs of shifting. After seeing the puffins (they weren't as good as those on the Farnes), I took a circular route back through farmland, to dodge retracing my steps and seeing the same people hogging the prime spots.

I left Bempton, drove north to Scarborough but didn't stop as parking was difficult, so continued to Whitby. The fish and chips at Whitby were the best I've tasted in England and I should know, I've given the subject extensive research. I successfully managed to eat the whole lot without being harassed by the patrolling herring gulls. Others were less fortunate.

I crossed the North Yorkshire Moors and wandered around Saltergate before returning to York, managing to hold myself back from an extra lap of the ring road. Typical, I'd got the hang of that just before leaving.

In the morning I drove west towards Leeds Bradford airport for the late afternoon flight. This provided ample opportunities to explore places en route and my first stop was Mother Shipton's Cave, beside the River Nidd. A dipper family gathered on the riverbank, a noisy crew making sharp sounds which cut through the background noise of the burbling water. River-dwelling creatures such as dippers, kingfishers and otters all have high pitched calls for this reason. Recent study has also suggested a higher pitch is now being used by urban songbirds, so they can be heard above the rumbling traffic.

One dipper fledgling perched close below, its eyes winking back and revealed a flashing white eyelid.

At Brimham Rocks the exposed millstone grit had been sculpted by the wind. Huge boulders balanced on narrow natural plinths which appeared to defy gravity. Time remained for one final stop at the Yorkshire Dales. At Stump Cross Caverns, a short-eared owl floated across the heather.

During this holiday I'd been blessed to observe both short-eared owls and marsh harriers in flight, graceful as ballerinas – the owl represents her dancing over the stage, while the harrier looks like her running through a crowd to catch a bus.

The strongest memories of this trip were the excellent locations, rather than specific wildlife, in particular the tranquillity of Lindisfarne, the lushness of the Wood of Cree and the majesty of Bempton Cliffs. The favourite place of all was the Farnes – a totally immersive wildlife experience, (being menaced by poo and pecks only boosted the encounter).

The decision to take a route with different start finishing point was also a fruitful one, and I'll repeat that tactic in the future. The final act of the holiday was to go shopping and buy a new coat. Even after two washes I wasn't convinced the smell of bird poo had completely gone.

White-tailed Eagle

Chapter 8

Skye, Harris and Lewis (2015)

I desperately needed a break, due to the stress of both my office work at the time and a part-time history degree. A wild and peaceful location was required to forget my daily routine. After consulting a map of the British Isles, I decided on six days exploring the Hebrides and northern Scotland. The circular route would begin in Glasgow, up to Skye, a ferry to Harris and Lewis, back across The Minch to Ullapool with a final stop at Grantown-on-Spey. The whole trip was organised at the last minute with no specific wish list. Scotland had previously been outstanding, so I was optimistic I would see a profusion of wildlife; but I could never have foreseen there would be so many memorable encounters.

The terrain on the A82 towards Glencoe was awe-inspiring; imposing mountains looming above the road like gathering giants. I wouldn't normally speak to myself, but on several occasions I emitted an audible 'Woooo.' Even though it was early June, winter endured higher up on the snow-capped peaks, while at lower altitude my car was hammered by rain. I was pleased to be in a warm dry vehicle, rather than outside with the soggy ramblers. They looked wet and miserable but I convinced myself that deep down inside they were having fun, and if I'd offered them a lift they'd have declined.

At Altnafeadh the weather cleared, presumably the low rainclouds couldn't get past the mountains. I parked in a layby, absorbed the scenery and felt tiny in comparison. Fantastic views were also provided at Mam Ratagan near my overnight stay; a glorious vista of lochs and mountains. Strong evidence that a journey can be just as wondrous as a destination.

My accommodation was in Glenelg, a small village beside a wide body of water called the Sound of Sleat with the mountains of Skye beyond. The hotel bar was lively with drinkers and throbbing with laughter. A local band thumped out cover songs and the walls trembled from their noise.

I checked to make sure it was Sunday.

Yes, it was.

I believe on Lewis and Harris they observe the Sabbath more soberly.

Evaporation from the hot sweaty crowd caused the windows to fog up with thick condensation; you could probably get drunk by licking the glass. Even for me it was too early for revelry, so my luggage was dumped in my room which had a vibrating floor as it was directly above the bar.

Two nearby brochs were visited – impressive and mostly intact. A lamb had managed to trap her head in a woven wire fence. She decided to resist my rescue attempts and lurched forward in an attempt to head-butt me between the legs. Eventually she was freed and bolted off to join a small gathering of spectating sheep. I got no thanks for my endeavours, not even a simple 'Baaaaa'.

Back at the accommodation, the bar was still hectic. I checked again, yes it was definitely Sunday. After dinner, a group of twenty-year-olds arrived, laden with camera equipment and they pitched up in the corner. The merry locals fancied a dance and tried to recruit me, but I resisted their approach – however the youngsters enthusiastically accepted the invitation. My decision proved wise as I watched the new recruits being flung around like ragdolls.

The atmosphere was quieter during breakfast and I recognised someone on the neighbouring table; it was Miranda Krestovnikoff, a BBC wildlife presenter on *The One Show*. I avoid imposing myself on celebrities, however I have no problem eavesdropping on their conversations. Apparently, a minke whale was spotted earlier this morning at the southern end of the Sound of Sleat. On the opposite side of the spectrum, some of their young team members were nursing bruises and hangovers from last night's ceilidh.

Breakfast was a delight, the sort of feast which makes lunch unnecessary (in theory). Afterwards, I went outside for fresh air in the hope it would aid my digestion. The view was stunning, a blue loch with a background of Skye's mountains dotted by cloud shadows. I tried looking for minke whales and might have had more success if I'd remembered to pack my binoculars. Thankfully the beautiful scenery calmed my frustration. After drawing a blank with whales, I wondered whether cetaceans would elude me once again during this holiday. How wrong I'd be.

The Glenelg ferry seemed a romantic way to approach to Skye, rather than using the new bridge, so I joined a queue leading down a winding road to the small port. The ferry was docked on the far side, giving me plenty of time to investigate the surroundings. Not all the activity in the channel was tidal; Atlantic grey seals were hunting in the quickening waters. They were very frisky; a female seal hurled herself above the water as she chased a fish.

Female grey seals are prettier than males, the guys have bulbous noses which make them look thuggish; like grizzled bouncers. One seal emerged with a fish in her jaws and three gulls plunged down on her, attempting to wrestle the prize from her mouth. The seal shook her head defiantly and submerged with her catch intact.

A crowd began to gather as the ferry returned, amongst them was the BBC team, but they remained behind as we boarded. A few weeks later their footage appeared on *The One Show*, which focused on Skye's white-tailed sea eagle population. They sadly omitted the ceilidh and whiskey drinking.

I was soon across the Sound, off the ferry and driving up a winding narrow road into the hills, rising up into Skye, before heading down towards Portree. After twenty minutes, the road cut inland and hugged the southern coast of Loch Ainort. Looming ahead was a skyline of green pyramidal mountains, while on the right the sea loch came closer to the road as I approached the tip of the bay. My peripheral vision is good and out of the corner of my eye I saw a huge black beast sweep above the waves. It was sleek and torpedo-shaped, like a small surfacing submarine; but

114

with a dorsal fin. I desperately needed to pull over. A gravel car park was spotted, I drove in and broke hard, causing grit to scatter.

A frantic rummage of my luggage ensued, scattering underwear and shirts unceremoniously across the backseat, until it resembled a jumble sale. Eventually my small handheld camera was found, I leapt out of the car and headed towards a high point on the left. Fresh air, remote landscapes and the chance of seeing a colossal sea creature – life doesn't get any more exciting than this.

The water was choppy which would make spotting marine life tricky, so I climbed the modest hill in the hope the elevation would assist my views. There was no path and I took long strides through the heather. During the stomp I pondered over what I'd just seen. I ruled out a prehistoric dinosaur as obviously they are only in Loch Ness. I was thinking basking shark; it was the right time of year for these summer visitors and it was big enough, but what I spotted for a split second (I was concentrating on driving, honest) surfaced like a very large dolphin. An orca could be ruled out as the dorsal fin I saw was too small; orcas have enormous black fins, particularly the males – they look like they're carrying upright surfboards on their backs.

But what else could it be?

I stood on the high point and hoped whatever I'd briefly seen would make another appearance. After ten minutes of nothing, doubts started to grow. Plenty of time had passed for it to have slinked back out of the bay. Patience is a vital commodity for a wildlife enthusiast, although the longer I waited the greater my pessimism grew. Then suddenly, I had a bolt of adrenaline as a black glistening cetacean emerged at the far end of the loch. It was not a shark and it was not alone. The handheld camcorder trembled with excitement as I filmed. The camera served two purposes: I'd get evidence of the sighting, plus I could use the zoom in the absence of binoculars. During the next surfacing I concluded there were at least four animals and they were long-finned pilot whales, a new and exciting species for me. They are called whales although, as with killer whales, they are actually dolphins (admittedly, big dolphins). All four dolphins kept in a close formation as they gradually moved towards my end of the bay. Occasionally they turned on their sides and displayed their long-pointed pectoral fins, hence their name. There were three large adults – the fourth was slightly smaller and presumably a juvenile. They rose closely together and floated at the surface like logs, before submerging again.

After twenty minutes of joyous dolphin viewing, I noticed something else: passing traffic. The big dolphins surfaced, while in the background people continued their daily commute, unaware of these incredible creatures beside the road. Do all these drivers lack peripheral vision? Are the passengers not glancing around at their surroundings? Are pilot whales so common around Skye that the locals find their appearances boring?

I finished filming and began watching the dolphins with my own eyes. It's always nice to get footage, but to truly appreciate a wildlife moment you have to give it your full attention. Five minutes later, I noticed a solitary car divert its journey and park beside mine. The driver got out, stood on the fringe of the car park and pointed binoculars in the direction of the pilot whales. Hurrah I thought, out of all the people to drive past, at least one person had noticed. It was time for me to go, plus I wanted to meet this person and share the experience.

After a clumsy stumble down the hillock, which was more of a controlled fall than a walk, I approached the lady and greeted her with a friendly, 'Hello.'

'Pilot whales,' she smiled.

After a brief introduction she revealed that she was a local wildlife expert. I love meeting local experts. She explained that 21 pilot whales recently stranded themselves nearby (subsequent research confirmed it was at Brogaig Bay near Staffin Island). With the help of volunteers, eighteen were re-floated and released into the sea. Later, more became stranded on Staffin Island and this resulted in the loss of six more. It's still not fully understood why some cetaceans behave in a suicidal way; but it's assumed they become disoriented and due to their strong social bonding, suffer a group fate. The dolphins we surveyed in Loch Ainort were presumably all from that original rescued pod and the lady was pleased I'd seen four, as she counted four the previous day; so no more casualties. She assured me that Loch Ainort contained plenty of pilot whale food, which consisted of cuttlefish and squid, and they wouldn't go hungry. We both shared our hopes that they'd feed well before returning safely to the open seas.

The greatest joy in observing the pilot whales was seeing their behaviour and sharing a small piece of my life with these magnificent mammals. The encounter was also tinged with sadness, as the dolphins were probably stressed. I'll never know the true feelings of this intelligent species, but I'm sure the recent events would've left some enduring emotional impact.

I continued to drive north and along the route I anticipated seeing mountains, seascapes and rugged wilderness. That all occurred, but viewed from behind a competitive unicycle race. After overtaking several one-wheeled racers I eventually arrived at the hotel in Uig (pronounced Oooick; well that's how I said it). My room was at the rear of the hotel and a window overlooked a backyard dominated by tree thickets. If I'd paid more for an expensive room, I'd have been rewarded with sea views. I decided to go to the front bar for some sea views, and a pint instead.

I introduced myself to the barman and four locals, and was soon on friendly terms. I took out my camera and showed the barman the pilot whale footage.

'Incredible!' he gasped, 'You saw those here?'

Perhaps pilot whales weren't so common in these parts. We discussed other local wildlife and I mentioned; 'Tomorrow I'm taking a boat trip to watch white-tailed sea eagles, have you done that?'

He shook his head. A red-haired local gent lent towards me and offered, 'He's a good lad, but not well-travelled.'

We chatted about Skye and the group recommended several nearby geological sites, including locations even the barman had visited. The Old Man of Storr and Quiraing were noted as worthy locations for exploring before leaving.

The friendly barman's evening shift ended and a new lad started. Within two minutes he managed to offend one of the ladies at the bar, with a brave but slightly foolish comment, 'Your blouse is the same colour as one of my goats.' I'm old and wise enough to realise that if you say something which upsets, either apologise or shut up and pretend it never happened. The barman did neither and fanned the flames of her fury, by trying to justify his comment. 'I don't know why you are getting so upset, my goats are very pretty', he remarked, a signal for me to move away from the bar and resume sea-watching from the large bay window. Later that night I retired to my room, peered out of the back window towards the trees and again regretted not paying for sea views.

****

The next morning it was bright and calm at Skye's capital Portree. Along the harbour front, different boat operators advertised eagle-watching trips. I chose to book a space on the biggest and most lavish boat. I'd already achieved cost-saving with the hotel room, so I could splash out on this outing. We left port, trailing behind a smaller competitor but we soon beat their craft for speed. I glanced back as the passengers on the other boat held on tight and bounced in our wake. The investment had already paid off. We were soon alongside a coastline fringed with overhanging trees. The skipper eagerly announced that a white-tailed sea eagle was high up in the woodland and a few seconds later he excitedly told us there was a second eagle in the trees.

I hadn't spotted the first one yet.

He offered directions based on the topography, 'Can you see the big tree with the t-shaped top?'

There were lots of trees.

He continued, 'There is a white rock to the left.'

I couldn't see a white rock from this distance, but I was able to borrow some binoculars and scanned again.

The skipper added, 'The female is on the left, she is larger than the male to her right, he's obscured by leaves.'

A guest cheered; he'd sighted them. He helpfully stood behind me, put his arm over my shoulder and pointed. I followed his arm down to the finger and immediately saw the female eagle. What a relief! It took another minute to see the male eagle; in my defence, he was hiding.

The guy next to me was looking in a completely different direction and said, 'Oh yeah, I see them now.' God knows what he thought was an eagle. A lady grabbed him by the shoulders and moved him thirty degrees, until he finally saw something which was actually an eagle, rather than a funny-shaped branch.

As our boat bobbed and drifted in the water, the skipper dragged out a chiller box, picked out a silvery fish and chucked it over the side. This offering would hopefully entice one of the eagles down. The eagles were unconvinced and continued to spectate from their lofty perches. The little craft we raced past at Portree eventually joined us and they also flung in a fish. Surely two fish would be too tempting for any eagle. The eagles showed little interest and stared down nonchalantly. The bobbing dead fish were moving about considerably more than the eagles.

A great black-backed gull circled above and plummeted onto the sea beside the fish, paddled closer and snaffled one. Antagonised by the gulls pilfering, the male eagle stirred, jumped from his perch and bolted down with heavy wing beats as if he was flapping two large sheets of plywood.

The skipper laughed, 'The male is going to teach that gull a lesson.'

The gull sensed trouble was on its way and gulped at the fish which went halfway down its gullet, creating a bulge in its throat. The bloated gull took off in the opposite direction to the eagle and an aerial race ensued. Both birds flew away quickly, the gull with a head start of twenty metres, shrieking at the chasing eagle. The gull's screams were undoubtedly an attempt to tell the eagle it was strong enough to fly, swallow a large fish and call; in other words too fit to be caught. The eagle wasn't convinced and maintained his pursuit. Eventually both birds disappeared across the loch, with only the faint cry of the gull still available.

Our boat circled the Sound of Raasay and an hour later we returned to the eagle roost. The male was absent, but the female remained in exactly the same spot as she perched before. I asked the skipper if she was just a plastic decoy, placed there to humour tourists. He laughed – but didn't deny my allegation. The smaller boat joined us again and each skipper threw in a fish. Throughout the entire time the female eagle didn't move, adding more weight to my argument.

The skipper explained that the clock was ticking and we'd soon have to return to Portree. The other boat headed off first; presumably it'd take them longer to get back in their slower vessel. We hung around for a couple more minutes while everyone forlornly stared at two bobbing dead fish. Not even a hungry gull was tempted; they'd all learned a lesson. A large shadow then shot over our boat and someone shouted, 'Eagle!' The female was still a statue – it was the male who'd returned. He swooped down at one of the fish, snatched it within his splayed talons, lifted on enormous wing beats, soared up to the trees and settled on a branch beside his partner.

No one expected the male eagle to creep up behind us in such spectacular fashion but we all saw it. which was more than could be said for those on the smaller boat; they'd already disappeared behind the headland. To add insult to injury, the eagle took their fish, not ours. As we left the eagles, the female moved towards the male and seized his fish, dispelling my theory that she was made of plastic. As we sped back to Portree we overtook the smaller boat again and their passengers bounced in our wake.

After an enjoyable trip, I toyed with the idea of driving back down to Loch Ainort to check if the pilot whales were still there. However, this thought went against my normal motivations for wildlife watching. I visit places in the hope of seeing creatures – if I went to Loch Ainort, I'd hope not to see them there because ideally they would be out of the loch and in the open seas.

Dunvegan Castle was my alternative destination and afterwards the Cuillin Hills. To call them hills was being modest; they are an impressive mountain range. Ramblers were jauntily hiking up a steep track to bag some Munros. If I tried to scale that slope it would probably kill me. I chose instead to return to Uig and walk over to the Faerie Glen, which was more within my physical limitations.

****

The next morning involved a lap of the Trotternish peninsula, where the geological highlights included the sheer cliff faces of the Quiraing and the upstanding rocky columns of the Old Man of Storr. I'm sure I've seen both locations in television series and films. They were stunning (particularly the spear-shaped Storr) but sadly I couldn't reach the summit joining hundreds of other tourists, as I needed to catch a ferry to Harris.

The ferry was a big vessel with a wide-open top deck and I stood on the starboard side to avoid facing into the midday sun. During the voyage I scanned for wildlife and while observing Harris in the distance, something halfway in-between caught my attention, the distinctive movement of marine mammals. I turned to a young couple sitting nearby and called excitedly, 'Dolphins!'

I received a gormless glimpse from the guy and the girl ignored me. Further behind them a lady heard me – she jumped from her seat and bent over the railings. She wore a large purple hat which caught the wind and nearly blew off her head. The dolphins approached and they revealed two features which helped confirm the species. First, their go-faster stripe flanks which were the colour of Dijon mustard and secondly the speed of their movement. They were common dolphins. If cetaceans were boats, harbour porpoise would be pedaloes, minke whales yachts, bottlenose dolphins those inflatable banana boats with people spinning off and finally common dolphins would be speedboats. Common dolphins are not as acrobatic as bottlenoses but their swiftness is just as exhilarating to witness. They slashed through the sea's surface like knives. The couple beside me remained static, but the purple-hatted lady acknowledged me with an appreciative smile. She leaned precariously over the railing to get a better view and held onto her hat. We both watched the pod of approximately ten dolphins dash closer, race from the bow, alongside the starboard, leap over the pulsating wake of the ferry and vanish behind. The whole spectacle lasted ten seconds.

The purple hatted lady walked around the people sitting and yelled through the sea breeze, 'What a fabulous start to my holiday!'

I glanced down at the couple below. The dull lad looked up at me and muttered, 'What did you see?'

'Dolphins,' I repeated wearily.

'Dolphins? Really?' He became a bit more animated and peered over the side of the ferry. 'Where?'

I shrugged. 'They went by, you missed them.'

'Oh,' he said disappointedly.

The lesson – don't ignore strangers if they shout 'Dolphins!' I felt no sympathy for the young couple. I tried to help them, but they snubbed me. I strode away to stand elsewhere, leaving the couple to stare at sea and its absent dolphins.

The ferry docked in the deep narrow berth at Tarbert and at the first junction I turned south. I intended to explore Harris before going north to Lewis. A short distance outside Tarbert was the beginning of the Golden Road (locals complained the cost of the road's construction was equivalent to its weight in precious metal). This narrow road was recommended for its scenery and it didn't disappoint. The route wove around inlets, over hillocks and cambered beside lochs, like a tame rollercoaster, sweeping and undulating through rocky coastlines. It was an absolute joy to drive.

Ten minutes later, I passed two people standing by the roadside, staring through binoculars at something on the hillside. If you ever see people behaving this way you should always stop and find out what's piqued their interest.

I walked over and used my regular opening line for such a circumstance, 'Hello, have you spotted anything?'

The lady turned towards me and breathlessly stuttered, 'There's an eagle up there!' I looked too, but didn't see an eagle. Wildlife knowledge is usually positive, but this particular moment it was potentially negative and I didn't have the heart to say her eagle was a common buzzard. I acknowledged seeing the bird, had a nice chat about how lovely Harris was and said farewell.

The road widened and swept northwards with a steep hill on the right, opening up to reveal magnificent views of turquoise sea, wide expanses of white sandy beaches and a backdrop of green mountains. It was breathtaking.

After Luskentyre the route rose into uplands, the traffic ahead met roadworks and we halted in front of red lights. I studied my surroundings, then gazed up. High in the sky was something twice the size of a common buzzard, with outstretched substantial wings fringed with finger-like feathers. Its silhouette was different in shape to yesterday's white-tailed sea eagle; this time the wings less square, tail larger, neck and head smaller. This led me to believe here was a golden eagle. Rarely do I wish traffic lights would remain red; sadly they changed to green and I had to move on. I took a final glance at the eagle while it soared above the mountain.

****

The following day the weather deteriorated and a powerful wind pulsated dark clouds above Lewis. It was like a gigantic sprinkler system, set to soak you every thirty minutes. With limited time to explore Lewis I went out regardless of the conditions. The landscape was similar to Shetland: wide moorlands dotted with modest houses, stunted tress and hardy sheep with wet miserable expressions. Does this breed of sheep actually enjoy being pelted by cold rain or would they prefer lazing in sunshine?

At the most northerly point, gales blasted me about at the Butt of Lewis. The wind grabbed hold of seabirds and flung them past at speed, while spume lifted off the waves and splattered the coast with a blizzard of dirty snow. The coastal path led over steep-sided cliffs cut by gullies and deep crevices. If anyone fell off the cliffs, the probable outcome would be death or at least a severe mangling between waves and rocks. It was safer inland amongst the machair grassland, which sparkled with yellow buttercups.

The drive along the north-west coast included seeing traditional one-storey rural cottages called blackhouses, and the impressive standing stones at Callanish. The afternoon sky thankfully cleared for my visit to Bosta Beach. The sand was as brilliant white as a Caribbean island, although the climate was not conducive for iced cocktails and budgie-smugglers and was better suited to hot toddies and thermal underwear. Terns stood on the white sandy shoreline and if I possessed binoculars, I might have been able to elaborate on the species. In the early evening I returned to Stornoway, my face glowing from the incessant wind and rain. It looked as if I'd spent the day getting my cheeks slapped.

Stornoway town centre reminded me of my home town Douglas; a safe, friendly atmosphere, with a blend of old and new. Modern architecture was adjacent to historic buildings, trendy restaurants beside old-fashioned local pubs, young executives swaggering around town while drunk elderly fisherman zigzagged. The nightlife was very familiar.

****

The subsequent day was calm and bright, good weather for exploring the eastern coast before departure. After strolling along a couple of beaches, I decided to stop at Tiumpan Head, as it had a lighthouse and I'm partial to lighthouses. This one was converted into kennels and it echoed with barks and howls. I moved away from the incessant din and rambled up a hillside pathway, where once again I was drawn towards two people with binoculars.

At the top of the hill, I greeted a gentleman and enquired, 'Hello, have you spotted anything?'

'Have we spotted anything?!?' he chortled deeply.

I waited for him to elaborate.

He turned to his partner who was busy gazing through binoculars. 'What have we seen so far today?'

She raised her face from her binoculars and blinked furiously, as though she'd been hit in the eye by an insect. 'Well, so far, minke whales, Risso's dolphins and harbour porpoise.'

The man interjected, 'And common dolphins.'

The lady checked her clipboard. 'Yes, of course, first ones we saw today.'

I turned to face the Minch. It was as though I was missing out on something happening behind me. The sea stretched over the horizon like a rippled blue carpet. Then from the offshore depths a minke whale rose and broke the sea's surface.

The man beckoned me closer. 'Feel free to use the telescope.'

I did.

I peered through the powerful optics at the sea, while we chatted about local marine life and their hobby. They were both members of a group called the Tiumpan Head Watchers which kept regular records of sightings – their list increased just then when a pod of Risso's dolphins appeared in the south, cornered the lighthouse and travelled north. Risso's are a similar size to bottlenose dolphins but with blunt flat noses, taller dorsal fins, and they become greyer and whiter with age. They also display scars, as if they've been in a knife fight. These marks are caused by interactions with their own species as well as their prey (squid will occasionally fight back).

I felt bemused by the whole Tiumpan experience and related my feelings to the lady, 'While researching Lewis I didn't see anything which mentioned cetaceans. I only turned up here to see the lighthouse.'

'That's a kennel.'

'I know,' I replied as the barking persisted in the background.

She chirped. 'We have our own Facebook group, and we are trying to spread the word.' I later joined the Tiumpan Lighthouse Facebook group and they continue to see spectacular marine life, including orca, fin and humpback whales.

The lady showed me some of their extensive recordings. While I read, I was alerted to the appearance of a pair of harbour porpoise below. If I'd known Tiumpan was so special, I'd have given it longer on my itinerary, but I needed to dash, just as another minke whale surfaced.

At Stornoway I boarded the ferry and gravitated to the top deck. Halfway across the Minch a pod of common dolphins leapt in our wake and later some bottlenose dolphins crossed south.

I've spent many hours staring out to the sea without success, so today left me in a state of disbelief. I never knew that anywhere offshore from Britain had such a vast amount of sea life. Why wasn't this abundance advertised? Are Hebrideans keeping it a secret to avoid the perils of mass tourism? After all, some Skye residents complain that since the construction of their new bridge they've been inundated with tourists. I suspect people live on these remote islands for the peace and seclusion. I guess it might be a problem if some loudmouth wrote a book and blabbed about all the Hebridean marine life. Next thing you know, Stornoway is crowded with people decked in camouflage clothing and carrying binoculars (if they remember them).

I completed the drive from Ullapool to Grantown-on-Spey and the following day headed down to Glasgow. The first scheduled stop en route was Loch Garten RSPB which would have been found sooner with better signage. Half an hour later than planned, I entered the visitor centre, manned by enthusiastic young staff. An expansive window overlooked hanging feeders and I studied the diners, hoping to see my first crested tit; instead there were coal and great tits, plus a female greenfinch. I overheard a father listing the bird species outside to his son and apparently my female greenfinch was actually a siskin – I couldn't tell the difference. The father's identification skills trumped mine because he possessed two attributes; extensive knowledge and binoculars. He explained that female siskins have paler chests and darker legs.

The communal feeding was convivial until all of a sudden the birds scattered. From the woodland a greater spotted woodpecker fired through the air and landed on the feeder with enough force to make it swing. Woodpeckers can deliver a nasty peck and they sometimes predate smaller birds, so they were wise to make way. Male woodpeckers have red plumage on the napes of their necks; this one didn't, so it was a female. She hammered away at the feeder and scattered peanut debris onto the floor; a godsend to the field mouse below.

Television screens provided live footage from nearby nests; one screen displayed a female redstart. Female redstarts resemble robins in shape, but they lack the same bold colours – they're like my favourite Lions rugby shirt, which after many washes has faded from red to a dull pinkish grey. The redstart nest box was located outside the visitor's centre, so I could stop and look at that before departing. In the meantime there was the main attraction to savour – an osprey nest. Occasionally I can be quite slow to catch on; it was a few minutes before I realised the osprey on screen was actually outside the window (in my defence, it was quite far away). With borrowed binoculars I gazed into the distance and studied an enormous nest with a large bird on top.

The guide explained that this was the female and her first batch of eggs had failed, but there was optimism they'd try again. I glanced between the screen and the actual nest and then a broad-winged brown-backed bird descended. For some reason I always thought ospreys were black and white, which is why I said to the guide, 'That's not an osprey.'

'Yes, it is,' she replied politely, 'It's the male returning.'

She was of course correct.

Ospreys might be smaller than sea eagles, but they are still massive. Everybody in the visitor's centre became excited by the male's arrival, even though some numpty had questioned his identity. He landed on the nest beside his partner; but perhaps they'd fallen out, because the female departed immediately. Possibly he was being blamed for the loss of their first clutch.

Upon leaving I stopped a safe distance outside the building and stared at the top corner of the roof where the redstart nest box was located. I hoped the male might return with food. However my tolerance for being bitten by midges was lower than my desire to see a redstart, so I scampered back to the car with flailing arms.

Argaty Red Kite feeding station was my final stop. I was under time pressure because my Glasgow flight was imminent, but I calculated I had thirty minutes spare. Sadly, my half hour didn't coincide with feeding time. It was nice to see approximately twenty red kites from a distance, as they gathered on trees and telephone posts. But it soon became obvious that none was prepared to shift any closer until the buffet was open, so I departed.

It was inevitable my luck would eventually run out.

This had been one of the most enjoyable wildlife trips ever. All my troubles were completely dispelled during my island-hopping adventure. Sadly, after a few days back at work, I felt as though I'd never been away.

Corncrake

Chapter 9

Orkney –
West Mainland (2018)

During my tour of the Orkneys I would try to achieve three specific wildlife experiences; all with potential in this region. Firstly, I wanted to discover an endangered species that's just beginning to show a small revival in numbers; corncrakes. I've never seen or heard a corncrake; they're very rare and have a habit of hiding in the undergrowth, so I'd be satisfied to simply hear their croaking call. Besides, they are not lookers – they resemble a juvenile pheasant. Secondly, I planned to spend a considerable time at the coast, so another otter would be great – it was more than ten years since my last one at Mull. The final item was ambitious: an orca. I've been very fortunate to glimpse an orca from the Isle of Man, but that sighting was distant and brief. I hoped to get a good view and for it to last longer than a couple of seconds. I was going in mid-May, so I also held expectations of seeing species beyond my wish list. I undertook significant research prior to departure and in addition to wildlife spotting, there were important historical sites worth exploring.

Accommodation was booked at four different locations: Stromness, Evie, St Margaret's Hope and Kirkwall. I'd organised a hire car, a tour around Hoy, and remembered to take binoculars. I was also going to be joined by my friend Joe for the second half of the holiday. He wasn't passionate about wildlife but I'd attempt to convert him to my hobby.

On the flight from Aberdeen to Orkney I had a window seat which initially presented the sight of murky thick clouds. Once at lower altitude, the Pentland Firth emerged and Orkney magically appeared; first the mole-hill shaped mountains of Hoy, scattered islands, then swathes of farmland across the mainland. The mainland was intercut with lochs and sea inlets so that I wasn't sure whether I was passing over sea or land. From height, St Magnus Cathedral dramatically dominated Kirkwall's modest housing; it was like the Empire State Building appearing in the middle of Croydon. The plane soon passed Kirkwall, swept low over fields and landed. The airport security process involved a nod from a bearded chap in a uniform.

During the bus to Stromness I gained my first impressions of Orkney. Lambs scampered across the fields and lapwings displayed in the air. Shetland ponies grazed in some paddocks, but Orkney was distinctly different to Shetland, the land was greener and it contained some trees. I am not claiming Orkney is blanketed by woodland, but it has enough trees to prevent them becoming a novelty.

At Stromness a hefty lad the size of one of the Stones of Stenness helped lift my suitcase off the bus. My evening's accommodation was a short stroll away, I checked in and took a diversion into the bustling bar to quench my thirst with their fine local ales. There appeared to be an equal split of tourists and locals, this ratio remaining a common sight throughout the trip. The locals seemed a jovial bunch and they dressed like me – scruffy. A pair of exhausted fishermen entered and sat down heavily. They had ruddy complexions, presumably from years of being scoured by the salty sea air; or they suffered serious problems with their blood pressure.

After a pleasant night's sleep, I was awoken by the rumbling noise of the departing Stromness ferry. It was an appropriate time to rise, so I got up and showered in a very confined cubicle – there wasn't enough room inside to swing an Orkney vole (if I had one).

The day of exploration began at a bus stop outside Stromness, which provided an unexpected opportunity for wildlife watching; nesting starlings. Starlings normally nest in holes in buildings or trees, but Orkney afforded limited opportunities for these; trees were still rare and the houses were sealed tight against the winter winds. Therefore, Orcadian starlings needed to be creative and improvise, and these starlings were nesting in a low stone wall adjoining the footpath, their entrance holes at knee height. Several parents zipped in and out of narrow crevices which chirped noisily with hidden chicks.

Surely this was a dangerous nesting choice? I asked myself how they could be successful. The first positive was that cats would avoid a busy road. Also, the local people seemed wildlife friendly, so it was unlikely they would go poking about and create disturbance. For twenty minutes I waited for the bus and was entertained by the starling parents' endeavours. When exiting the walls they seemed to co-ordinate with passing traffic, flying perilously close to the bonnets of vehicles – perhaps this was another canny tactic to cause pursuing birds to be squashed on a car windscreen. What I initially considered a foolish nesting choice might actually have been quite astute.

The starling viewing was interrupted by a male chaffinch in a nearby shrub emitting a loud, 'Tzzzeeee'. This was his warning call. One of the most rewarding skills for any wildlife enthusiast is to learn warning calls, which are usually sharp, high pitched and repeated after a pause; and crucially they can allude to a passing bird of prey (sometimes you'll be unlucky and see a crow or a cat). I stood on the pavement's edge, investigated the surroundings and then looked up. A peregrine falcon was heading for Stromness town centre. Its appearance disturbed the rookery behind the main street and they rose en masse and went berserk. Rooks display collective aggravation better than most. The peregrine swerved from the unwelcoming committee and it was a few minutes before the rooks settled back onto their branches, to continue crapping on the parked cars.

The morning brightened at Kirkwall where I visited the tourist information centre; I'd arrived on Orkney without a map. There were detailed ordnance survey versions, but I discovered a free map. Job done. Next, collect the hire car. While driving about Orkney, I realised I would struggle to hide the fact I was a tourist. The car was emblazoned with large lettering advertising the hire car company.

I drove the mobile billboard west for its first promotional gig at the Cuween chambered tomb. It was here I heard a cuckoo (in my childhood this sound was a regular feature of the countryside, but sadly it's become a rare treat). A farmer stopped fixing his tractor and listened too; he told me it'd been calling all week. Orcadian farmers appreciate the sound of a cuckoo and they also retain ponds in their fields. The only negative I found was their extensive use of wire fences instead of hedgerows; however, on such a windy island, fences were probably more practical.

The Ness of Brodgar was a short distance away, the location for several Neolithic sites, first the enormous Stones of Stenness and behind them the remains of an early settlement at Barnhouse. A bird hide was found on the banks of Loch of Harray and I crossed through a swarm of midges, heard a reed warbler and quickly strode back with midges still in pursuit.

The footpath to the Ring of Brodgar led beside an uncultivated field. Redshank parents chirped at their two fluffy chicks, as they bumbled between cuckoo flowers. The precocious youngsters were already independent feeders, probing into the vegetation for insects with their stubby beaks. Some tourists paused to photograph a sizeable mound of wild primroses; pale yellow petals and deeper coloured centres. I was aware of a local species of Scottish primrose, but wasn't sure what they looked like, maybe it was only a small regional variation. I struggled to see anything unusual about these primroses.

After visiting the prehistoric village at Skara Brae (it was reminiscent of Jarlshof in Shetland), my final destination of the day was Yesnaby. The car park was busy and an elderly gent in a fluorescent tabard directed me to park further along the headland.

'Can I park anywhere?' I asked.

'Yes sir, just stop before you go over the cliff.'

I heeded his advice and parked a safe distance from the edge. The majority of the tourists were north, milling around information boards and coaches. To the south was an outcrop of ochre rock with fewer people, so I explored there instead. I ambled across the sandstone headland, while being thumped and buffered by the wind. I perched above the cliff and soaked up the Atlantic views while the wind continued to shove me about. In front of me, fulmars bounced up as if they had a trampoline beneath. A large fly whizzed over my shoulder and headed offshore, unaware that in that direction, its closest landfall was Greenland.

Great skuas were on regular passage. I'd never previously given them credit for their grace in flight; I was impressed by the way they swept nimbly above the waves. The skuas all flew south; presumably there were seabirds down there in need of harassment. Further out on the open sea, there was a seabird feeding frenzy – hundreds of distant white specks swirling above the water, like someone had shaken a large snow globe. Using binoculars I identified herring gulls and kittiwakes, but couldn't see any cetaceans.

A solitary puffin peered from a crevice in the cliff below, conceivably trying to avoid becoming a target for a passing great skua. I was full of admiration for the gliding great skuas, until I returned inland and their flight paled into insignificance against an elegant Arctic skua. A crow appeared and was hounded out of the area by double-teaming lapwings and an oystercatcher. A crow's life on Orkney seemed to have a lot more hassle than back home.

As I departed Yesnaby the large crowds of people were still congregating in the north. I discovered the reason later when I reviewed Orcadian locations online. The cause of the north's popularity was a short distance around the corner – an amazing sea stack with a hole at the base. That was an irritating realisation; I would have loved to have seen that with my own eyes. After all the hours of preparation prior to the holiday, I was still able to cock it up during the trip.

It was late afternoon when I returned to Stromness, and retired early in preparation for a 6:30am start.

****

At daybreak I drove to Houton for the Hoy ferry to join a guided tour. The road was quiet in terms of traffic, but it was rush hour for wildlife – on two occasions I stopped for jay-walking fledglings. I waited for them to flutter back into the verge before continuing.

The morning was cold and misty, but the greeting from the ferry staff was warm. I boarded the large vessel and followed signs to the passenger lounge which led me into the bowels of the boat. The lounge was reminiscent of a school classroom, colourful and welcoming. Sadly it was windowless and I always feel claustrophobic in rooms without windows. I clambered back onto the top deck and sat on a cold damp bench. I endured these conditions throughout the trip with my backside getting gradually more chilly and damp. Two locals were sitting in their heated truck cabin and regularly glanced in my direction. I could occasionally hear them laughing; in all likelihood joking about the idiot sat outside. I pulled the coat lapels up around my nose, hat down and between my letterbox view I spotted a passing great skua. Its head turned and inspected me then decided to fly off and ruin the morning for a nearby tern colony.

The ferry journey was scheduled to last an hour. Halfway across the western side of Scapa Flow, the weather improved and I emerged from under my hat. I hoped to do a little wildlife watching but sadly the sea state remained too choppy for spotting cetaceans. Nonetheless, I had a fantastic sighting of the distant silhouette of a white-tailed sea eagle. The huge bird flew amongst gulls dwarfed by its size. It was probably one of a pair of eagles who recently took up residence on Hoy, knowledge I'd garnered the previous night while in the pub. Pub customers usually feed me a load of tripe; but for once, I'd been granted accurate information.

It wasn't long afterwards that the ferry arrived at the port of Lyness, in Hoy's south-eastern corner. Terns were nesting on a dilapidated pier detached from land, making it safe from land predators such as stoats. I met the tour guide and fellow tourists; all genial and chatty and I looked forward to being in their company for the day. The itinerary involved visiting Hoy's historic sites and important local landmarks. The schedule omitted any reference to wildlife, but the tour would be outdoors all day, so I was optimistic I might glimpse some nature during our travels.

Hoy would be a brilliant place for a childhood home, lots of wartime naval base buildings, now abandoned and derelict, all waiting to be turned into hideouts and dens. The wild landscape contained the raw beauty of moorland with regular sea views. Farming and housing were minimal, particularly in the mountainous north. We parked opposite the Dwarfie Stane and met a RSPB warden; she had her eyes on an eyrie. She pointed to the white-tailed sea eagle nest, high up on the opposite hillside and advised us where to walk to avoid disturbance. She also highlighted a few other things of interest, including flowering lousewort. While rambling through the heath I spotted clumps of pink petals: lousewort! I announced this to the rest of the tour group. In acknowledgement I received feigned enthusiasm, a smattering of dismissive glances and one shrug followed by, 'That grows on the hillside behind my house.' I slunk to the back of the group as everybody else walked off.

The Dwarfie Stane was a large lump of rock, the size of a big limousine, with a chamber cut inside by early settlers. No one took the initiative, so I was the first to crawl through the narrow entrance. It was a cramped dwelling with sleeping areas for small people, probably Hobbits. I heard excitement outside, so I slowly extracted myself from the rock (delayed when my belly became wedged). As I fought to squeeze my gut through the gap, apparently the eagle left its nest, circled above and revisited its eyrie. After eventually freeing myself, one guest turned and asked, 'Did you see the eagle?'

Clearly not. I'd been stuck inside a rock with no windows during its performance. I shook my head while trying to disguise my annoyance.

Shortly afterwards a female hen harrier cruised over the moor, which took the edge off my disappointment. I then spotted more lousewort, but decided not to share it with the others.

Our guide was an expert on naval, maritime and military history, including the military bases and war graves. He was passionate about his island home and in particular the RNLI. On the heather upland we passed a pool and in the middle was a red-throated diver.

I remarked, 'There's a diver in that pool.'

The tour guide replied, 'That's strange, people normally dive around the Scapa Flow shipwrecks,' and he drove on.

I suspect local wildlife was not his forte.

We continued north to Rackwick Bay, where the long, rugged beach was exposed to everything the Atlantic could throw at it. The bay was bookended by high cliffs and the shore was strewn with debris from those cliffs. The weather was pleasant, but the cliffs continued to be battered by waves; they probably never got a day's rest. Some guided tours offered the opportunity to go from here to the Old Man of Hoy but that would require a hike and we'd selected a less strenuous itinerary. Besides, after Yesnaby I'd begun a theme on this holiday: to miss out on impressive sea stacks. We visited abandoned crofts, heard cuckoo above and reed bunting below, and an inquisitive lamb approached me and bleated repeatedly. I didn't understand her issue.

Back in the minibus, we travelled across a causeway to the island of South Walls, stopping at a nature reserve called the Hill of White Hamars. 'Hamars' is Viking for hammers and based on the ferocity of the waves; I guess the 'white' was the frothing sea which struck the cliffs like a mallet. The coast was deeply cut by the sea and over many years this action carved out caves. The roofs of some caves had collapsed inland, creating deep sink holes in the fields, one wide enough to swallow a bus. In strong storms these caves would surge with incoming waves and send explosions of frothing water into the air. There were no geysers of spray today, but we found evidence of previous tempests, as the grass fringes were burnt with saltwater and scattered with seaweed. It wouldn't be a safe area to wander around in the dark, but it was good habitat for Scottish primroses, pointed out by one of the other tourists who knew her botany (even though she'd earlier dismissed the lousewort). She pointed to a tiny clump of flowers (Primula Scotica) amongst the grass, significantly smaller than my garden primroses, with bright purple petals and yellow centres. It was an unexpected treat, although I worried that before I realised what they looked like, could I have accidentally stepped on some?

The tour was a varied and enjoyable eight-hour outing. On the return ferry we all sat on the top deck in sunny conditions and I commented that I hadn't noticed any of these fair-weather travellers on the outbound journey. We said our farewells at Houton before I drove to my new accommodation at Evie, north of the West Mainland.

The guest house was on a sloping hill facing a channel of water called the Eynhallow Sound, with the hills of Rousay beyond. The landlady Denise and I hit it off immediately, mainly because we both had the same sense of humour. Denise quickly identified two of my greatest pleasures – good food and the 'occasional' drink. Dinner was served on a large table and all six residents gathered together like a family. A feast was placed in the middle of the table and we helped ourselves. The ravenous crowd only needed thirty minutes to polish off most of the food, but a quarter of a bottle of red wine survived. Denise picked up the bottle and passed it around the table in an anti-clockwise direction. I would be its last stop. Everyone politely declined the opportunity to finish it off before it was eventually pointed at me.

Denise gave me knowing smile.

'I'd better drink it then,' I said. 'Otherwise it'll go off.'

She emptied the bottle into my waiting glass.

Later I rested in the front room beside a large window, a cold beer in one hand, a pair of binoculars in the other. It felt like heaven as I stared across the fields. Hares danced a spiralling chase and oystercatchers foraged for worms. The distant sea once again provided no dolphins, even though I maintained a steady watch throughout the evening. As the sun fell low in the clouds the windows became caked with midges. Mercifully they remained outdoors.

****

After a wonderful night's sleep (the best for several days), I ate a delicious breakfast before departing on a new day of exploration. The sights during the early morning drive included a hare jogging down the centre of the road. Further along a tabby cat was being subjected to an aerial assault by starlings and swallows.

The first destination was the Earl's Palace at Birsay, which had been neglected and required restoration – two centuries ago. The walls chirred with young starlings and sparrows, while parents commuted to the nearby beach for insects from a strandline deep with seaweed. Above the tidal line were manmade stacks of balanced rocks, each over a metre high, like large stony traffic cones. They reminded me of the French wedding patisserie called croquembouche, consisting of dozens of profiteroles stacked to a peak. I continued thinking of profiteroles as I strolled inland, but all thoughts of chocolate and cream vanished when I was confronted by a huge black bullock. He stared directly at me and huffed loudly. He did a very accomplished job of being intimidating. Thankfully he was behind a fence, although as I approached closer, I realised it wasn't a sturdy barrier. The bullock lent forwards and the fence shifted a few centimetres. The track diverted sharply right and I was relieved to escape bovine threat. I left Birsay with plans to return later during low tide to explore the offshore Brough. I wanted to cross the causeway on foot, rather than swim.

A pastel floral display greeted me at The Loons RSPB – carpets of pink cuckoo flower, yellow marsh marigolds and white bogbean. I stood in the arc of an architectural concrete wall which had been built there to amplify the sounds of the reed marsh habitants. A skein of greylag geese passed overhead and the concrete construction lifted the volume of their honking. A lapwing chased a common gull and once the gull was successfully evicted, the lapwing emitted a celebratory high-pitched Yorkshire call, 'Eey upp, eeeeey upp!'

A bird hide was situated around the corner and inside three people were silently observing nature. I never engage with people unless they show signs of sociability – and there was no indication of that. I sat quietly in the corner and overlooked a wetland habitat with little grebes and tufted ducks floating on a large pond. A shoveler emerged from the reeds – a duck with an appropriate name – its beak perfectly shaped to scoop pondwater for plants and insects (or clear small snow drifts).

I opened the window to listen out for bird songs. A reed warbler unleashed its rasping call while clinging to a swaying lanky blade of grass. It was a peaceful location to sit and absorb nature. A swirling mass of midges formed outside and I hoped they wouldn't come indoors and bite someone, especially me. When I left, I exchanged smiles with the others, then drove to the next destination. Five minutes down the road, I remembered I'd left the window open in the hide and could imagine the scene now – three people cursing me as they were devoured by midges.

At Marwick Head I parked south of the beach and walked towards the headland. A large object had been washed onto the strandline which from a distance looked like a battered thick tree trunk, but closer inspection revealed it was a large dead cetacean. The animal was significantly decomposed and the air was heavy with its smell. Based on its size, it was possibly the remains of a pilot whale. I didn't stay long as I found it difficult to breathe. Further down the beach, a couple of lads approached from the headland. When we crossed, I pointed out the dead cetacean and they were intrigued and went over to investigate.

A raft of eider ducks gathered in the bay, the drakes serenading the females with calls of, 'Oooh er!' like Frankie Howerd in the *Carry On* movies. In the background there was another sound, that of lads coughing – the smell of decaying cetacean had just hit the back of their throats.

The path took me upwards; it was steep, but made easier by frequent stops to watch razorbills, fulmars and kittiwakes. On the headland's summit I sat on a rock and gazed down at cliff ledges lined with guillemots, like queues of suited office workers. A couple with a dog sat nearby and we exchanged nods. The collie scampered to my side and she dropped a stick by my foot. Normally I'm an enthusiastic stick thrower but I was fully aware of an eighty-metre sheer drop beside me. I had a terrifying premonition of me chucking the stick, it catching the wind and disappearing over the cliff with a collie in pursuit. With that in mind, I tentatively threw her stick a couple of metres inland. The dog stared at my pathetic throw, retrieved the stick and returned to her owner. If she could speak, she'd have probably said, 'Nice throw fatty.'

The sea yielded up no dolphins, although the seabirds were excellent. Fulmars floated on the updrafts, while guillemots bombed back and forth to the rocky shelves but after twenty minutes of sitting on the rock, I had a numb bum, so I stood up, had a stretch and a waggle then walked off towards the Kitchener Memorial. At the back of the tower a plaque remembered the poster boy of World War One and the crew of *HMS Hampshire*, who lost their lives off this coast in 1916 when they struck a German mine.

A short distance beyond, a path led inland; I much prefer circular routes to straight ones, so took it gratefully. Diurnal rabbits bounced over the thick grass as I ambled down a track between large fields. An abundance of skylarks fired out their trilling songs like a heavenly choir and escorted me through the pastures. The sky cleared and the sun warmed the landscape but the heat also lifted the smell of the dead pilot whale, which achieved a more nauseous pungency. I quickly got into the car and departed for somewhere fresh.

Back at Birsay it was now low tide, I parked at the tip of the peninsular and crossed the exposed rocky causeway to the Brough. The waft of rotting seaweed made a welcome change to decomposing pilot whale. Children excitedly explored the rock pools, so I knew the joy of tormenting sea creatures in nets was alive and well. A small girl caught a shore crab and waggled it by a back leg. I'm sure I did the same at her age. I reached the Brough without slipping or plunging my foot into water and was greeted by a mass of yellow flowering birdsfoot trefoil, before walking among the foundations of an old Viking settlement. Once across the central hump of the island there were more cliffs.

Orkney seemed to be a paradise for fulmars – they were nearly as numerous as the starlings. One flew close and gave me an eye-shadowed glance. They are glorious birds despite their Old Norse name meaning 'foul gull'. It relates to a fulmar's ability to vomit fishy oil over anything threatening it while on the nest, a cunning deterrent to falcons, great skuas and human rock climbers.

Further along the coastal path, a plump female eider duck appeared from the grass. We exchanged looks and both wondered what to do next. I took the initiative and decided it was a pleasant place to stop and sat on the grass, leaving the duck to waddle off at her own pace. It was a comfortable seat and I settled down for a little sea watching.

The viewing provided no dolphins or whales. I was surprised I hadn't spotted any yet but perhaps my expectations were unrealistic. Orkney was a new location and whereas I know the best places and times of year on the Isle of Man, I was a beginner here. Maybe there were more sightings first thing in the morning or later in the evening, or perhaps during June the feeding was better offshore.

Maybe they were hiding around the corner, so I went around the corner to find out. No dolphins were there either, but it was the location of a murder. In old black and white movies, a human crime scene would be indicated by the white marked outline of the victim, but on this occasion we had had an avian assassination and it resembled the explosion of a feather cushion. My detective work determined that the victim was a pigeon and the feathers had been plucked by a bird rather than chewed off by a mammal, so the killer was undoubtedly a bird of prey.

I carefully walked back along the rocky causeway and drove inland to RSPB reserve on the moorland hills at Cottascarth. The stroll from the car park to the bird hide was a fair distance but worth it when a male hen harrier flew past. They are smaller than female harriers but make up for lack in size with their good looks. When there is gender distinction in species, the male is usually the most handsome (because they need to impress the ladies) and the female is drab so that she is camouflaged on the nest.

This is particularly apparent in hen harriers: the male has silvery white plumage with black wing tips... the female is brown, with other brown bits. He tilted, dipped and scoured the heather for prey. I hoped he might pounce on one of the plentiful pipits, but his talons went empty as he disappeared over the ridge.

The interior of the bird hide was modern and comfortable – it seemed better constructed than my home. A couple of birdwatchers soon joined me and we chatted about our combined wildlife adventures on Orkney. They had experienced a great encounter the previous evening, a family of otters splashing about on a glistening shoreline. It sounded like a beautiful moment; I wish I'd witnessed it myself. They had friends on holiday with them who were also disappointed at missing out – so much so, they were apparently no longer speaking.

A bird of prey emerged high above the ridge and we started an enjoyable game of 'guess the falcon'. Twitchers can get stuffy and competitive when it comes to identification but when the participants are genuine wildlife enthusiasts, it's great fun. We aired our thoughts without risk of humiliation. Based on size, shape and movement, we came to a general consensus: peregrine falcon.

A few minutes later, frenetic squawking was heard above our hide, loud shrieking noises on the roof then a bird of prey made an appearance. It flew away at speed, pursued by two starlings. 'It has a bird!' the lady called out. Grasped in the raptor's talons was a motionless feathery bundle which we assumed was a young starling. We had another entertaining game of 'guess the falcon' and after a short debate the agreement was: merlin (because it was smaller than the earlier peregrine). The merlin left its pursuers behind and darted down the valley.

It was also time for me to leave so I said farewell and went for a final stop near to the Evie accommodation. The track up Burgar Hill crossed between fields, and along an overgrown fringe a lapwing approached a brown hare from behind. The lapwing crept closer and closer. Once in range she stretched out her beak and delivered a sharp peck to the hare's backside. The startled hare scampered off and the lapwing returned to her nest, content that her family was now free from disturbance.

An enormous wind turbine towered above Burgar Hill car park; I stood beneath the blades and felt their movement as they whooshed like a Ferris wheel on steroids. An elderly couple walked into the bird hide. I followed and greeted them once inside. All the bird hides on Orkney were comfortable and sturdy buildings, I imagine because flimsy hides would be blown to Norway in a winter storm.

The main attraction was twenty metres outside the hide's big windows. Stretching across the moorland basin was a peaty-coloured pond and immediately two large birds glided down and landed with a splash in the middle of the lagoon. The lady chirped, 'Red-throated diver.' The birds were obscured by a faint mist which prevented me noticing any obvious red-throat markings, but I agreed with the lady, as this was their typical habitat and they had the sleek profile of divers. Additional supporting evidence was provided by artwork on the walls, presumably by local children. Amongst these pictures were several red-throated divers. Well, some were a bit dodgy; one resembled a red-necked crocodile while another could have been the mutant offspring of a robin and an emperor penguin. Neither of these hybrids are expected to be seen around Orkney, so I'll stick with red-throated diver.

The divers climbed inelegantly onto a small island to the right of the pool. They hunkered down in a patch of marsh marigolds, the male climbed on top of the female and they mated amongst the flowers. How romantic.

A short time later a male hen harrier passed through and disturbed a flock of greylag geese who had previously been relaxing on the bankside. The harrier disappeared with three geese in tow. The lady then spotted a great skua lurking on the opposite ridge, possibly sitting on a nest. This was bad news for the red-throated divers if they choose to nest here too – it would be like living in a house made of straw with neighbours who are arsonists.

I was soon back at the B&B and sat in my comfortable chair, gazing out of the big window with both hands busy holding beer and binoculars. A Belgian couple were staying that night and they joined me. When I began scanning outside with binoculars the gentleman asked if I was bird watching.

'Yes but unfortunately there's not much out there at the moment.'

He leaned closer. 'We saw birds today, could you help me name them?'

Normally this would entail the retrieval of a phone and me being shown the distant image of a badly focused brown blob, but fortunately, today was going to be different. He embarked on a surreal game of charades. The Belgian stood up and imitated the first of his mystery species, by making a waddling movement across the room.

I was about to call out, 'Ring-tailed lemur', but he spoke before I could comment.

'Brown bird, quite tall, beak long, not straight.' He put his hand to his face and with his hooked finger stuck on his nose, pointed downwards and pecked at the bookshelf.

'Curlew,' I said while opening the bird book and presenting him with a picture of the curved beaked wader.

He nodded. 'Ahhh, curlew.'

I glugged a mouthful of beer ready for the next challenge.

The Belgian became more animated for this one and he strutted along the carpet like a constipated speed-skater. 'Noisy, black and white, very noisy, whay whay whay…. red beak.'

'Oystercatcher.'

I showed him a picture and he agreed. While he was close to my face he stared at my nose and commented, 'Your face is as red as an oystercatcher's beak. Have you been sunbathing?'

I suspect it was a result of the wind at Yesnaby, rather than any sunburn. Sadly, no other species required identification as I was quite enjoying the challenge.

If only he'd seen an otter. I'd have loved to have witnessed that impersonation.

Merganser

Chapter 10

Orkney –
South Ronaldsay and
East Mainland (2018)

After departing the home comforts of Evie, my morning drive featured a domestic cat and some sparrows, thankfully, both were at different locations. I also saw my first blackbird of the holiday; they seemed to be an Orcadian rarity. It raced across the road and narrowly avoided my windscreen (maybe that's why they're such a rarity). Blackbirds either possess a very finely-tuned talent for judging distances or a reckless approach to road crossing. The bird turned sharply and disappeared into a hedgerow, which made me think of home and the blackbird nesting in my allotment hedge.

In January I had fitted two bird boxes, one at the side of my fruit cage and another in a hawthorn hedge (the installation of that one caused me blood loss). The birdlife snubbed my kind efforts and chose naturally available sites instead – chaffinches moved into a goldcrest conifer tree and a solitary female blackbird was busy in the hawthorn hedge (three foot from the bird box which caused me great hurt). My neighbour had more success with his bird box, as great tits regularly commuted to his with food. When I saw my neighbour next, I remarked, 'Have I mentioned – you've got great tits!'

He laughed, which was polite of him.

From the middle of my plot I'd sit and watch the three nest sites; chaffinches left, great tits ahead and blackbird closest to my right. I probably should have been busy gardening. The initial joy from all the nesting activity was tempered in early May when the eggs hatched and the parents became increasingly wary of my presence. I'd be at one end of my plot being scolded by a chaffinch, then I'd move away and get clucked at by the blackbird. I came to the conclusion they'd have to get used to me – eventually they did.

One sunny day I heard the clucking female blackbird (I never once saw the male – he was probably deceased or a slacker). Her return to her nest wasn't achieved by a direct route; there was always considerable faffing about beforehand. She'd land on the fence (five metres from her target), hop onto the ground and begin a prolonged approach to the hawthorn hedge in a series of running bursts. She regularly clucked, not for my benefit, but to warn her youngsters to keep quiet. She also delivered a mean stare, the sort that interrogates your soul. I avoided looking directly back, as animals have learned that being watched with interest by a human face can be dangerous (in the old days when we put four and twenty blackbirds in a pie). To observe her I'd tilt my head and glance through the corner of my eyes, my face pointing away. This ploy seemed to put her at ease.

Once at the base of the hawthorn she'd give me one final check, before elevating in a flurry of wing beats and disappearing amongst the leaves. How did she manage to slip into the hawthorn hedge without any bloodletting?

I never once approached the hedge to peek inside, even though I'd have loved to have seen the hatchlings. My inquisitive nature was curbed by a desire to avoid creating disturbance during a delicate time. The allotment was no longer mine, but I was happy to temporarily relinquish it to my seasonal feathered guests. After a week, the female blackbird eventually realised that the beardy guy wasn't a threat. She became more relaxed, her approach shorter and straighter. On one occasion she scurried right past my feet, eyeballed me and pattered off.

I then did something which wildlife filmmakers try to avoid; I became involved. This blackbird family had grown on me, and I had emotional interest in their wellbeing. I learned the mother's warning call; sorrowful and high-pitched. Once heard, I'd investigate the cause of her anxiety. I became an expert at shooing-off jackdaws and hooded crows. She allowed me to walk straight past her to do this, although I remained under surveillance by one of her inquisitive eyes. I admired her maternal energy every time she returned, whether it was because of potential danger or a wriggling worm delivery.

The day before departing to Orkney my crops were treated to a soaking and afterwards I sat down and relaxed. Out of the corner of my eye I saw a blur of dark feathers as the blackbird fluttered down, landed with wings splayed, then ran directly up to me and stopped – this was the closest we'd ever been. I froze as she stopped beside my right foot, probed the path with her beak and drew out a very long worm. The worm took a vicious beating before it was coiled it into a neat package, like a mini Cumberland sausage. I turned my head and faced her directly. She didn't flinch and remained close. We both had a moment together (the worm didn't participate). It was one of the most powerful and emotive wildlife encounters I've ever experienced. I felt part of her life. This was more than just seeing a blackbird; she had my personal affection. In all probability she just saw me as a stupid beast whose purpose in life was to scare off crows or dig up worms (when I eventually got round to some gardening). But I'm no stranger to unreciprocated love.

Thoughts of back home filled my mind as I left Evie and drove to the airport to collect my best friend Joe who feeds the sparrows in his back garden but complains about the cost. Some bird species annoy him, such as herring gulls and feral pigeons, and most of all, he has a deep and irrational hatred of penguins. Apparently, they've hijacked Christmas, they smell of fish and their only useful purpose in life is to feed leopard seals. If I ever happen across two tickets to Antarctica, Joe wouldn't be my first choice as travel companion.

Joe was waiting outside the airport terminal as I parked alongside him. He read the large lettering emblazoning the side of the hire car and exclaimed 'You couldn't lose this in a car park, could you!'

I omitted to declare that three days earlier I'd managed just that!

We travelled south and visited the Italian Chapel – the creative accomplishment of Italian prisoners during WW2, who successfully turned two Nissen huts into a glorious place of worship.

Causeways provided convenient routes to island-hop down to South Ronaldsay. On the southernmost tip we called in at a Neolithic site called 'The Tomb of Eagles'. The staff at the site spanned several generations and they made the whole experience more wonderful with their enthusiasm. This ancient burial place was recently unearthed and amongst the archaeology they found human remains and white-tailed sea eagle talons.

Along the path to the tomb, an unaccompanied springer spaniel scampered past, squeezed under a gate and ran into an adjoining field. She poked her nose into the entrance of a rabbit burrow and her stumpy tail wagged excitedly. She then scuttled over to the neighbouring warren and did the same. We continued along the route while I regularly checked the dog's progress.

I commented to Joe that it was nice to hear so many skylarks.

'They go on a bit,' he replied.

Sometimes I wonder whether his dismissiveness towards wildlife is just to annoy me.

A skylark descended and before touchdown its singing ceased and everywhere fell silent. From behind us another noise gradually grew louder. The pattering of feet and panting of a spaniel; she overtook us with a large object in her mouth – a recently killed rabbit. The dog trotted proudly in the direction of an elderly lady who glared down with a shocked expression at the dog's dead rabbit. We continued in stunned silence: even though we'd just encountered Orkney's apex land predator.

At St Margaret's Hope we checked into our B&B, dumped our luggage and freshened up. The owner David and his son Will were welcoming hosts and both delightfully eccentric. The hotel overlooked the harbour and the coastal town was charming – it reminded me of the location for the film *Local Hero*. During a solo stroll around the village, I discovered a community garden bathed in afternoon sunshine. It was a peaceful venue with a welcoming bench for visitors to relax. A collared dove started to sing – sing is probably the wrong word for the repetitive 'doo doooooo doo.' The calling dove was perched on a roof, and unsurprisingly its partner was nearby. Doves make happy friendly pairs; roosting together tightly like snuggling couples and flying in close formation. Seeing two doves is always a peaceful sight; the exact opposite of seeing two robins – if you put two robins in close proximity, it usually results in GBH.

I reunited with Joe, we got into the car and began an exploration of the surrounding area, but unwittingly ended up in a traffic jam for the ferry. The free map was to blame according to Joe, as it only featured the main roads and not the minor ones and Orkney is predominantly minor roads. I performed a U-turn while the ferry guard watched. The guard read the large lettering on the hire car and came to the correct conclusion that we were lost tourists, and bestowed on us a jolly wave.

The subsequent stop was intentional; the Sands o'Wright, which was a pristine beach presumably named after one of my more illustrious ancestors.

Evening was spent back in St Margaret's Hope where we chatted to locals and visited two of the three pubs (we were warned off the third – no idea why). At sunset on the harbourfront, the bay shimmered in pinks and blues, an anchored yacht swayed and oystercatchers piped loudly. The serenity of the calm horizon was entrancing.

****

The following morning the harbour was sunlit and the coastal air imparted a crisp salty perfume. Barn swallows chattered above the B&B, while I awaited Joe's arrival.

As I drove I explained to Joe that the Orkney morning commute usually involved wildlife on the road, and sure enough, within a minute we met the day's 'beast on the boulevard' – a common gull. I swerved from its path. Joe swore.

The old churchyard at Old St Mary's contained headstones with recurring local surnames, the older stones cloaked with crunchy pale-green lichen, an indicator of Orkney's clean air.

Burwick's port was filled with parked cars and mobile homes awaiting the ferry to John O'Groats. At the end of the car park, Joe saw an information board and he loves information boards. Unfortunately, behind this one was a man in a flat cap having a pee. Joe turned to me and commented loudly about the close proximity of the public toilets, but it failed to distract the man in the hat from his business.

We rambled up the coastal path. Once on the headland, the clifftops were lined with red campion. Joe spotted a puffin and I explained how it used its tongue to gather small fish such as sand eels, before clamping them in its thick multi-coloured beak.

Joe's contribution was, 'It's currently using its thick multi-coloured beak to scratch its arse.'

I tried to think of a witty comeback, but became mesmerised by the sight of the puffin satisfying its itch, and the moment was lost.

The coastal footpath contained exhilarating moments when it bothered the cliff edge. We both gingerly glanced forty metres down to the sea; thankfully neither of us have a fear of heights. The headland offered panoramic views. South was the Scottish mainland marked by Duncansby Head lighthouse beside John O' Groats, separated from Orkney by the Pentland Firth, Britain's most dangerous stretch of sea. Today it looked relatively benign. To our west were the mountains of Hoy, while in the foreground a handful of freighters and an enormous oil tanker commuted into Scapa Flow.

Seabirds were drawn to a patch of sea which was criss-crossed by tidal currents. Herring gulls are good indicators of food bounties – in urban areas it's usually an overturned bin, but while at sea they swarm above shoals of fish. Occasionally the fish are driven to the surface by dolphins; therefore such gatherings are worth close inspection. I studied the gulls through binoculars as Joe walked off – it was as if he knew I'd be wasting my time. On this occasion he was correct.

Next on the itinerary was Herta Head. A large mobile home was spread diagonally across all the parking spaces so we had to park near a ditch. We rambled up the headland, which was one of those inclines where you reach the top, perceive a higher peak further along, scale that, only to reveal another higher point beyond. Apparently, a broch was in the vicinity; we never found it (unless it was the pile of rocks beside the path) and eventually we accepted defeat on the never-ending-summits.

The coast was visually stunning but sadly the wildlife highlights were plenty of fulmars and two rabbits having a quickie. When we returned to the road, the owner of the mobile home appeared and he apologised in a French accent for blocking all the spaces. We recognised his hat; he was the same bloke from Burwick who had been peeing behind the information board. We politely accepted his apology and never mentioned the earlier incident.

While crossing the Burray causeway, Joe called out that something moved in the sea below. We entered the village, parked outside the seafront hotel and looked for marine life. Nothing was seen during our initial viewings. The front door of the hotel opened and a lady approached and she spoke in a soft Scottish accent, 'Have you boys spotted anything?'

To call us boys was flattering to say the least.

The three of us stood together and she enthused, 'We occasionally see dolphins out here.'

At least somebody sees bloody dolphins on Orkney.

After five minutes she went back inside, then Joe got bored and went to inspect the shoreline and its profusion of crustacean shells scattering the beach. 'Look, it's crabmageddon,' he said.

There were three explanations to consider, other than 'crabmageddon';

a) the shells could have been discarded by crab fishermen

b) crabs could visit this area and moult their old shells

c) there was a massive resident otter with a penchant for crabs

I stared forlornly at the sea for a few more minutes before we left and explored the peninsular at St Mary's. A male red-breasted merganser bobbed on the sea, identified by its dark back, black head and red bill. This species is usually found at the coast, unlike the similar-looking goosanders who prefer freshwater habitats.

Joe took a different route back to me because a mute swan gave him 'a look'. Perhaps he thought swans could break your arm with a flap of their wings (an inconceivable story, but one which has undoubtedly saved many swans from being hassled by children). I enjoyed the rest of the walk alone and at no point felt at risk of being beaten up by a large waterfowl.

We subsequently tried to find a little island called Hunda; instead we discovered a road which looped back on itself and a couple of dead ends. Joe was becoming increasingly annoyed by the lack of detail on the free map, and I stirred things up regularly by asking him to refer to it for directions. During another U-turn my navigator eventually exploded and the map suffered one heck of a beating, the crumpled mass dumped unceremoniously in the footwell beneath Joe's feet. We finally saw Hunda, at another dead end with no obvious parking places or path.

I asked Joe if he wouldn't mind referring to the wrinkled map. If looks could kill, my adventures would have ended abruptly in Orkney.

Herston was significantly more positive; a sprinkling of modest houses lining a rocky shore, with views over Widewall Bay to the Sands o'Wright. But this area provided something more than its splendid scenery – a wildlife rarity. I had never considered adding this species to my wish list, as I thought it was unlikely to be seen. It's an animal which resides nowhere else in the UK: an Orcadian vole. One theory is that Belgian traders brought them during the Neolithic period. Was the Belgian staying at the Evie B&B a modern-day vole smuggler?

The vole sighting happened while I drove us out of Herston, when a mammal took a dash across the road. The animal had a blunt nose, stubby tail and was larger than your average vole; enough information for a positive identification. The moment was brief as it scampered over the tarmac and disappeared into the opposite verge. I was delighted to see a rarity; Joe was more concerned in claiming he saw it first.

Joe directed us to Northfield where the beaten map implied the location of another broch. Once again, the broch was nowhere to be seen. Somewhere around Orkney there was possibly a mass gathering of dolphins, whales and brochs; all hiding from tourists.

The evening comprised a substantial dinner, numerous pints of local ale (our favourite was called Corncrake) and concluded with an argument regarding the primacy of the vole sighting, the accuracy of the map and whether the Sands o'Wright was a quarry. We ambled back to the B&B and halted on the harbour front to admire the seascape. The bay was millpond flat, dappled yellow by the setting sun. A solitary tern flew over the bay's centre and plunged for a fish; the impact causing a ripple of delicately expanding circles.

****

The following morning, I arrived for breakfast as Joe chatted to an Australian couple on the neighbouring table and was surprised that it concerned local wildlife. Joe confessed later he instigated the dialogue by boasting about 'his' sighting of an Orcadian vole. This backfired when the Australians assumed that Joe was a wildlife fanatic. I got on with my breakfast while they bombarded Joe with details of their visit to the island of South Georgia between the Antarctic and South America. Joe was shown countless photographs of penguins, his arch-nemesis.

We checked out and left the southern chain of islands for the mainland. I was reluctant to leave St Margaret's Hope; it'd been one of the most charming places I'd ever visited.

On the drive north a suicidal brown hare dashed in front of our car, causing an emergency stop which woke both of us up – and possibly the lucky hare too. Our second stop was the beautiful churchyard of St Nicholas, bedecked with colourful wild flowers. Joe managed to pass four mute swans without incident and I identified a raft of eider ducks. Joe claimed that all ducks were just ducks and separating them into different species was making life unnecessarily complicated. A female Atlantic grey seal appeared in the bay and Joe used his simplified terms; he pointed to her and said, 'Seal.' Seals feature in Orcadian folklore as 'selkies'. They are believed to have the ability to change into human form.

Using the remnants of the map, we travelled north-east to Deerness and took a break at Dingieshowe to admire the pristine white beach. Only a couple of gulls were presently on the shore; if Dingieshowe was two thousand miles south it would've been packed with holidaymakers. It was considerably more pleasant at its current location.

We continued to Mull Head Nature Reserve where there were several things of interest to me, including a collapsed sea cave called The Gloup and the possibility of eventually spotting cetaceans. Joe was keen to visit the Covenanters Memorial, a monument marking the loss of life of Scottish Covenanter prisoners who were being transported to America as slaves in 1679. Their vessel sank during a tremendous storm with them trapped inside, and a monument was subsequently erected near the shipwreck site.

After consulting the information board's map, Joe stated that all items of importance were within walking distance, so we set off along the eastern coast. First was The Gloup, a deep cavity created by a collapsed sea cave, substantial enough to swallow a double-decker bus.

Bordering the path were more manmade columns of rocks, stacked a metre high. They were prolific around Orkney and created by many visitors. I found them interesting, but others consider them annoying additions by people spoiling the landscape. Joe was of the latter opinion and contemplated kicking them over.

At the Brough of Deerness a wide opening between the cliffs was the dwelling for a meadow pipit. The bird beat its wings furiously to reach an elevation ten metres above, then it cupped its wings into a parachute shape, spiralled down and the surrounding cliffs amplified its trilling call. At this time of year pipits are no longer just little brown jobs – their territorial performances stop me in my tracks and warm my heart. They easily rival skylarks with their summer displays. Sadly during winter they revert to being little brown chirpers.

The Brough was reached along a precipitous path, aided by a chain railing drilled into the rock, but still not a route for the faint-hearted. The flat top of the Brough was thickly matted with grass, forming a soft and bouncy mattress, and if I'd been alone I might have enjoyed a lie down. At the northern tip I scanned the wide seascape. Expectations of cetacean-spotting had fallen considerably during the holiday – I'd now be delighted to see a harbour porpoise, let alone an orca. I examined the entirety of the 180-degree coastal views and witnessed only waves and the occasional gull. Something else was noticeably absent and greatly pleasing; the lack of pollution in all its forms. No annoying noises from traffic or planes, the air was fresh and crisp, and Orkney seemed mostly free of litter.

On the return I passed an elderly couple on the narrow cliffside path and we carefully squeezed past each other. 'This is interesting,' commented the lady.

I scanned the coast for the Covenanters Memorial. A structure was visible on the next promontory so we rambled towards it for twenty minutes and found a concrete triangulation station. In the far-off distance a tall chimney-shaped structure poked above the remote headland. Through binoculars I studied the square-sided monument and confirmed it was the object of our search.

'It seemed closer on the information board,' sighed Joe. 'I'm not walking all that way.' Once again, his plans had been foiled by a map. He immediately headed back in the direction of the car park. Even though I had great sympathy for the Covenanters plight, I didn't fancy hiking a mile for a close-up experience with their chimney, so I followed Joe.

The route led over moorland as a blanket of sea mist blew in from the east. In the fringe of the mist, two small birds circled and emitted a vibrating mechanical buzz. They were male snipe and this was part of their courtship;

they were drumming. Snipes look similar to woodcocks, but woodcocks aren't percussionists. It was an exciting and completely new wildlife experience for me. As they dipped and circled, they sounded like tiny jet planes. Snipes generating the winnowing noise by vibrating their modified tail feather were similar to me during childhood when I'd put cardboard strips against my bicycle spokes to make it sound like a motorbike.

'Drumming snipe!' I exclaimed excitedly.

'Yeah, I've heard them now,' said Joe as he marched off.

I relished watching the snipe for five minutes alone. Once I'd had my fill, I caught up with him at the car park as he strode off to remonstrate with the information board map. His positive attitude towards it had definitely waned.

We drove a short distance before making another emergency stop for the local wildlife. A small bird came so close to the windscreen I could identify it by its pink legs: 'Meadow pipit.'

We reached Kirkwall at 5pm, which in most towns would be rush hour. The congestion consisted of four cars waiting at a roundabout. After an arduous ten-second wait, we continued to our hotel, checked in then explored the town centre in beautiful sunshine. In the middle of the high street was 'The Big Tree'. It was definitely a tree; however it was an exaggeration to claim it was 'big'. Despite its stunted growth, the sycamore was very old and added a pleasant piece of greenery to the town centre.

It had been unusually hot and dry on Orkney; gardens with burnt brown lawns, veg patches with bolted rhubarb and tall flower spikes. It was as warm as summer, but spring was still ongoing in the cathedral grounds, as a pair of rooks noisily coupled in the trees.

The locals were friendly and we chatted with a chap called Andrew, from a remote northern island called Sanday. We talked about the Orcadian winter; I assumed the long dark winter nights would be their greatest grievance. He explained they were more concerned by the gales, which were so bad that cattle were housed indoors to prevent them being hurt by gusts over 100mph. Andrew mentioned he'd recently heard corncrakes near Scapa, so visiting there would be part of tomorrow's itinerary. As for the rest of the evening, that would involve beer. I stumbled into bed at 11pm, moderately merry.

I was awoken at 6am by an American in the neighbouring room yelling out, 'Honey, I need my pants!'

After a disrupted night's sleep, I went for breakfast and was relieved when Joe requested a relaxing final day. We toured the museums, palace and cathedral, before going to Scapa.…… which wasn't exactly reverberating with the 'Crex crex crex' call of corncrakes.

It was soon time to depart Orkney and the taxi journey to the airport was livened up by a hare in the middle of the road. It must have mistaken the car for a springer spaniel as it zigzagged in front of the bonnet before dashing into a field. It confirmed one thing; all wildlife jumps out in front of vehicles in the Orkneys.

A couple of hours later, we were airborne. As we departed Kirkwall, I stared out of the plane's window and reflected on a brilliant holiday. Orkney was blessed with stunning scenery and wonderful people. My favourite places were Rackwick Bay on Hoy, Mull Head at Deerness and all of the RSPB reserves. We'd been very lucky with the weather, and the accommodation was divine in Evie and St Margaret's Hope. It was a place I would love to revisit in the future, perhaps to explore the islands north of the mainland, and try once again for corncrakes, otters and orcas. I might also have another attempt at witnessing the sea stack at Yesnaby.

Even though I'd expended a lot of time watching the sea, I had failed to see a single cetacean. This was by no means wasted time. All my cares in the world are forgotten while immersed in this relaxing pastime. Around Lewis dolphins had been leaping all over the place. The barren times on a wildlife safari are important – they serve to amplify the joyous moments when you hit jackpot, and make them more magical.

I may have failed to achieve any of my ambitious wish list, but I was jubilant to find Scottish primroses, hear drumming snipes and of course see my first Orkney vole.

Once home I had one final wildlife experience to complete – to confirm the well-being of the nesting birds on the allotment, in particular my beloved blackbird. The first thing I noticed was how well the allotment had flourished in my absence. It was like missing a party and finding out everyone had a great time without me. I sat in my chair and watched the nesting areas. The great tit parents were still busy feeding their young, but there was no activity at either the chaffinch or blackbird nest sites.

After several hours without seeing or hearing birds, I could be sure that both nests were vacant, so I approached the conifer. All was quiet and I checked where the chaffinches regularly vanished inside the tree. The lime-coloured foliage parted to reveal the dark interior. There was nothing inside. I stepped back, looked down and saw a green nest on the path, packed with grass and moss and intricately woven with spider silk. The central cup was lined with downy feathers and must have been a snug home for chaffinch chicks. I picked up the nest and gave it a squeeze – it was spongy to touch. But why was it on the ground? My immediate thought: this was a crow's doing. It's always a good starting point to blame a crow. The nest could have been discovered, pulled from the conifer and the vulnerable occupants eaten. I later learned that crows weren't to blame (on this occasion). After chaffinches fledge, the parents remove the nest from its original position to prevent the site being noticed by a predator (thwarting the devious crows), allowing it to be used again in the future. Chaffinches then often recycle the nesting material to build a new one elsewhere. On the whole it all seemed like good news.

With some trepidation I then approached the hawthorn hedge. I dreaded discovering a nest full of dead blackbird chicks. I put on thick gloves, as the hawthorn had already caused enough blood loss, parted the shrubbery and peered inside. A V-shaped branch in the top half of the hedge held an empty nest, woven with twigs and strengthened with dried mud (a blackbird's upbringing lacked the comforts afforded to a chaffinch). Then I walked back and found a dead blackbird fledgling on the floor, a sad revelation. The dead bird was half the size of an adult; it had feathers but was probably too young to fly. It may have been the runt of the litter and not strong enough to survive.

I told myself that the other youngsters successfully fledged, even though I didn't have any evidence to back this up.

Sand Lizard

Chapter 11

Dorset – Poole (2018)

I tell people the fact that I'm a wildlife enthusiast, but it can occasionally create problems. For example, my colleague Geoff always refers to me as a naturist, rather than a naturalist (there's a serious difference). Another friend, Mark, asked if I knew anything about wildlife and I replied in the positive. He then asked me to come to his flat and rescue a herring gull stuck on his balcony.

Sometimes my friends are helpful, particularly when they encounter a special wildlife event and let me know. In August I received a text from my friend Neil saying he was at the Manx coast observing dolphins so I immediately drove to meet him south of Douglas. I found Neil and a pod of Risso's dolphins leaping, tail slapping and splashing about happily (the dolphins, not Neil). After a sensational show, the dolphins went south and I followed. We met again at Langness, where the dolphins swam alongside a group of kayakers before coming closer to shore. This completely made up for not seeing any cetaceans on Orkney and I wouldn't need a dolphin fix during my Dorset trip.

In the mid-1970s, my childhood was spent in a landlocked corner of Cheshire, but once a year we'd have a family outing to the seaside. The initial sight of wide blue waters was always joyful, especially when my dad placed a 10p prize fund for the first person to spot the sea. Big money in those days. The sea has continued to be a source of pleasure for me, even without the financial incentive. Nothing beats the scent of salty air, soft sand pressed underfoot and shingle crackling amongst waves. Family holidays were often spent in south-west England and our adventures would begin with a day's travel in our spluttering old family car. I'd have my I-Spy nature book on my lap and gaze out of the window. The most exciting spectacle was seeing a kestrel hovering above a motorway embankment. It was always a source of complaint when our chugging old Austin-Morris Princess passed before the kestrel pounced on an unsuspecting rodent. My parents were adamant, even in the face of my loud protests, that the hard shoulder was not a place to park up and watch kestrels. Grown-ups were such spoilsports.

Another sight which brought great anticipation was a triangular red road sign depicting a galloping deer. This promised an encounter with Bambi and his family (sadly with his mum absent). I would be fixated by the woodland bordering the road and prepare myself for wild animals to energetically charge from the undergrowth. My parents also rejoiced at the appearance of a deer sign; they knew it'd shut me up for at least twenty minutes. I still get the same buzz now when I see a deer sign, even though during my entire lifetime, not one single sign has resulted in a subsequent deer sighting.

Childhood holidays would be in Cornwall and Devon, but we never stopped at Dorset. That would be remedied this year. The seven-day trip would take place at the end of August, mostly on the southern coast around Poole and Weymouth, chosen by me for their abundance of nature reserves, diverse coastlines and the neighbouring New Forest.

The first two items on the wish-list were sand lizards and any snake. The Isle of Man has lots of common lizards but no other reptiles, so I was hoping for something new. The third creature was wild boar, before I realised they were usually found in the Forest of Dean rather than the New Forest. So, I swapped wild boar for Dartford warbler, a more realistic target. I tried to organise a couple of guided tours without success; however, my schedule was already busy.

On my wildlife trips I usually go alone. With independence comes freedom and I don't have to compromise my schedule. However, Joe was joining me again after Orkney – admittedly we did a lot of bickering, but we also had plenty of laughs. Joe is fascinated by history rather than wildlife, therefore to accommodate us both, during the daytime I'd visit nature reserves while he'd explore local landmarks. In an attempt to get Joe more involved in my wildlife hobby, I gave him a challenge. Every evening when we'd meet, he was to provide me with his 'Wildlife Moment of the Day'. I'd already foreseen this might cause problems and so it did on the first evening. At 7pm we flew into Bristol airport, drove through Somerset to Wells and Joe announced his wildlife moment – a dead badger by the roadside.

He noted sadly, 'That's the first badger I've ever seen.'

'They are usually more active and less flat,' I replied solemnly.

The day concluded with a pub crawl around Wells, given added interest by being the outdoor location for the excellent film *Hot Fuzz*. In the morning we explored other attractions in the charming city (we'd done the pubs sufficiently), and visited the cathedral and Bishop's palace. Wildlife spotting was limited to ducks and swans in a moat, surrounded by signs warning people not to feed bread to the waterfowl. Apparently since my childhood, ducks have gone gluten-free.

I presented Joe with our excellent holiday map – one photocopied sheet of A4 incorporating the whole of Dorset. It was in colour with additional sites of importance written in pen. In my opinion, it was more than adequate for our purposes.

Joe snatched the map from me. 'Is this it?'

'Yep.'

'Has an ink-covered spider crawled across it?'

'I've written on some places of interest.'

'The scale of the map is tiny, I can hardly read the place names.'

'Is there a problem with your eyesight?'

'No!' he snapped, 'We are currently in Somerset. Do you have another sheet with Somerset on it?'

I shook my head. He seemed difficult to please this morning.

We continued south for a scheduled stop at Garston Wood RSPB and became lost in a maze of Somerset A-roads.

Joe muttered, 'If we had a map containing Somerset it would've helped.'

I ignored his negativity and stopped at a petrol station to get local knowledge. I asked the young member of staff to point me towards Shaftesbury, but she shrugged. I asked for the quickest route to Dorset – I might as well have been talking to a mannequin. Fortunately, a more worldly customer, who was familiar with the existence of neighbouring counties, pointed us in the right direction.

Before the holiday I researched all the nature reserves and the online details for Garston Wood displayed it in spring, blanketed by bluebells. It was now August and the floral display had diminished. The summer highlights included the possibility of rare butterflies, such as purple emperor and silver-washed fritillary, but I only saw a common species called speckled wood.

A gang of long-tailed tits chirped around us, communicating with each other to make sure everyone was present. A little further along an unfamiliar bird call echoed around the canopy. I walked towards the noise and stood in the shade of a tall tree as the bird continued to belt out its call. Unfortunately I couldn't see the performer and my phone was still in the car, otherwise I'd have recorded the call. Instead I tried to memorise the loud repetitive chirps which resembled a fire alarm. Four resident species at Garston Wood had unfamiliar calls: bullfinch, nuthatch, spotted flycatcher and marsh tit. I listened to recorded versions of all their calls later, but was unable to match my memory to exact species. Nuthatch seemed close but I wasn't 100% confident, so it'll go down as an 'unknown'. I have lots of 'unknowns'.

After my futile attempt at bird watching in Garston Wood, we sat on a bench and scoffed lunch, then continued towards Poole, passing several recently manured fields. The smell in the car became so pungent it caused us to cough and grimace. This raised the perennial dilemma; do you raise the car windows to keep out the ripe smell, or is it best to lower them in an effort to aid ventilation as you drive through? This subject requires further scientific study.

The blue waters of Poole appeared on our right before we arrived at the harbourfront – I expected salty fishermen, sailors and perhaps gangs of pirates but instead it was a popular place for families and yacht owners. Our hotel was on the harbourfront which was well serviced by restaurants, pubs and dotted with palm trees. In the evening we sat outside in the evening sunshine while Joe revealed his wildlife moment of the day, a cat sitting on a cushion in Wells Cathedral. I remarked that it was a *'wild life'* challenge and yesterday's badger had no *'life'* and today's cat wasn't *'wild'*. He refused to concede and my challenge was becoming less successful than I'd originally hoped.

****

The following day, I drove into Hampshire on the A31, which became the M27 and I waited in anticipation to see an exit mentioning the New Forest – none did. When I feared I'd soon end up in Southampton, I took the next turning and joined a miserable queue on the A36. Thirty minutes of mind-numbing gridlock passed before I was released onto open road, where I celebrated seeing a sign welcoming me into the New Forest.

At the beautiful village of Nomansland, ponies grazed open fields beside the road. I was close to one of my desired destinations; Bramshaw Wood. The woodland possessed the deep musty scent of an ancient forest and consisted of a good mixture of trees including beech, oak, ash and holly. The breeze rustled leaves and caused an ancient oak to creak. A fallen tree was smothered with yellow bracket fungus; possibly the edible species chicken-of-the-woods. A few years earlier I was given chicken-of-the-woods by Kelvin, a work colleague. I was dubious about his identification skills and researched it before cooking. He was wrong – it was a Dryad's saddle which was apparently still 'edible' so I cooked it. It tasted foul and I played merry hell with Kelvin afterwards. My friend Erica once ate a mushroom she was given by an 'expert'; its consumption led to her sight turning blue and she went into hospital to have her stomach pumped. With those incidents in mind, I didn't forage any fungi.

After an enjoyable thirty-minute stroll, I returned to the car park as a band of feral children were unleashed into the countryside, screaming and crashing through the undergrowth. The timing of my departure was impeccable.

The journey south was enlivened by livestock on the road: a drove of donkeys, three horses and two saddleback pigs. I suspect it'd be cheating if I claimed the highway hogs were wild boar. Road signs warned of deer (not livestock) but I saw no deer.

At Brockenhurst I stopped to buy lunch from a shop and asked for directions to my next destination, Rhinefield Drive, a scenic driving trail. The route was dotted with wild New Forest ponies, some on the road while others adorned garden lawns like living statues. I had to navigate around one white mare in the middle of the road and looked at her face – she didn't care one jot she was blocking traffic. Her attitude was admirable.

The road was flat and scenic, with open heathland stretching into the distance. I was eager to stop and explore on foot, but there was nowhere to pull up. It would have been bad form to abandon the car on the roadside and obstruct traffic, particularly as the ponies were already performing that role. Parking was eventually found at a woodland called Hinchelsea, beside more deer signs, and no deer. The swathe of heathland was dappled purple with flowering heather and buzzed with bees as they gorged themselves on the abundant nectar. In the middle of the heathland, something sizable moved out of the gorse ridge ahead, a doe fallow deer and she sauntered gracefully like a model on a catwalk. The chestnut-coloured beauty turned in my direction, stared and angled her ears toward me.

I'd been spotted.

She then pranced off to demonstrate she was in prime condition and an unsuitable chase, oblivious to the fact that I couldn't even chase a very old deer. She vanished behind a bank of gorse. I'd experienced a lovely wildlife encounter; and this was the first time in my entire life that I'd passed a road sign warning of deer and actually *seen* a deer.

It was a sunny afternoon and a pleasure to be in a peaceful heathland. There was a tooting sound in the distance, which I initially dismissed as a child blowing a whistle, but realised the noise appeared to be coming from a circling buzzard. It was different to the 'mewing' calls I normally associate with common buzzards; but since they are a fairly new addition to the Manx countryside, I'm unacquainted with all their vocalisation. August was after their nesting season, so I assumed this was a juvenile begging food from its parents.

Later I mused over the possibility it could have been a honey buzzard. I checked the various calls and the notion had potential, but I wasn't confident. To add to the difficulty, the bird was distant and had flown away before revealing any distinctive markings. I'll take more interest in the future if I hear a tooting buzzard and in the meantime it'll go down as another 'unknown' on my increasingly long list.

An alternative footpath led back to the car park, with the main objective to hunt reptiles. I focused on the square metre around my feet as I walked, in the hope of stumbling across a coiled snake or a basking lizard. Staring at the ground meant I'd miss seeing anything above – a goshawk could have been chasing a nightjar overhead and I'd been none the wiser.

It was a while before I came across anything and even then it was a quick glimpse. Something scurried between the heather and vanished into the undergrowth. The fleeting sighting was reminiscent of when I've previously disturbed common lizards, so it was treated as nothing new. I had more success with insect spotting; a brown butterfly with wings camouflaged like rippled bark – a grayling.

Study of a small mound revealed the entrance to a wasp nest. I deftly moved closer, trying to avoid disturbance and an angry response. A couple of wasps were busy on a fresh papery layer, which was brown and intermittently dotted with white stripes like finger nails. I applaud wasps when they eat the caterpillars on my allotment cabbages and I rarely get stung as I'm relaxed in their company. People usually get stung when they turn into whirling dervishes.

I finally returned to the car having failed to identify any new reptile species. I'd only scraped the surface of the New Forest but it was late in the afternoon and time to head back to Poole.

Once back, I was greeted by the sight of Joe sitting outside the hotel bar; his natural habitat. I waited in trepidation for his wildlife moment of the day.

'Sandwich tern,' he said.

My jaw dropped.

He explained he'd been walking along Poole harbour watching seabirds and saw something he considered unusual, describing it as, 'Not a ****ing seagull'. He subsequently located one of his beloved information boards and made an accurate identification. I was so glad, especially after he told me if he'd not seen the Sandwich tern, his wildlife moment of the day would've been a '****ing seagull pecking a dead fish'.

****

The following morning was sunny for our afternoon excursion to the opposite side of Poole harbour. Joe first embarked on a steam train trip from Corfe Castle to Swanage, while I drove to Arne RSPB. We arranged to meet four hours later and it was mid-morning when I arrived at Arne. The large car park was already half full – this was clearly a popular place. The visitors centre had good display boards showing recent sightings and I was thrilled to see ospreys on their list. I chatted with a reserve manager and he helped devise a route which included tip-offs for wildlife at various places. He explained the timings between each area and it dawned on me that Arne was an extensive site: I'd only anticipated a four-hour wander in the countryside, but this might escalate into a speed walk. The visitor centre was at the centre of a network of paths which wove either north-east or south.

I rambled north-east to begin with, saving the ospreys in the south for later. On the fringe of the woodland there was a raised bird hide and from here I sighted sika deer. They are bulky animals, similar in size to fallow deer but with darker fur. Seven stood grazing on the mudflat grass and further study revealed three more in a gully, their antlers giving away their presence. The name sika is the Japanese word for deer. Japanese names for creatures in English are sometimes the Japanese word, followed by the English word, so koi carp, when translated, is 'carp carp'. The 'deer deer' were impressive. It would be great to observe them during their autumnal rut. However, it was August, their testosterone levels were low and they seemed relaxed.

Further away on the mudflats a host of birds were feeding: curlews, oystercatchers and little egrets. Little egrets are a welcome recent addition to our waterways and coast; smaller than grey herons and brilliant white. A flock of terns swirled in the distance and I wondered whether one of them was spotted yesterday by Joe.

The next stop was Shipstal Beach, a short stretch of golden sand and a place the warden suggested for sand lizards. The first thing I detected was a European hornets' nest, the first I've ever seen. A stern face peered back at me, like a gladiator in a shiny yellow helmet. I know wasps quite well, but I had no idea of the tolerance levels of hornets to people. I didn't want to be chased across a pretty beach by a swarm of large angry insects; it would ruin my day, although had he been there, it would probably have made Joe's wildlife moment. The hornets' nest entrance had a papery wall with a circular access point in the centre; like a wasps' nest but larger. I began to appreciate how big hornets were as they bustled inside. One flew in my direction and I froze. It harmlessly buzzed above my head. A hummingbird hawkmoth was feeding nearby on overhanging heather, its long proboscis dangling down to the nectar source. This moth was potentially a hornet's lunch but I didn't have time to wait and see.

The search for sand lizards continued and I scanned a steep sandy bank dotted with clumps of vegetation. Lizards always like to bask near a place of safety, so they can dash to cover from predators such as kestrels. While perusing the bank above me, I was surprised to hear a noise down by my feet; the distinctive sound of a scurrying lizard. On the border between vegetation and beach, a lizard lunged out, snatched an ant and dived back into the undergrowth. I crouched down slowly and waited for it to re-emerge. From the quickness of the sighting I didn't know if it was a sand or common lizard. I've been fortunate to see hundreds of common lizards on the Isle of Man, and I hoped this knowledge might help me tell the difference. The lizard reappeared and allowed a closer view. It was similar to my known species but there were important noticeable variations – it was larger and its flank displayed vibrant green stripes and bright white speckles. It was definitely not one of my common friends. The sand lizard retreated back into the grass and vanished.

A little further along there was another – this one didn't have bright green markings, but it did have silvery white specks. She was a female sand lizard, a very neat little reptile. What differentiated her most from a common lizard was her size; she was noticeably wider around the neck and body. It was great to watch her for a few minutes, but it was time to move on.

Back in the woodland a family paused to watch three sika deer and they were delighted when I mentioned the sand lizards. From an oak tree a green woodpecker called loudly; I waited for it to show its face but it didn't, so I continued south through a silver birch woodland towards Coombe Heath, where the staff had mentioned ospreys.

At the end of summer, ospreys often stop over in Poole Harbour to nourish themselves before continuing their long southern migration to Africa. A recent project supported by the legendary conservationist Roy

Dennis involved the release of Scottish juvenile ospreys near Arne, in the hope they'd adopt Poole Harbour as their new home. Therefore, I had the chance of seeing one of the new residents, or Scottish birds passing through on their annual migration.

Typical of me, whenever I have a time-critical situation, I take a wrong turn. I realised I was on the wrong track when it aimed towards a distant woodland. I turned and selected an alternative route east. I'm not a speed walker, particularly in hot weather – by the time I reached the first bird hide I was dripping with sweat. Inside, four birders gazed aimlessly in different directions. This indicated there wasn't anything interesting to be seen here. I sat down, mainly to recover from the route march, but also to scan the surroundings; perhaps the other people were missing something. The scenery was wide and uninterrupted across Middlebere Lake ('lake' was a misleading name for an inlet of Poole Harbour). The tide was out and the lake was mostly mud. Binoculars picked up distant gulls, curlews, cormorants and crows. There weren't any ospreys, unless one was disguised as a cormorant.

Once I'd recovered from the stomp, I left the hide and walked westerly to the next viewpoint. The valley swept into shallows cushioned by woodland. A bird hide was tucked amongst the trees facing the lake, the destination for my earlier aborted route. I absorbed the landscape and lent against a bench inscribed with a plaque which read; 'This is a good place to view ospreys.' I gazed upwards and saw an osprey! Unlike white-tailed sea eagles, an osprey in flight doesn't have square broad wings and it more resembles a giant skua. It drifted effortlessly above Middlebere Lake, before heading towards the shallows. Once at the end, a second osprey lifted from an artificial nest and they both met in the air. The ospreys spiralled together before moving in unison towards the woodland. Those inside the bird hide must have enjoyed magnificent views.

I continued further to spectate from a contrasting angle and something fluttered between nearby conifers. I suddenly saw a Dartford warbler. It was phenomenal to have a Dartford warbler in the foreground and ospreys in the background.

Dartford warblers have dark plumage and a downward-angled beak, their facial characteristics reminding me of Gonzo from *The Muppet Show*. The warbler made a mechanical sound as though it was saying, 'Meh, meh,

meh.' Then its tail lifted, shaped like a black lollipop stick, which it flapped up and down. It was joined by another Dartford warbler and they both disappeared behind a conifer.

This was probably the second time I'd seen Dartford warblers. I'm sure I've seen one of these birds previously on the Isle of Man. I'd been strolling around Langness, with no camera or anybody to help verification when one crossed my path and landed on a gorse bush. As with previous unusual sightings, I reported it to our local birding group. When I logged onto their database they had three options – 'Possible', 'Probable' or 'Definite'. I chose 'Possible' as it was a first for me, plus I had no photographic evidence. I thought nothing more of it until a few hours later I was contacted; apparently it was the first ever reported sighting of a Dartford warbler on the Isle of Man and crowds of birders had been dispatched to spot it for themselves. Unfortunately none of them had any luck. Based on my 'possible' report, the decision was made not to log it as their first ever local sighting. Maybe somebody else will get a positive Manx recording in the future, and certainly the warbler I saw at Langness looked just like those at Arne.

Two people approached and they were transfixed by the ospreys so I also mentioned to them the Dartford warblers which had reappeared and we all stood together, eyes flitting between warblers and ospreys.

Another sweat-drenched route march ensued and I remarkably added a kestrel and a sparrowhawk to my day's sightings. Both birds of prey were in the air and although a similar size, they form different shapes in flight. Kestrels are sharply cut and sleek, like a lady in a figure-hugging black dress, while sparrowhawks (notably the females) are slightly ruffled like a lady in a flowing cape.

Arne was a truly magical place and I was very fortunate to see so much during a hurried stay. It ranks as one of the best reserves I've ever visited. I felt exhilarated and smiled all the way to collect Joe. We both travelled south to Studland and parked at Shell Bay; a fine stretch of sand dotted with holidaymakers. Joe took a paddle in the blue waters while I read my guidebook; it mentioned the heathland behind the beach and said: 'Adders are quite common here, so be careful'. I went off to be 'careful' while searching for venomous snakes.

When I scanned the New Forest for reptiles, a common lizard crossed my path and that caused me no alarm. The same thing happened here, but this time a scooting lizard made me jump. I'm not a skittish person, but the potential for an encounter with a venomous snake put my senses on high alert. Wildlife watching can be an adrenaline-charged hobby.

There were numerous small red damselflies but sadly, no adders.

Joe went to the public toilets and came back complaining that his flow was hindered by house martins fluttering above the urinals. For the birds, I guess it was a safe place to nest in close proximity to flies. We crossed by ferry to Sandbanks and gazed across the harbour towards Brownsea Island; we'd seen it from all sides but never had time to visit and search for red squirrels.

That evening we sampled local ales in several pubs, including one called the King Charles which was advertised as being haunted (it had a wide selection of spirits). It was soon time for Joe to announce his wildlife moment of the day. He explained it happened during his steam train trip to Swanage when a lady felt an insect on her chest, gave it a slap and was stung on her boob by a wasp. After yesterday's Sandwich tern, we'd taken a step backwards.

Great White Egret

Chapter 12

Dorset – Weymouth (2018)

Breakfast was devoured beside a large window overlooking Poole's quayside. A mixed flock of turnstones and starlings were working the jetty for scraps, while I tucked into a full English. I felt I had the better deal.

We checked out of the hotel and drove towards Weymouth, with a couple of stops planned en route. Our first quest was to find a wildlife reserve north of Poole called Lytchett Bay; my research suggested the possibility of spoonbills. We didn't find Lytchett Bay or any spoonbills, and in any case subsequent research revealed the spoonbills were more likely to be seen during winter. We did however discover Upton Country Park, which seemed more popular with dog walkers than wildlife. We're both dog-lovers, but decided to leave after it felt like we'd gate-crashed Crufts.

Proceeding west, at Bovington I had hoped to find a reserve called Higher Hyde Heath. Instead we found Monkey World. I was driving so we didn't stop and continued to the Tank Museum, which contained lots of tanks. After seeing three hundred large metal vehicles, I asked two members of staff about the whereabouts of Higher Hyde Heath.

One replied, 'The only place I know for wildlife nearby is Monkey World.'

We left the museum without any guidance regarding Higher Hyde Heath, but went in its potential direction in the hope of stumbling across a road sign. The only sign of note advertised the River Piddle. We passed Monkey World again and drove straight to Weymouth.

Later, Joe announced his wildlife moment of the day, which was a Tiger (in the tank museum's German section). I had an early night and hoped the next day I'd have more fortune with wildlife sightings. It'd help if I actually discovered a nature reserve.

The Weymouth herring gull population were early starters and woke me at 6:30am. I felt sufficiently refreshed to get up and have a morning stroll – Radipole Lake RSPB was nearby. On the walk to Radipole I stopped by a garden to observe a hanging bird feeder. Feeders have an energy and excitement that's difficult to replicate in the British countryside. Various tits came in for their breakfast and the pecking order was dominated by great tits, with blue tits second and lastly the diminutive coal tits (identified by the white stripe on the back of their heads).

The smaller birds were continually chased off by the great tits and I wondered how they survived. It's not just at feeding times when great tits bully their way to the front, I've also seen them chase blue tits from nest boxes. Perhaps great tits are kept in check by predators – for example a sparrowhawk might target a more sizeable meal when given a choice (a great tit is nearly twice the weight of a coal tit). If I'm offered a small or large ice-cream – I'll usually go for the bigger one. However, I suspect a hawk on a high-speed raid would grab the first and easiest target, irrespective of its size.

My walk continued through a strip of parkland which ran alongside a large reed bed. The thatched roof of the RSPB welcome centre appeared but it was closed. I consulted my watch – 7am – fair enough. I wouldn't describe myself as a morning person, but I do know an early start has its rewards. The main benefit is that nobody's already scared off all the wildlife. The mallards were a bit disgruntled at my early arrival and they quacked while making way for me on the path. I crossed the footbridge and ahead of me a squadron of sand martins performed a free air show above the reeds.

A screech emanated from deep in the undergrowth, the piercing noise like a piglet being throttled. This was the call of a water rail, a rare wetland bird found in similar habitats back home on the Isle of Man. They are usually heard rather than seen, and add an element of spookiness to a walk, particularly when out exploring alone. I was out alone, in a strange place in the early morning light; I glanced about nervously and moved on.

Behind a bank of rustling reedmace (bulrushes), a pair of great crested grebes and their youngster travelled together into open water. All three grebes swam in a tight formation towards the middle of the pool, then the adults shepherded their offspring away from a great black-backed gull, who was probably disappointed at being denied breakfast.

The reserve was a decent size and it took twenty minutes at a pleasant pace before the path looped back in the direction of the visitor's centre. An egret was disturbed, it made a loud call, rose on strong wing beats and elegantly flew upwards. It was closer than any of my previous little egret encounters and I was surprised by its size. I was also confused by its bill colour; I thought their bill was dark but this one's was yellow. It flew away, drifted in an arc and landed in a deeper patch of reeds. The early morning start paid dividends – if anyone else had gone this way before me, they'd have scared it off first.

A short distance away I stood on an area of decking, lent over the wooden railing and heard a 'plop'. A plop noise could be insignificant at other venues, but at Radipole it hinted at the possibility of a rarity. After a few seconds, I ruled out the culprit being a coot or moorhen. When waterfowl are disturbed they usually move onto open water or take flight. Nothing came out, which indicated this was a mammal which chose to hide rather than flee, providing further evidence of it being a water vole. They make a 'plop' after they jump into the water. Water voles have become rare due to habitat loss and predation from an alien invader – American mink. I knelt down and checked the reeds for gnawed grass, a sign of vole activity. There was nothing obvious. I waited for several minutes until the likelihood of a water vole sighting faded completely.

Back at the hotel, I showered, had breakfast and prepared for another reserve. I'd learned from yesterday's mistakes and researched the exact location prior to departure. While driving along a dual carriageway, a banner advertised my target: Lorton Meadows Wildlife Trust. The banner didn't indicate whether I should turn left or right at the subsequent roundabout, so I chose the wrong option. Eventually I arrived at Lorton Meadows and met a Trust volunteer as he opened the visitor's centre; we had a quick friendly chat and I followed his guidance on a route.

The meadows were natural and undamaged by modern agricultural practices. Deep hedgerow boughs were weighed down by abundant blackberry and hawthorn fruit, just like the countryside of my childhood. It was cheerfully nostalgic. The grassy areas fizzed with stridulating crickets; they were prolific here – it sounded like Spain or France. Unfortunately I have little expertise when it comes to crickets – I know a cricket as well as I play cricket (which is very poorly).

The leisurely walk through the buzzing grassland contributed a hovering kestrel and stonechats calling with clicks. The bottom of the field bordered a woodland and I decided to explore inside. After taking a few strides into the interior, I was plunged into darkness by the thick canopy above. It was a little time before my eyes acclimatised; the woodland was reminiscent of the film *The Hobbit*'s gloomy forest Mirkwood. Unlike Mirkwood, this place contained decent footpaths and no giant spiders.

But I was given a fright by a grey squirrel. There are no squirrels in the Isle of Man so I'm unfamiliar with their ability to jump out from nowhere. I returned to the meadow, where tree rodents were unlikely to spook me.

Back at the visitor centre, I met the reserve warden again and asked him about the crickets. I was intrigued to know the name of the noisiest species. To help him I provided some highly accurate descriptions: 'Intermittent fizzing like changing channels on an old telly... or when you pass under a pylon and you hear the power lines hissing.' He had no idea what I was talking about. However he was a very accommodating and retrieved a thick book from behind his desk. This tome contained records of local sightings and I flicked through. No crickets were documented, but something else was much more interesting – several observations of grass snakes. I mentioned the snakes to the chap and he replied nonchalantly, 'Oh yeah, under the corrugated iron sheet over there,' and pointed me outside. Surely my first wild snake wasn't going to be so easy. His directions led me to a paddock with a corrugated sheet lying in the corner. Reptiles warm themselves by resting beneath sun-warmed metal, similar to humans on cold days when they come indoors and press their backsides against radiators.

I stood above the sheet and felt a rush of adrenaline. It was reminiscent of my childhood, when I'd reach under the Christmas tree for the largest gift. I took a deep breath and set the camera to film the event; if a snake was to bite my face, I'd want to capture the moment for posterity.

As I lent down a cricket hopped onto the corrugated sheet. It made me stop in my tracks. Film footage of it increased my knowledge of crickets 100%. It was a dark bush-cricket, but subsequent investigation revealed it didn't make a fizzing noise; that had probably been generated by great green bush-crickets.

Anyway, back to the snake hunt. I held the bottom of the corrugated sheet with one hand and filmed with the other. The dark bush-cricket was dismissed and hopped off. As the sheet lifted, the sun cast itself over the brown ground beneath; behold, a snake! Spherical jewel eyes, yellow neck banding and a black collar. A grass snake. Clearly no fan of publicity it slunk off quickly into the undergrowth, while at the same time something else stirred and followed. Both creatures disappeared in less than five seconds – five awesome seconds. I was focusing on seeing the snake with my own eyes, the filming was secondary, so I was unsure whether the camera had captured anything.

Later, I was delighted that the footage confirmed the grass snake sighting. Importantly, it also helped identify the reptile beside it; a legless lizard called a slow worm (there was nothing slow about its dash for cover). A fantastic result, which means Dorset had already successfully delivered one snake and all three British lizards (sand, common and slow worm). Only the rarer adders and smooth snakes remained elusive.

Lorton Meadows had been enormously rewarding and I proceeded in high spirits to Lodmoor RSPB, on the eastern end of Weymouth beach. Lodmoor consisted of a vast reed bed, nearly as substantial as Radipole. Weymouth is blessed to have such an abundance of wildlife reserves on its doorstep.

The first noticeable birds were high-pitch screeching black-headed gulls, having a heated conversation limited to vowels. A lower tone was provided by a gaggle of Canada geese having a honking competition. At the northern end of the reserve, a road was fringed with snowberry trees, laden with white fruit. They looked unappealing to eat but apparently, a few people have ignored the obvious message, consumed some and spent a day projectile vomiting. One or two have even died. I gave the berries a miss; even I'm not that stupid.

An information board displayed a map showing various paths, including one which led back to my earlier destination, Lorton Meadows. Different conservation charities had procured interconnecting plots to make a large area of joined-up habitats. Nature loves those corridors and so do wildlife enthusiasts. The path returned south into Lodmoor where a gathering of birders overlooked a flock of waders and my old nemesis; the godwit. I stood by the lagoon and eyed up my old foe but once again I couldn't determine whether these were bar or black-tailed godwits, so I stopped beside a lady and asked the standard question when faced with this adversary, 'Hi, I'm not good with godwits, do you know which type they are?'

The lady replied calmly as if reading from a field-guide: 'To tell the difference at this time of year between the bar-tailed and black-tailed godwits, you should examine their legs. Both species have knobbly knees. If the distance above the knobble and the base of the bird is long enough to write "black" it is a black-tailed godwit, if it's only short enough to write "bar" then it is bar-tailed.'

At first, I thought she was pulling my leg; but I considered her advice and again turned to the godwits. The distance between the knee and the body of these birds was perhaps long enough to write 'black', so I asked if my assessment was correct, 'So, they are black-tailed godwits?'

She nodded.

At last! I'd established a way to identify godwits. Well, so long as I can see their legs. I left Lodmoor, felt proud I may have got the godwit monkey off my back. The real test would come when I next met a godwit. Would I correctly ID them without any assistance?

In the afternoon I joined Joe, drove to Portland Bill and en route stopped at Chesil Beach. It was a warm day and I was sweating after wading to the summit of the moving pebble ridge.

The resident little terns and wader species had finished nesting around the beach and lagoons. Only one creature was spotted – a mackerel being landed by a sea angler. Even without wildlife watching, it was nice to sit in the sun and observe the world. Gentle waves danced across a shore, fizzing, like a freshly poured glass of lemonade.

The spit of sand we sat on stretched westerly for eighteen miles and was reminiscent of Blakeney Point. I didn't want to relive that exhausting trek, so after sufficient relaxation time, I recommended we return to our car.

We were soon driving up the rocky mass of Portland. The road wove up a steep hill and we overtook two cyclists struggling against the incline. Further along Portland there was cliffside parking at Cheyne Weares. We enjoyed lunch and admired the blue sea; it was like being beside the Mediterranean. Joe was drawn like a magnet to an information board and he read out, 'Common lizards can be seen here.' I went into the undergrowth to explore. After a couple of minutes one was spied, perched on the chalky cliff edge, which posed for us both before it scampered off. A minute later, Joe spotted another common lizard which he claimed was larger and more majestic than my measly example.

The two cyclists we overtook earlier then peddled past looking shattered. We passed them on route to Portland Bill lighthouse and stopped in a football pitch-sized car park. Portland Bill has featured in several wildlife programmes, but this didn't seem to be the right place; it was far too open and lacked vegetation.

Even so, the coastal area was still worth exploring. We aimed for the most southerly point, but the only route down was by clambering over boulders. I'm not as nimble as I used to be: in my youth I'd have skipped down these enormous rocks like a mountain goat. Now I slumped downwards like a fly-tipped mattress.

This shoreline contained no sand; every grain had been ripped away by the raging waves. Only hard chert remained and it was constantly battered by the sea. Fossilised oysters were embedded in the sturdy rock – to collect fossils around here you'd require a pneumatic drill. One huge slab called the Pulpit Rock had broken at the base and fallen diagonally, resembling a bible leaning against a pulpit. Beside the rock was a Health and Safety notice, warning visitors not to climb the steep sloping stone. The thought of scaling a large rock over a rampant sea never crossed my mind. I prefer my body parts in their current positions.

On our drive back we slowed outside the second lighthouse where there was a bookshop which had piqued Joe's interest, so it seemed a good excuse to call in. The shop was closed and parking was for members of the Portland Bird Observatory only, so we left. On reflection I should have gone inside and asked about becoming a member; it's easy to be wise after the event.

That evening we ventured into Weymouth – our hotel was at one end of the long beach – the town centre at the other. By the time we trekked across the seafront we were parched and found respite in the first pub, where I awaited Joe's wildlife moment of the day. It was a common lizard; not the one I showed him, but his 'superior' specimen.

****

The weather so far during the holiday had been excellent, but on our final full day it took a turn for the worse. I revisited Radipole during the morning, parked outside and I ran (like a wounded bison) into the visitor centre through lashing rain. Two RSPB volunteers gave me a friendly welcome before we chatted about the reserve. It was pleasing to be in a warm hospitable shelter with good company. The sweeping windows provided splendid views of the waterfowl on the river and surrounding pools. I stood admiring the sights as water dripped off my clothing and formed a puddle around my feet.

One of the volunteers pointed to an egret opposite. 'Good timing,' she said. 'The great white egret is still here.'

Wow. I'd seen this species yesterday and incorrectly deduced that Poole's little egret population was well fed. I felt a bit foolish; this was obviously a separate species – a little egret stood further away and it was half its size. I avoided confessing my earlier misidentification and decided to make myself appear more knowledgeable by saying, 'The beak is a different colour.'

'Yes,' she replied. 'These have yellow bills and the little egret's is black.'

I nodded.

She continued, 'It is also significantly bigger, it would be difficult to mistake the two.'

Quite.

I thought I'd better change the subject. 'Yesterday I was at the far end of the reserve and heard a 'plop' noise.'

The gentleman chirped, 'Water vole! Excellent.'

I felt redeemed. I wasn't such a bad wildlife watcher after all.

He plotted my 'plop' on his map while I studied the chart, making me aware of more pathways at the top of the reserve which I'd previously missed. I glanced out of the window at the pelting rain and windswept reeds, and came to the conclusion: 'maybe later'. I found a chair, pulled it towards the window and spectated the wildlife being lashed by rainfall. Rather them than me.

The lady approached with a mop and removed my puddle.

On the riverside, a gathering of grey herons huddled together like grumpy pensioners at a bus stop. Cormorants perched on individual posts, and even during the heavy downpour, the sand martins continued their aerial ballet over the water. One swooped towards a tufted duck and nearly hit it in the face. The duck seemed unamused by the stunt; the way that ducks do. The group of tufties drifted past on wind-generated waves and joined a family of mute swans as they bobbed beside the window. The cygnets were the same size as their parents, but with soft grey plumage. Juveniles often have dowdy plumage because they need to grow feathers quickly, using limited reserves. When three years old they reach breeding age, and before then they'll moult into the same plumage as their showy parents. A juveniles' appearance enables them to avoid conflict with adults, who might otherwise mistake them as a territorial threat.

The swirling birds above consisted mostly of sand martins, with a handful of house martins – identified by their white bums. They were not the only white things; the great white egret flew off with its neck tucked in, like a fat chin.

Shortly afterwards, a group of birders arrived and they joined me by the window. I decided not to mention they'd missed the great white egret by minutes. More people arrived and we formed a friendly gathering.

A great crested grebe wafted past; they are handsome birds. Then something moved in an area of cleared reeds which caused momentary excitement. Using my binoculars I focused on a small dark creature scurrying on the ground; I was thinking water vole. But it was a coot.

It was a very enjoyable hour in the visitor centre, probably the best place for a wildlife enthusiast in that weather. Lots to see, knowledgeable friendly company and it was dry.

Joe spent the morning with the intention of getting wet, swimming in the hotel pool. In the afternoon our destination was badly signposted but after several wrong turns we eventually found the Cerne Abbas Giant shrouded in mist. We both sat in our car and stared at the huge chalk image of a naked man with a notable phallus. A couple were bravely trekking up the hillside. Folklore implies that visiting the giant can aid fertility; they must have been keen in this weather. I lowered the window, took a photo of the chalk giant, got drenched, checked the photo, it was rubbish, deleted it and we left.

Back at Weymouth the weather began to ease, so I decided to revisit Radipole for the third and final time, to explore the paths I had previously missed. There was still a bit of Dorset mizzle in the air, but it was definitely more amiable than earlier. At the reserve entrance I once again disturbed the mallards feeding on a pile of seed beside the footbridge.

The rain weighed down the vegetation; reed mace leaning and twitching in the breeze. A bold dunnock joined me for part of the journey. They used to be called hedge sparrows until someone finally realised they weren't actually sparrows. Dunnocks are dull coloured and have a dreary song; similar to me. What sets us apart is they have an interesting sex life with both sexes mating with two or more partners.

Further along there was a wall of reeds and at ground level I noticed a dark circular hole the size of a small dog. Due to all the surrounding watercourses, it would have been a great habitat for otters. The hole was otter-sized, although no spraint (otter poo) or footprints were nearby – the earlier deluge would have presumably washed away any evidence.

The sky cleared and this presented the welcome opportunity to finally walk outdoors without getting wet. After a pleasant thirty-minute stroll I returned to the footbridge beside the RSPB visitor's centre. A bird of prey flew low, swooped upwards and landed on the thatched roof; it was a male kestrel; bronze back speckled with black spots, bright orange legs and a silvery head. He looked in my direction and I froze. I was fortunately far enough away to not be of concern; he altered his gaze from me and scrutinised the footbridge below. He continued to study the ground while fluttering along the thatched roof. Once he'd shuffled to the top corner, his eyes locked on the ground, staring down fiercely as the wind ruffled his plumage. He resembled a feathered gargoyle. I edged closer and instantly the kestrel plunged to the ground like an arrow, disappearing for a split second, before returning to the roof with a mouse gripped in his talons. He dispatched it with a sharp peck before flying off. It was a wonderful experience to witness – probably less so for the mouse. It completely made up for all those times in my childhood when I'd travelled hundreds of miles along motorways with my I-Spy books without seeing a kestrel pounce.

I crossed over the bridge and glanced at the area scattered with seed for the ducks. The free food must have drawn out the hungry mouse for its last meal. A female mallard was just sitting there: she must have seen the whole incident at close range, but she nonchalantly returned to her seed. No other mice braved the outdoors. I imagined them cowering inside a nearby wall, one asking the others, 'Where did Paul go?'

Predator and prey encounters are the most exhilarating and emotional experiences for any wildlife enthusiast. I don't have a morbid preoccupation with death; I've only great respect for the participants in their daily struggles. The process creates natural balance and means the best animals survive. Without kestrels and their fellow hunters, we'd be overrun with mice. I admired the kestrel's skill and appreciate that mice have to be eaten for him to exist. If there's reincarnation and I came back as a mouse, that's how I'd want to go, a swift end, much preferable to being one of the mice flattened under the metal grip of my granny's mousetraps.

I met with Joe that evening and he gave me his final wildlife moment of the day – apparently in the hotel swimming pool he'd spotted a whale. Had he faced a mirror? But the evening was young and if we were going to fall out, I'd prefer it to happen later, so I said nothing.

The next morning, we returned to Bristol airport and on the way, Joe saw his second-ever badger; it was dead beside the A37. During the holiday I never saw a single hedgehog, perhaps they'd already been wiped out by careless inconsiderate drivers.

When I returned home, I reflected on another special holiday. The only negative was missing out on some reserves because of the lack of signage. Did they want to keep their locations a secret? However, I have to accept it was mostly my fault – I should have researched their whereabouts in greater detail rather than relying on signs. Neither of us considered Sat Nav as a solution – we're both too old for that new-fangled technology (particularly Joe, who's owned a convertible car for six years and still hasn't learned to remove the roof).

There was a long list of positives for Dorset. Poole and Weymouth were convivial venues to stay, with impressive nature reserves nearby. My favourites were Arne and Radipole RSPB. If you ever visit Arne, dedicate at least five hours to inspect it properly. Before the holiday, I thought I had given myself an ambitious wish list. I smashed it. In addition to discovering a grass snake, a slow worm, sand lizards and Dartford warblers, I had succeeded in seeing so much more. The biggest bonuses were ospreys, great white egrets, roe and sika deer, plus a hornet's nest. Dorset would be a tough act to follow; I needed to think of somewhere with lots of contrasting habitats and a wide diversity of wildlife. Wales appeared to be the perfect choice.

Hobby & Dragonfly

Chapter 13

Wales – Powys, Gwynedd and Ceredigion *(2019)*

I was travelling in May but my planning began eight months earlier – I was taking this holiday seriously. Some of the itinerary was based on Iolo Williams's book *Wales' Top 40 Nature Sites*, plus additional ideas provided by the *Visit Wales* website, which claimed that in Cardigan Bay 'Bottlenose dolphins are so common here, you'd be unlucky not to spot one'. I planned to test that theory. My wish list contained ring ouzels, ospreys, adders, redstarts and those unmissable dolphins.

I succumbed to buying a detailed map of Wales rather than using something photocopied onto a tatty piece of paper. I would start in the north-east of Wales and zigzag to the south-west. An eclectic mixture of accommodation had been booked, ranging from pubs, B&Bs and hotels; each destination with nearby nature reserves. I didn't research the reserves too deeply; I only noted the potential species. I prefer arriving at new places and being surprised.

On the first day, I crossed into Wales on the A483 towards Wrexham. My newly crumpled map had the name of a nearby woodland reserve; Maes y Pant. It eluded me but I found a shop to buy wine (I was staying with relatives that night and alcohol is always good currency). Before meeting them, I went to Fenn's Moss near Whitchurch, where sheep jaywalked and the hedgerows prolific with birdlife. The reserve was sign-posted; an unusual extravagance based on my Dorset experience.

I drove tentatively over a steep hump-backed canal bridge before pulling into the reserve's car park.

Chatting to a local walker, I learned that the fens were currently patrolled by birds of prey called hobby (its Latin name is *falco subbuteo*; because it is a 'hobby' it has provided the name for the table football game).

I followed his directions between fields and woodland. Chiffchaffs, robins and a blackcap were all singing. It wasn't long before I reached the open fens; a brown landscape with the colour palette of a wholemeal loaf. In foul weather, fens are bleak, the sort of place where escaped convicts might lurk. Thankfully, today was warm and flashes of sunlight broke through the overcast sky. The paths were bordered with stunted trees and ditches, with cut bracken littering the verges. The fronds of the dead bracken formed zigzag patterns like snakeskin; on several occasions I hoped I'd seen an adder, but only succeeded in staring at bracken. A sign indicated that raft spiders lived in the surrounding pools – they were apparently big, chunky and difficult to miss. I missed.

I was soon distracted from my futile search for snakes and spiders by something in the sky; an unusual bird. Binoculars revealed it as a bird of prey; it was a hobby! The hobby's plumage is reminiscent of a peregrine falcon, particularly the white bib, however the body is sleek and slender like a large swift. They hunt swifts and swallows, but their diet in May consisted of dragonflies, picked up during fast swoops over the wetland. The hobby descended and streaked through the fen like a tornado jet-plane on a bombing raid. A second hobby circled high above but declined to join its flying partner.

Stonechat and sedge warblers sang, while further ahead a gentleman with a long lens camera was attempting to photograph a moving object. The man stalked around the base of a silver birch while the song of a whitethroat rattled from the top. He aimed his lens up at the bird, it flew further away, he cursed. This game continued four times while I kept my distance and watched with growing amusement. Eventually the photographer fist-pumped, which indicated a successful snap and it was safe to approach without disturbing the whitethroat. The man was in good spirits and he provided directions to an area where the raft spiders skulked. I didn't get the opportunity to meet him later and thank him for the duff information. However, I did find plenty of dragonflies (a.k.a. hobby food) including one sporting a white face – it looked like it'd bumped into a recently white-washed wall. Later on, I met a wildlife warden and described the species in my own special way; apparently the 'Tipp-Ex headed dragonfly' was better known as a white-faced darter. The warden also mentioned that every time one of her colleagues visited, he usually saw adders. Bully for him.

That evening I sat with my host in their garden sipping a glass of wine (my gift didn't remain unopened long). We watched a buzzard circle above the neighbouring field, before a starling landed on a nearby birdfeeder. My uncle glanced at it and said, 'Oily vermin.'

Animals have no voice of their own, so I often speak in their defence, although, as a gardener, I struggle to put forward a positive case for slugs, apart from saying, 'They are hedgehog food.' I tried to persuade my uncle to see the positives in starlings: they eat pests, have a skill for mimicry and their murmurations are beautiful. His facial expression suggested that I'd failed to sway the jury.

****

The following day I headed west towards Welshpool and during the drive became aware of an annoying feature of the hire car; it had possessed a very small engine and disliked hills. Even the slightest gradient would cause it to slow and force a change into a lower gear. During a gentle slope the car struggled in third gear and I was overtaken by a moped. On the positive side, the car's carbon footprint was minimal, so I was doing my bit for the environment.

The map was scribbled with names of several worthy locations in Welshpool's vicinity. The first was Llanymynech Rocks – found after asking directions from a Pant man who was cutting his hedge (the village was called Pant; he wasn't gardening in his underwear). He managed to decipher my badly pronounced attempt at saying Llanymynech (apparently it should sound something like clanee-my-netch) and pointed me in the direction of a narrow unsigned entrance.

Llanymynech's car park rang with chiffchaff and blackcap songs, while the air was filled with the zesty fragrance of elderflower, reminiscent of my favourite gin mixer. A small friendly lady with an enormous angry dog approached; I took a diversion from its snarling, which led to a 200-foot vertical wall of ochre rock. Historically this was a busy quarry, but today there were no sounds of industry, just the squawking and chirring of jackdaws. The jackdaws became uppity with an approaching kestrel which evaded their mobbing and swung into a crevice. Presumably this was the kestrel's nesting site. I couldn't fathom why a kestrel would choose this place for a home. It would be like living beside a rowdy nightclub.

A short exploration of the quarry failed to reveal any interesting new plant species (you can occasionally discover floral rarities such as bee orchids on disturbed soil). It was nevertheless a pleasant stroll and I headed back to the car.

A decision needed to be made on the next destination. I could continue searching for the smaller reserves scrawled on the map, but that would undoubtedly require signposting, local help and an element of luck; or go west to Lake Vyrnwy which was recommended by Iolo Williams.

I decided to follow Iolo's advice. Surely I couldn't fail to discover a lake the size of six-hundred football pitches. After a thirty minute drive I located the lake… the impressive dam wall was a giveaway. It resembled a jolly version of Tolkien's Black Gate of Mordor, with orcs being replaced by cycling families and brightly dressed ramblers.

A single-lane road led above the dam to Coed Y Capel RSPB. Coed in Welsh means trees, while Capel is chapel and one was outside. The bird hide's interior was big and empty, with benches facing a sloping woodland. A token piece of wildlife greeted me – a wood pigeon.

A few minutes later a small grey bird flew from the undergrowth like a thrown lump of potter's clay, and stuck against the birdbox's side. The bird shuffled to the round opening and disappeared inside. I snatched my binoculars, watched the circular hole and waited for the bird to re-emerge. Seconds later I saw a nuthatch, a smart-looking bird resembling a little grey woodpecker.

I don't have a bird list and I'm also slightly forgetful, so I can't remember all the species I've spotted. My list of 'maybe seen, although can't remember' has four members – whinchat, marsh tit, yellow wagtail and nuthatch. I was pleased to move nuthatch into my 'definitely seen' list. Unless I forget again. The nuthatch flew away and once again it was just me and the wood pigeon. I looked at the pigeon. It looked at me.

The door opened and a gangly man appeared. He was smartly dressed, as though he'd just stepped off a yacht. He ducked under the doorframe, stood for a moment and perused the scenery. He eyeballed me, took a weary breath and asked nonchalantly, 'Anything about?'

Sometimes I enjoy pointing out the bloody obvious. 'There's a wood pigeon.'

He shook his head, slightly frustrated by my impertinence. 'Anything other than that pigeon?'

'You missed a nuthatch.'

He shrugged dismissively, as if nuthatches regularly visited his yacht. 'Any pied flycatchers?'

'Not unless there's one hiding behind the pigeon.' I lifted my binoculars and pretended to peer around the pigeon. 'Nope, none there.'

He sneered, gave the pigeon a final glance and departed. I decided to leave as well and search for pied flycatchers; they were on my 'definitely not seen list'.

At the RSPB shop I chose not to buy a puffin hand puppet and instead took a clockwise drive around the lake. Lunch was consumed at a huge picnic table, perfectly designed for any touring basketball teams. Then I headed to a car park signposted for Rhiwargor Waterfall. A footpath followed a stone wall and halfway across the field I heard a new bird call. I followed the noise and stood beneath a majestic oak and listened, before realising I was under the wrong tree. The song continued to resound, 'zunk... zunk... zunk... zzzeeeee... zee'.

After inspecting the leafy canopy of the neighbouring oak, I eventually picked out a male redstart, giving it loads. This was the first time I'd heard a redstart calling (a few years earlier I'd sighted a silent one in Bordeaux). Redstarts are uncommon migratory summer visitors to Britain, but mid-Wales is a hotspot. Redstarts are the same shape as robins with the same red bellies but male redstarts have a striking black face. I quickly grabbed my camera, pointed it at the tree, but the bird had flown off. A minute later I heard its distant call on the opposite side of the river. There was a crossing further up, but I decided to return to the car – once sat inside I realised I'd been so distracted by the redstart that I'd forgotten about the waterfall. I decided to give the waterfall a miss; I wasn't sure where it was and convinced myself that reaching it would involve a hike.

The Lakeside Hide was my next destination, where a meandering path cut between bluebell-scented woodland. As I entered the bird hide, a couple broke from their conversation and welcomed me. After our introductions they explained that no wildlife was currently around the lakeside. I asked if there were any other locations worth visiting.

'Rhiwargor Waterfall,' the woman replied immediately.

I tried to think of a suitable excuse to explain why I'd just been there and not seen a waterfall, apart from me being forgetful and lazy. I was rescued by the man who added, 'If you are birdwatching, go beyond the RSPB centre in the direction of the sculpture park...'

The woman interrupted, 'It doesn't have any sculptures.'

He ignored her interjection, 'There's a fork in the road with bird boxes... It's a great place to see fried piecatchers.'

She turned sharply towards him and laughed in his face. 'Fried piecatchers!?!'

'I'd love to see a fried piecatcher,' I enthused.

The man was flustered and tried to bring order. 'No. Not a fried piecatcher, I meant to say...' He paused, took a breath and corrected himself, 'Pied.... flycatcher.'

I left them to their banter and drove to the recommended area near the sculpture park (where I also didn't see any sculptures). An interesting path led beside a wide burbling river. A young couple strolled ten metres ahead, the girl's clothing was unusual for someone on a country walk; she wafted along in a bright summer dress while her high heels clattered over the uneven ground. Why was she dressed this way? Perhaps her boyfriend said they were having a wild day out – and she misinterpreted this as a party invitation. Her boyfriend was a BIG lad, a rectangular unit, large enough to play for the Welsh rugby team... as the entire scrum. He wasn't overweight, but I suspect he possessed a good appetite. Was he the fried piecatcher?

Their pace was much slower than mine and the path wasn't wide, and they (particularly him) blocked any opportunity to overtake. Rather than attempt to barge past, I leant on a fence and studied the river for dippers. Once I was confident there were no dippers about, I resumed my walk and soon caught up with the couple as she tripped around in her inappropriate footwear and he waddled. I decided to stop again and watch the river. This routine continued until the path was wide enough for me to pass.

I enjoyed the open road for a minute until something caught my attention – another nuthatch. The bird defied gravity as it scampered like Spider-Man on the underside of a branch. I was so entranced by the nuthatch's movement that I failed to notice I'd been overtaken by the Piecatcher and Party-girl. I followed in their wake for a short distance before another opportunity to overtake presented itself, I then picked up my pace and discovered a steep path into the woodland. I was confident this route would be too much for Party-girl's footwear and the Piecatcher's girth. Halfway up the slope I stopped to take a breather – in my lifetime, I too had caught too many pies.

The path was signposted as the Craig Garth Trail; it joined a road and further ahead it forked. A small bird flitted upwards, snatched a flying insect and landed on a wire fence – it was a pied flycatcher! I moved into the undergrowth to disguise my approach. This ploy provided close views of this brilliant male bird as he snacked on passing insects or chirped happily. Flycatchers are similar in size to goldfinches, with a stubby black beak, plumage black on top and white underneath.

The flycatcher was very content in his location and never moved more than a metre from his original spot. This enabled me to observe his behaviour, which became mesmerising. When I finally emerged from the undergrowth it caused the flycatcher to emit an alarm call. Further down the road, I stopped to look back and he'd happily resumed his previous routine, and seized a passing fly.

The drive to Welshpool led between lush green fields intersected by thick hedgerows, dotted with white pompoms of flowering hawthorn. I found myself behind a tractor and knowing the hire car lacked acceleration, waited for a long straight before attempting to overtake. Eventually an opportunity arose, I pulled out, dropped it into third, put my foot down and started a painful crawl alongside the tractor. Ahead of me, a car immediately cornered and approached quickly, I slowed and returned to my original position behind the tractor and its laughing driver.

Even though an annoying proportion of the return journey was spent staring at the backside of a Massey Fergusson, there was still time for other reserves. The map was marked with three places en route – Dolydd Hafren, Red House and Pwll Penarth. I'm not sure how the Welsh conceal their nature reserves, but they were successful in their endeavours. I eventually found Llyn Coed y Dinas reserve – sadly the bird hide was closed for repairs, which left distant views of black-headed gulls.

Before the day ended, one final opportunity for a reserve remained – Severn Farm Pond – within walking distance of my Welshpool hotel. I checked-in, enjoyed the pictures of sheep in my bedroom, got lost in a maze of hotel corridors and belatedly exited the building. The evening sunshine offered some warmth and swifts screamed as they crossed the skyline. I quickly got my bearings and wandered in the direction of 'the pond'. My route was soon blocked by a familiar adversary – the considerable frame of the Piecatcher. At first I didn't notice Party-girl because the Piecatcher blocked her from sight, but when she emerged, her attire was more subdued than earlier. She dressed up to explore the countryside but for a night on the town she had dressed down. I'll never understand ladies' fashion. I also struggled with the Piecatcher's evening apparel – he sported a shiny navy-blue tracksuit which made him look like the TARDIS.

****

The following morning I finally discovered the Severn Farm Pond in a large industrial estate, where the dawn chorus struggled to be heard above the rumbling traffic. Near the entrance, blue tit chicks called from inside a nest box. Would they be so chirpy in an open nest which was accessible to predators? I think not!

In the centre of the reserve a large pond was encircled by willows. The trees had shed their thick brown and white cottony catkins onto the water's surface, making it resemble a large bowl of creamy chicken soup with croutons. I decided to leave for somewhere more remote, tranquil and less soupy.

After a picturesque hour-long south-westerly drive, I began searching for Carngafallt RSPB near Rhayader. A narrow lane led through ancient woodland with gnarly trees festooned with lichen; and the calls of cuckoos and wood warblers rang from the deep wilderness. At no point did I find a sign for the RSPB reserve and instead parked at Elan Village for a stroll beside the river. I didn't realise until later, but I'd actually been in the reserve.

At the Rhayader Red Kite Feeding Station I was disappointed to discover raptor lunch wasn't served until after 1pm. Instead of waiting two hours, I headed north towards my evening's accommodation at Machynlleth.

As I drove, a red kite passed above, presumably on its way for lunch. Its wide wingspan tilted and caught an updraft, circled and lifted higher. Kites are large, majestic birds, a sight to make other thoughts disappear. I tried to concentrate as much as possible on the road ahead, while this beautiful distraction continued above.

The next stop was a remote upland reserve at Gilfach Farm. The information board didn't mention the mountain-dwelling cousin of the blackbird, the ring ouzel, but to my untrained eyes this upland habitat seemed perfect ouzel territory. Sadly the information board was correct: there weren't any there.

From Gilfach the road progressed north-west to the acclaimed Wildlife Trust site at Cors Dyfi, where ospreys nest. The footpath to the main bird hide was a boardwalk fringed by darkened timbers. The dark strips of wood soaked up the heat of the midday sun and drew in sun-worshippers; common lizards. Dozens of lizards draped themselves over the boardwalk edges like holidaymakers on deck chairs.

The assent to the top of the bird hide was breathtaking (I really need to improve my fitness). The structure supported a spacious room manned by four volunteers and we chatted about ospreys, the reserve and surrounding places. Every time I named a local town or village, the Welsh contingent helpfully corrected my pronunciation. The elevated lookout provided the sight of a local celebrity, Monty, a male osprey first recorded here ten years ago. He's regularly appeared on *Springwatch* and it was a pleasure to make his acquaintance in real life. However, *Springwatch* never featured him perching motionless for an hour. I suspect it wouldn't make entertaining telly. Even at first-hand viewing it wasn't enthralling. The eggs were also static, although the wardens hoped they'd hatch in a couple of days. I gave the statuesque Monty a final glance before I decided one of us should make a move.

On the walk back there were stops for flowering ragged robin, two noisy jays and a chirping reed bunting. A warbler was knocking the crap out a large green caterpillar; it was either trying to dislodge irritating hairs off the caterpillar's body or tenderising it like a steak. The warbler swallowed the caterpillar; the equivalent of me gulping a baguette down in one mouthful. Because its beak was full, it wasn't singing and the warbler's plumage was my only guide as to its identity. I noted a light line above its brow, checked my bird book, and discovered that many British warblers have that marking, so it didn't help at all.

Around Machynlleth there were opportunities to stay in tree houses or tepees, but apparently they were targeted at family groups rather than single middle-aged men, so instead I booked into a countryside hotel beside the Afon Dulas (afon is Welsh for river). The beer garden rewarded patrons with generous unobstructed views across a valley and my evening was spent gazing across this landscape. Strange-shaped hawthorn bushes dotted the fields – the local farmer had given them a flat top haircut with his tractor strimmer and underneath they'd been closely grazed by sheep. Their combined efforts created a topiary of bare hawthorn trunks which resembled legs with green bodies above and four pints of local ale made them to look very strange creatures.

Suddenly a sparrowhawk crossed above with a disgruntled finch in tow. Shortly afterwards a carrion crow landed in a nearby tree, causing all the jackdaws and blackbirds to take umbrage. Their agitated chatter only ceased once the crow had enough of their noise and departed. I pondered over the contrasting reactions of the local birds to these two separate threats. This was the breeding season, and while a sparrowhawk might take one bird, a crow could wipe out an entire nest. Therefore in spring, other birds rightly deemed crows the biggest threat and worthy of the noisiest protest.

Before sunset I strolled around the hotel grounds, down a path between mature oak trees and along the steadily flowing Afon Dulas. There was a pied flycatcher, another nuthatch, a treecreeper and two dippers (which appeared to be nesting under the railway bridge). Imagine having all those at the bottom of your back garden.

****

The following morning I visited Ynys-hir RSPB, a large reserve with mixed habitats. It had potential for a couple of personal firsts, including garden warblers and the outside chance of a spoonbill. After the usual enquiries with the welcome centre staff, I headed north into the woodland where I encountered another pied flycatcher and once again cherished seeing this charming little bird. A blackbird scrabbled in the leaf litter, scattering dead plant material into the air.

Further along, something disturbed the undergrowth and a small mammal bounded closer as it cut a path through the leaves. It revealed itself in one leap as a weasel with something in its jaws. The plump bundle was a dead rodent, presumably a vole. The weasel was unable to see me with such a sizeable object in its jaws and it continued to approach, until belatedly screeching to a halt in a flurry of leaves. It snorted a nasally grunt, before turning sharply and diving for cover beneath a log pile. That was a once-in-a-lifetime experience for me – and for the vole.

The woodland walk further rewarded me with a drumming woodpecker, sounding out its territory on a tree. At Cuddfan Marion Mawr bird hide (Cuddfan is Welsh for 'hidden'), a whitethroat lifted on frenetic wingbeats, held in the air and belted out its scratchy jerky song. In Britain there are two types of whitethroat – common whitethroat and lesser whitethroat; as you would expect, both have white throat feathers and the lesser is the smaller of the two. I'm only familiar with the song of common whitethroats – lesser whitethroats have different vocalisation but they remain a mystery.

Dozens of Canada geese busily swam in the pools and strutted among the grassy banks. They were noisy this morning, as though they'd been aggravated, but there were no signs of the culprit. My attention was diverted by a scratching noise at the front of the bird hide. I followed the sound to its source and discovered a wasp. It was chewing the wooden exterior, gnawing away at the window frame like a dog on a stick. I watched engrossed as it gathered woody pulp in its jaws, before it flew off with new building material for its papery nest. The wasp's departure left me with the din of the Canada geese who sustained their boisterous mood.

Amongst the honking rabble I spotted an outsider; a waterfowl which wasn't a familiar British species. My first incorrect guess was Egyptian goose, but this bird didn't have the eye colouration of Rocky Balboa after twelve rounds. I wondered if it was a harlequin duck, however this was more goosey than ducky. I eventually identified it as a red-breasted goose and subsequently researched this bird's appearance at Ynys-hir. I was interested to know what birders thought of this unusual sighting, but they were all dismissive – it was labelled as an escapee and therefore unworthy of their lists. If I had a list it would have been on mine.

In the centre of the wetland was the hide Cuddfan u Morfa Heli (I didn't attempt to pronounce that) where redshanks chimed and shelducks dabbled. A pair of lapwings took to the air and chased a passing carrion crow, which dodged its pursuers and fell into the reeds. I peered over the bank to see where the crow landed and my appearance caused the crow to return to the air. This enabled the lapwings to finish off their work. I hadn't meant to wreck the crow's morning, but the lapwings seemed happy with the outcome.

I left the wetland and entered deep woodland, where a grey squirrel watched me suspiciously. I hailed the squirrel with a jovial, 'Good morning!' The squirrel sat upright like a gnome and gave me a steely scowl. Near the southern section of the reserve, a bank vole scrabbled in the leaf litter, a plump snack for any weasel breezing past.

The Cuddfan Ynys-hir hide was at a high point in the woodland, with views through mature trees to the wetlands below. A buzzard used the thermals to gain height and once above me, I noticed something dangling from its talons. At first I thought the worst; that it was snared in rope or wire, but as I studied the coiled object, I realised it was a snake. The sky was overcast and the snake's silhouette failed to offer any pattern or colouration, so it was impossible to distinguish what species of snake. The buzzard crossed overhead and disappeared behind the trees, presumably delivering lunch to its young (they were getting snake, I was having a sandwich). Adders were on the reserve's species list, so perhaps that was my first ever sighting of an adder. I'll never know.

A bird sang nearby and its melody was unusual, reminiscent of a blackcap but the tune was more hurried, abrupt and concluded with a meandering finish. I recorded the sound on my phone and discovered later I'd heard my first garden warbler.

The footpath looped clockwise through a wetland dotted with the skeletons of dead trees and grazed by white horses (it reminded me of the Camargue in France). An information board listed local species and displayed a real-life two-banded longhorn beetle – in person! Adders were listed, but absent in the surrounding undergrowth – maybe they'd been eaten by buzzards.

A couple of guys stood on a grassy hill overlooking a patch of wetland; apparently they'd spotted something other than the pair of orange-tip butterflies above my head. The younger of the two men pointed at the swathe of vegetation and said, 'There's a grasshopper warbler out there.'

I heard its zinging call, aptly reminiscent of a chirping grasshopper, but I couldn't see it, so I asked for his guidance to gain a sighting.

He gazed over the featureless green scrub and tried to find an object to pin directions from. 'Arrrr,' he muttered. 'Can you see that tall brown twig?'

I raised my eyebrows and replied, 'It's a bit like looking at a lawn and asking if I can see a particular blade of grass.'

He sighed. 'Okay, see the tallest tree on the horizon? Go slightly left of that and down.'

I followed and a moment later chirped, 'Oh, I see it.'

'Great.'

'Well… I can see the tall brown twig, where's the bird?'

He replied wearily. 'To the right.'

'Bingo!' Through binoculars I saw the little greyish-green warbler holding its beak wide, throat throbbing from its vibrating call. It was a real treat to watch one performing. I thanked the birder for his patient help, then moved on, accompanied by a fluttering Speckled Wood butterfly.

That evening while relaxing in the hotel's beer garden I chatted with other guests. One of them thought he'd heard a nightingale the previous night but he wasn't sure, as it sounded different to his ones in Kent – did it have a Welsh accent? I never got to hear any nightingales myself, but at dusk I watched several herons returning to roost in the conifers across the valley.

Something else caught my attention. A sheep was lying in the middle of the field with her legs in the air. There was no way I could reach her due to the railway line, otherwise I'd have gone into the field and tried to flip her over (occasionally sheep become stuck on their backs). As she was motionless, I suspected it was too late anyway.

A blackbird turf war diverted my attention. One blackbird took prime position on a pole and competed in song with another across the garden. The blackbird on the pole was louder, had a wider repertoire of melodies and absolutely thrashed his competition. At one point he even sang over his rival. It was therefore a surprise when the superior bird flew off first. Perhaps he felt he'd made his point, or maybe his missus was expecting him back earlier with some worms.

Then I witnessed the 'Miracle of Machynlleth'... the sheep which I thought was dead, suddenly resurrected herself, waggled her legs, righted herself and trotted off to join the others. It was a happy ending to a delightful stay in Machynlleth, a place I never once pronounced correctly. The next day I planned to head south towards Pembrokeshire and explore the coast.

Water Shrew

Chapter 14

Wales – Pembrokeshire (2019)

During my morning bath, a bar of soap shot out of my hands, flipped into the air and landed in the toilet bowl like a well-aimed basketball shot. Little did I know this incident was a portent for what was to come...

The first hour of the morning's drive was spent pushing through horizontal rain, causing the abandonment of my original plan to visit the sand dunes at Ynyslas. I'd intended to search for reptiles – but they're fair-weather friends. Thankfully the showers lightened further south and by Aberporth there was only light drizzle. On a headland north of Aberporth Bay, fine views were presented over the crescent-shaped cove, containing a harbour nestled beside a golden beach. This area was recommended for dolphins, but I felt pessimistic about my chances due to the weather. Why did I think a bit of drizzle would deter a creature which spends the entirety of its life being wet? Within a minute a pair of bottlenose dolphins emerged on the far side of the bay; they swam about briefly before departing. I was very pleased to be proven wrong.

A footpath wound down to Aberporth beach and beside the grassy verge a small mammal scurried. It was a water shrew, identified by its pale belly, darker upper fur and size (they are slightly bigger than common shrews, which in turn are a smidge larger than the aptly named pygmy shrews). The water shrew scampered onto the path and began a fidgety circular movement. This seemed unusual behaviour. Maybe it was poorly or perhaps it wasn't as keen on the wet weather as dolphins (even though you'd expect a 'water' shrew to thrive in damp conditions). Sadly I was powerless to help, due to my limited knowledge of shrew ailments and cures.

A young couple approached and gave me a glance which suggested, 'What are you looking at?'

'A shrew,' I said.

The lady bent down to take a closer look of the furry little animal 'Aww, he's cute.' She leant directly over for an intimate peek.

'Watch out, they have a terrific leap and will go for your face,' I said.

She immediately backed off while her partner roared with laughter.

'Oh, shut up!' she retorted in her strong Welsh accent.

The shrew dashed back into the undergrowth not ill at all – and I made a less speedy return up to the car park.

From Cardigan, road-signs led me to the Welsh Wildlife Centre and Teifi Marshes; a large reserve with several footpaths. I went to the visitors' centre for a map to aid my navigation. The paths were designated colours. The receptionist gave details on each route. She pointed to the yellow path beside the River Teifi, 'The yellow route is difficult to negotiate, so we recommend visitors avoid it.'

'Is it closed?'

'Some of the path has eroded, plus a tree has come down. Best take the green route instead.'

I can understand cautiousness on the part of a reserve representative – no one wants to be liable for somebody injuring themselves. However, if you explore woodlands on a regular basis, you'll occasionally find Health and Safety notices unnecessarily spoiling a good adventure. I'm sure there are benefits of being told if a particular route will bring you into contact with a rabid fox or a party of schoolchildren, but usually the dangers are far less perilous. Previously I've crossed beyond coloured warning tape and discovered nothing more than a fallen branch. Everyone needs to take responsibility for their own safety and I assess the dangers based on the available information. If I'm out alone and it goes wrong for me, I'm to blame and I'll suffer the consequences. I live life on the edge – I don't keep the protective lens caps on my binoculars, which any self-respecting wildlife watcher knows is hardcore.

Feeling buoyant with adventurous spirit, I was soon on the yellow route, adjacent to the River Teifi, cushioned either side by a valley of thick woodland. True, some of the track had slipped away through water erosion, but I easily overcame this minor obstacle. A bird flew above the river and I paused to get a better view – it was a grey wagtail not a kingfisher. Around the corner, the river continued to flow between the lush sloping woodland and I found four people staring at the river. A few seconds of eavesdropping revealed the subject of their conversation was otters, and I soon established they'd not seen any.

The path forked, one route led upwards into the woodland, while a more interesting track hugged the river. I guessed both were versions of the same yellow route and they'd converge later. I decided to follow the riverside path which offered greater possibilities for kingfishers and otters. Rainwater from the earlier deluge had soaked the vegetation, and as I brushed through the leaves, my legs became sodden. A fallen tree lay across the route; I climbed over unperturbed, glanced back at the obstacle and thought to myself, 'That's what the lady warned me about'. I laughed in the face of the Health and Safety, and continued merrily along.

A long thin flying insect bobbed through the air: a blue damselfly with wings patterns which looked like they'd been smudged by a criminal's inky fingerprints. Subsequent research confirmed it was a banded demoiselle. The demoiselle landed on a tall iris blade and I waited for its pretty wings to be displayed again, but it decided to stay put and would not entertain.

A willow tree hung close to the river's edge and behind it a patch of sticky mud sloped into the river. It was squelchy by the riverside and my feet splatted and sank, so I strode onto higher ground which soon became firmer. I stopped to consult the reserve map, which indicated that the yellow route converged with the green route where the river turned left. I peered through the willows and could see a sharp bend in the distance. I persevered between more fallen branches as a bird flew down the river – *déjà vu*; it was a grey wagtail, not a kingfisher.

Behind another willow tree, some resemblance of a path continued through the undergrowth. Several stings later I realised the greenery concealed nettles. The nettles became deeper and taller, so I forged on with arms aloft – this failed to prevent stings penetrating my shirt and attacking my midriff.

I heard footsteps above and I thought to myself, 'Thank God, I'm not that far from the other footpath.... there's somebody up there'. After twenty minutes I'd endured enough of the mud, nettles and fallen trees. I yearned to be reunited with civilisation, although I desperately wanted to avoid retracing my steps. This led to my absurd decision to navigate the steep 45-degree steep woodland bank. I gave up on the river and carefully edged upwards on all fours over wet rocks and vegetation. My progress was slow as I gradually climbed higher in search of humanity and the other path. No obvious signs of a path or people were seen, so the laborious crawl continued upwards. The footstep noises didn't seem too far above. Once a couple of metres higher, I stopped, faced by the originator of the footsteps – a sheep.

I wondered, 'What are you doing on this woodland slope?'

The sheep's expression suggested she had the same thought.

Startled, I lost my footing and tumbled down the bank like somebody on a water slide. I grabbed a branch halfway down which halted my fall, but the branch broke from the tree and joined me for the rest of the descent.

Three things I should be grateful for – firstly, the muddy hole I plunged into was a soft landing; secondly, a rock which I displaced on my highspeed slide missed me by inches; and thirdly, I was wearing thick jeans which protected my rump from gravel rash.

While easing myself out of the mud, I was met with a welcome distraction. Otter footprints! I followed the evenly-spaced webbed toe markings, which traced the otter's route from the trees to the river (the otter's approach was probably more elegant than mine). After studying the footprints, I turned around, extracted myself from the mud with squelching steps headed for more nettles. My whole body tingled with pain.

I realised that rock climbing was no longer an option, so I continued along the riverside. I checked my map again. Somewhere up the slope, where sheep lurked, I knew there was the green route and I anticipated my yellow route would soon climb and we'd meet like old friends. I gave my boots a shake, offloaded some of the mud, plucked vegetation from my hat and shirt and noticed my arm was bleeding. The branch must have sliced me during the fall. I hadn't noticed at the time, mainly because my body was already suffering misery from nettle stings.

A tawny owl flew past. Tawny owls are portly birds and it bobbed along like a ball on a string, weaving through the riverside trees. The owl didn't notice me, covered in so much woodland and mud that I blended perfectly into the undergrowth.

I crossed behind another willow tree, walked over a mound and froze in my tracks. I'd reached the end of the line. The path ended abruptly at a sheer rockface and the river diverted sharply left at this unpassable barrier. I sighed. I hate being defeated, but I'd gone off-piste. This was definitely not the yellow route and from this moment onwards this gloomy cul-de-sac would be known to me as 'the brown route'. I glanced down myself; bottom half caked in mud, leaves and twigs poking from my clothing, my body throbbing from nettle stings and a bloody sleeve. Some people might consider this character-building.

The tawny owl passed me again, chased by a blackbird.

It was time to admit defeat and retrace my steps. Failure sapped my energy as I trudged wearily back through the mud and undergrowth. On the protracted, painful return, I revisited the nettles, branches, mud and fallen trees. There were the otter prints, with mine next to them – no one else stupid enough to add their footprints. This was a place where only otters, owls and fools dwelled. A grey wagtail mocked me from the river, it wasn't joined by any kingfishers.

I plodded onwards and finally saw people on the official yellow route. The sight filled my heart with joy. I picked up my pace and reached the fork in the track where I'd gone off-grid.

The family coming down the track saw me and stopped; parents shielding their children from the approaching Creature from the Black Lagoon.

I ignored their concerned stares and greeted them with genuine happiness. 'Afternoon!'

'Hello,' replied the father tentatively.

I hoped my next comment would explain my dishevelled muddy state, 'I wouldn't go down the riverbank route.'

One of the children chirped up, 'We went down there when Tommy took us gorge walking.'

This was of interest, so I asked the boy, 'Did you find a route through the woodland?'

'No, we crossed the river. We had wetsuits.'

That's why the route petered out beyond the mud bank. I squelched on and continued up the track into the woodland. At the summit, I sat down wearily and caught my breath in a sunny glade. Steam wafted up from my clothing; water and sweat evaporating in the midday heat. The darkness of the woodland gorge was below; the unforgiving place from which I'd escaped. There was clearly no way from down there to up here, other than the final route I'd just undertaken.

The exploration of the remainder of the reserve was far less eventful. From the mallard hide, I saw mallards. The kingfisher hide in contrast, was guilty of false representation. I've visited several kingfisher hides – none has yet yielded a single kingfisher.

I drove north to New Quay with one important objective – to change out of my filthy clothing. I didn't want to rock up at this evening's B&B in Llanarth like a vagabond. Thankfully, there were toilets by a large car park at the top of New Quay. I rummaged through my suitcase and gathered a bag of fresh clothing before going into a toilet cubicle. While undressing I noticed stings everywhere and examined the cut on my arm. It wasn't deep and had stopped bleeding, which was a relief. I gathered my grubby clothing and shoved it in a bag, before noticing leaves peeking out of the dirty shirt's top pocket – a souvenir from the wilderness trail. I reached in and grabbed the foliage.

Nettles!!!

A stream of swearing echoed around the cubicle.

I shook my hand which smarted like I'd been electrocuted, and opened the cubicle door. A man at the urinal was staring in my direction, no doubt wondering what had happened in the toilet to cause such a torrent of expletives. I declined to say I'd just been stung by nettles – that'd only raise more questions than it answered.

A steep path wound down to New Quay harbour where I stopped above the breakwater and sat on a low wall. A beautiful view: to my right a golden beach bustling with holidaymakers, next to a blue sea dotted with swaying little boats. Immediately three bottlenose dolphins surfaced beside a pair of paddleboarders. I looked around and noticed most of the surrounding people were facing in the same direction; everyone delighting in dolphin-watching. A brilliant shared experience and credit where credit is due… the *Visit Wales* website was spot-on about dolphins being abundant in Cardigan Bay.

The dolphins didn't care about the large audience or sea traffic, and happily swam around the harbour. They splashed about for twenty minutes before disappearing beyond the southern headland. That made up for the earlier jungle exploits, although it provided little comfort to my knees during the steep trudge back up to the car park.

The next morning I drove south to Carmarthen and collected Joe from the train station. We visited Castell Henllys and walked through the ancient woodland of Pengelli Forest. Joe had earlier downloaded a free app on his phone to identify flowers. I was delighted he'd taken an interest in nature and he deployed his new toy on some foxgloves. The app then said he'd need to pay to continue. He cursed it as a 'catalogue of s***' and it was uninstalled. His enthusiasm for botany had been short-lived.

The woodland birdwatching was more rewarding; it included a rumpus between two blackbirds and a jay, while dippers bobbed along the stream. I was treated to a blackcap sighting; they usually hide in thick undergrowth. The male blackcap revealed himself on the edge of a thicket, his black head cut in a Peaky Blinder hairstyle. The blackcap made a loud sharp clicking noise which resounded like a hammer striking a stone – his alarm call. Potentially I was the cause of his concern, so I moved away.

The rest of the day was spent sightseeing before retiring to our accommodation in Newport (an attractive little coastal village, rather than the larger city with the same name). It didn't take us long to discover a beer garden. A confident robin came close to Joe and he fed it a crumb.

But a moment later a crash of thunder sounded above – it was as though the clouds were packed with dynamite. Everyone in the beer garden expressed a collective 'Oooooooh!!!' We scrambled under a canopy before a lake fell from the sky. Sadly, this and gales were the beginning of a deterioration in the weather which scuppered my boat outing to Grassholm's gannetry. It was annoying to miss out on something I specifically wanted to see, but two days later I'd scheduled a Skomer trip which would hopefully be more successful.

Instead of Grassholm, we explored St David's. In the cathedral grounds a noticeboard mentioned the presence of hairy-footed flower bees. I saw a wasp. The sun reappeared and a red kite crossed above.

The beaches along this coastline were stunning and we stopped at Newgale for a wander over a wide stretch of pristine sand. Gannets dived offshore. Dinas Head provided some welcome sunshine. Inland from the secluded beach there was a wetland wilderness containing umbellifers and yellow flag iris. It was quiet and relaxing in the wetland. The beach was pandemonium. Dozens of children splashed each other in the sea and practised their shrieking. Even the genteel game of cricket was reduced to a shouting match. Dogs bounded in the waves, apart from a pug who was less enthusiastic about taking a dip in the cold waters.

We sat on a low stone wall and watched the frenzy of screaming excitement, flying cricket balls, manic barking and random chases. It was difficult to tell who was having the most fun – the kids or the dogs. Sat around us were the parents, watching at leisure, undoubtedly hoping their children would burn themselves out and gift them with a peaceful evening.

A brace of buzzards circled above, using the thermals to gain height. Joe suggested they were hunting the pug. He then claimed to have seen a red kite, but I corrected him – it was an orange kite and it didn't count if it was attached by string to a youth.

The evening beer garden entertainment involved a child being stuck up a tree. I offered to give the trunk a shake to dislodge him, but my services were not called upon.

****

The following morning the rain belted down for our trip to Cardigan. We parked near the river and admired a sculpture of an otter but no otters appeared in person. Cardigan Castle dominated the riverfront and thankfully most of it was sheltered. Then we went to Cemaes Head and in drier weather trekked up the headland. Joe objected to the hill halfway up and said, 'This is madness,' turned around and went for a stroll on the flat beach. He subsequently missed seeing a dolphin from a high viewpoint beside the youth hostel.

The dolphin was a positive, the big negative was my decision to make this into a circular route. I dropped down through a steep woodland to the shore and discovered the tide was high (two metres high in places). There was no alternative but to return up the hill and go all the way back (Joe would've been intolerable if he'd been subjected to this).

My misfortune with footpaths notwithstanding, I was luckier with bird sightings. A white-rumped bird flew from the hedgerow. A white backside is something I associate with wheatears, but hedgerows aren't typical wheatear habitat and this bird was noticeably stockier. I tracked the bird by slowly moving along the hedgerow. Once within a few metres, I recognised the thick beak and rosy chest of a bullfinch, a happy reminder of the bullfinches of my childhood.

At Ifor Forest, Joe saw a genuine red kite (not attached to a child) and he correctly identified another bird after hearing it calling, 'Chiffchaff.'

He impressed me, so I asked how he knew its name.

'It's the one which goes; flip flop, flip flop.'

Thankfully Joe wasn't given responsibility for naming birds.

As we rambled around Ifor's undulating forest, Joe mentioned he wanted to see a nearby Neolithic tomb called Pentre Ifan. We drove there.

The tomb had three large upright stones supporting an enormous capstone boulder – and two small children. The children scattered off the top after being shouted at by their parents. Later, in the beer garden there were more untamed children, while dogs (releasing streams of slobber) watched their owners eating. Lurchers seemed to be a prevalent breed and we questioned whether Newport was holding a lurcher convention. It wasn't.

The next day we headed towards Tenby and Joe questioned the car's horsepower. 'Do you still have the handbrake on?'

'No.'

'Try using the accelerator.'

'My foot is flat to the floor.'

'Can you knock it down a gear?'

'I'm currently in second.'

'Jees, this is a crap car.'

At last we agreed on something.

A year earlier I'd taken a Pembrokeshire resident called Katherine on a guided tour of the Isle of Man. I mentioned I'd be visiting her patch in the future and she recommended Bosherton Lily Ponds near Stackpole. It was an excellent tip-off. The large freshwater lake was filled with white flowering lilies. A quick detour into the trees revealed purple orchids, while the lake's overgrown fringe contained reed warblers. At the beautiful sandy beach, Joe went for a paddle and I began a circular walk over the headland.

At the summit of the cliffs, the coastal flowers included scarlet pimpernel (I've always considered them more orange than scarlet), sea pink (definitely pink) and birdsfoot trefoil (named because the seed pods resemble the three toes on a bird's foot). Offshore was a pinnacle of stone named Church Rock. When a rock formation is claimed to resemble another object, the comparison is usually dubious, however this little island made a very convincing shape of a church.

Jackdaws flew above and further inland a small gang of choughs poked their curved red beaks into the ground. Choughs are snazzy crows; they have red legs and black plumage like shiny PVC. Through the blustery wind I could hear them calling 'Cheow'.

Along the sea cliffs, razorbills tucked themselves into the crevices as a ferocious wind whipped off the coast. Spring squill and buttercups danced to the rhythm of the blustery wind, while a buzzard used the updrafts to hold its position in the air, like a large hovering kestrel.

The circular route looped back through fields grazed by cows. One child didn't realise that, where there's cows, there's always pats. His mother sighed. 'Oh Jimmy, what have you stepped in now?' The path crossed over a magnificent eight-arch stone bridge, then returned to the freshwater lake and its lilies. Small fish darted amongst the sub-aquatic vegetation, but no prowling pike were spotted.

I picked up Joe from a nearby pub which he'd 'accidentally' found. Afterwards we headed to our accommodation in Tenby – a charming coastal town, with friendly bars and good quality eateries. However, Tenby wasn't flat. This was emphasised after we trekked down fifty steps to a beach, realised the tide cut off our onward journey and had to climb back up again. The ascent involved numerous mutterings about bad backs, sore knees and burning hamstrings.

After an early night I woke at 7am, scoffed a quick breakfast and drove to Martin's Haven for a boat trip to Skomer. Arriving early was important because only the first 250 people would be allocated a space. There was no pre-booking or reservations, so I was in a race against other enthusiasts. It was a lengthy and slow drive (thanks to the car), and I eventually got to the bookings desk at 8:45am.

The staff member said, 'Sorry, the final two spaces for landing on Skomer have just gone. Do you want a boat trip around the island instead?'

I was deeply disappointed at being denied stepping foot on Skomer. The boat trip seemed poor consolation; but I accepted their offer. My melancholy increased after I sat down on the 'booby prize' boat. It rocked and on the opposite seat a young girl whined to her mother, 'We're all going to die.'

Two other passengers were chatting, one man said it was the second time he'd tried and failed to get onto Skomer; the first time he arrived early, got a space but the boat was subsequently cancelled due to a rough sea state. Another man commented that people arrived as early as 6am to guarantee their places. I was kicking myself – I should have got up earlier or hired a faster car. I should definitely have hired a different car.

In all fairness the boat trip was fun, the skipper was enthusiastic, we saw hundreds of puffins – and the little girl was wrong – we didn't all die. On Skomer's headland the lucky beggars who bagged landing spots walked above the sea cliffs. Could they sense dozens of envious eyes staring up at them from our boat?

Afterwards I contemplated driving all the way to the Llanelli Wetland Centre, but the A40 traffic was abysmal so I returned to Tenby. I crossed the beach to St Catherine's Island while the tide was out. Yellow blooms of sea radish sprawled across the headland – their leaves are apparently edible and taste similar to cabbage-flavoured radish (I'm in no rush to try that). Below in the shallows a barrel jellyfish pulsated. Most jellyfish don't have eyes; however they can sense light. It established the close proximity of the rocks, squeezed its bell-shaped body and propelled itself from danger. I joined a tour of the island and this included a slideshow. The tour guide mentioned local wildlife and he alleged that whale sharks resided off this coast – I was sceptical, but didn't air my doubts.

That evening, Joe joined me in a beer garden and we sat in the warmth of the sun. Throughout the holiday the Welsh weather had been mixed, but when sunny it was glorious. On the opposite table, a family departed, leaving the remnants of their meals. Within seconds a herring gull dropped from the sky and plonked herself among the leftovers. She quickly perused the culinary choices; the gravy-soaked crust of a meat pie, a salad, a bowl of chips and half a battered fish. The gull immediately opted for the fish, gulped it down and jumped in the air as a waitress ran over with her tea towel swirling. This confirms that when given a choice, gulls choose their traditional seafood diet – with additional crispy batter.

****

The next morning, Joe was in good spirits because Jan the landlady used the local phrase, 'Tidy.' He'd been waiting all holiday for someone to say that. His positivity dwindled during the long drive to Malvern, particularly after we were overtaken by a large motorhome. Joe sighed loudly as the vehicle hurtled past us at speed.

We eventually crossed into England and arrived in the spa town of Malvern, situated on its steep hilly ridge. Malvern is well-known for its natural beauty and as the destination for a large vegetable competition. I considered asking Joe if he wanted to enter the big turnip contest; but he was still grumpy about travelling the width of Wales in the automotive version of a slug, so I decided not to antagonise him further.

The hills provided a great viewpoint for gazing across the Severn Plain, a wide expanse of farmland dotted with trees. From this lofty position I observed several birds flying high in the sky. Much like learning bird songs, recognising birds in flight requires a little time and effort, but it has great rewards. To become successful, you need to test yourself every time a bird crosses the skyline (admittedly this will result in seeing lots of crows and pigeons).

Identification is made easier by the fact that most birds don't venture high. The majority prefer to stay closer to the ground, either because they aren't strong flyers or they prefer the safety of undergrowth. For this reason, migrating thrushes and waders usually fly high during cover of darkness.

During daylight the sky is only a place for the bravest, fastest, largest and toughest. Brave birds are the little ones (such as pipits, whitethroats and skylarks), who make fleeting ventures into the open air to attract a mate or defend a territory. Fast ones include pigeons, swifts and swallows

– quick and agile so they can evade avian predators. Large ones include geese, swans and herons, while others opt for the safety of numbers, such as starlings. The last and most interesting category are the toughest, which includes crows, gulls and (the main reason I study the sky) birds of prey. I've spotted highflying peregrines, kestrels, buzzards, harriers, kites, eagles and sparrowhawks in flight; they are all up there if you care to look.

Usually I'm alerted to a bird of prey by the reaction of other birds; such as mobbing crows or noisy gulls. Other times I've only noticed them by keeping an eye on the sky, and this happened once again when I noticed a single bird circling above Malvern. This lonesome wanderer could immediately be separated from gregarious birds such as crows and pigeons. Its shape was different to the thin narrow-winged gulls. The bird held in the air and only two large British birds regularly hover; kestrels and occasionally buzzards. There's a size difference between the two, but from this distance it was difficult to discern. Kestrels hover with energetic flapping, while buzzards have a lazier wing movement. The bird then flew closer, tilted and revealed pale patches on its wide underwings; the final piece of evidence which confirmed it was a buzzard.

The buzzard gained height on the thermals and a single crow exited the nearby trees to give it some aggravation. Maybe this lonesome crow was expecting backup from his mates, because once he reached the buzzard, he quickly aborted his solo mission and pegged it back.

A moment later a bright white bird circled at speed. Could this be something rare, perhaps an egret or an albino crow? Inspection through binoculars revealed it was a domestic white dove, which was disappointing.

St Ann's Well was housed in a pretty building amongst the trees. Above the marble drinking font, a large stone plaque promoted this 'fountain of crystal water'. I cupped my hands and swallowed a deep refreshing mouthful, then noticed behind a vase of flowers a smaller notice from Malvern Hills District Council stating the water should be boiled before drinking, due to its dubious purity. I next went to nearby public toilets (nothing to do with the 'pure' spring water). On the wall above the urinal, an emerald moth rested. I pulled out my phone, switched it to camera mode and focused on the subject. The light was poor and the camera struggled to take a sharp picture, so I took a dozen snaps to help identification later. A flushing noise rumbled from one of the cubicles – I was unaware of there being anybody else in the toilets. The cubicle door opened and a man walked out and delivered me 'a look'. He appeared to be insinuating that taking photos at a public urinal was strange behaviour. I was going to say I was photographing a moth, but decided not to give him the satisfaction.

As a wildlife enthusiast, getting odd looks from strangers is part of the territory. I've received several raised eyebrows from strangers while I've been inspecting animal droppings, bird pellets and squashed roadkill. Other enthusiasts take it to the extreme; a biologist I knew collected dead wildlife to dissect and determine the cause of death (including checking the digestive system for plastic). The last time I saw him he was strolling around with a deceased seabird poking out of his jacket pocket. Even I raised my eyebrows at that.

In the evening I sat with Joe outside our hotel and I reflected: I'd had an adventurous and fascinating holiday. There were some negatives, mostly my choice of calamitous footpath routes, failed boat excursions and a car with the horsepower of a lame pit pony. The positives outshone those adversities. The Welsh were incredibly friendly (even though I couldn't pronounce their place names). The countryside boasted extensive woodlands and superb nature reserves managed sympathetically for nature. This provided rich biodiversity and rewarded me with wonderful bird encounters. The highlights were pied flycatchers, hobbies, bullfinches, a tawny owl, redstart, grasshopper warbler and garden warbler. Plus bottlenose dolphins, water shrew, a weasel with a dead vole, a live vole, and a banded demoiselle.

I would recommend anyone to visit springtime Wales – and I wish you better luck with the footpaths and boat trips.

Red Squirrel

Chapter 15

Northern Ireland (2019)

Prior to my previous wildlife safari holidays, I've created wish-lists containing star species such as dolphins, whales and eagles. This time I had modest ambitions, based on the fact I was visiting in August and spending half the holiday inland. Nonetheless, I wanted two firsts; Irish hares and wood ants, plus two species for repeat viewings; red squirrels and otters.

My route was spread across the southern counties, starting at Strangford Loch on the east, before going westerly inland to Enniskillen and Armagh.

Flights from the Isle of Man take 25 minutes – mine was slightly delayed by a stowaway bumble bee in the cabin. I was happy for it to have a free lift, but other passengers were less considerate. An elderly lady screamed as it landed on her head and a fight ensued until the poor insect was squashed. She announced to everyone, 'Don't worry, I've saved you all.'

One hour later I was driving from Belfast International Airport to Strangford. A rolling road crossed between lush open countryside and lovely overgrown paddocks. At Lisburn, the Mourne Mountains appeared on the horizon, which confirmed I was going in the right direction. Then

I caught my first brief glimpse of Strangford Lough – mature woodland overhanging a wide stretch of calm water. It looked magical.

Strangford was my kind of place; colourful terraced streets with history and character, beside a tranquil blue lough. Early evening was spent walking a circular footpath north of the village, through a long avenue of trees bursting with wildflowers and surrounded by golden wheat fields. At the coast, an Atlantic grey seal bobbed in still waters, while on the rocks, little egrets and oystercatchers foraged. A heron took off and emitted a noise like a hacking sneeze.

In Strangford's centre, over a hundred people gathered around a triangular village green between two pubs. The reason for the get-together: their summer festival. Three days of music, sports, tournaments, dancing and drinking. Everyone seemed to know each another and generations of families formed large groups. A grandfather lifted the youngest of his tribe onto his shoulders for a higher viewpoint, while friends were received with hugs and smiles. At first I felt like a wedding gate-crasher, but soon became a welcome invited guest.

I stood on the front steps of the Lobster Pot pub beside the bouncer; a short middle-aged lady who was very amiable until crossed, then it was as if you'd released the Kraken. She spotted a miscreant and bellowed ferociously, 'No glasses outside Niall, get yourself back here!'

Niall – three times the size of the bouncer – cowered, exchanged his glass for a plastic version and apologised.

Shouts of encouragement echoed around the village green as a peloton of cyclists appeared from the top road. As they passed through the cheering community, I sat on a bench with the local newspaper. *The Down Recorder* was an interesting read, particularly the sports section which had a full page dedicated to pigeon racing.

At dusk, hundreds of crows flew to their roost at the rear of the village. They spiralled down like roof slates in a twister before 'carring' and 'carricking' from the treetops.

****

The following morning I drove south along the Mourne Coastal Road and parked at Cloghy Rocks, where gannets and terns plunged into the frothy tidal waters. Closer to shore, harbour seals were hauled onto rocks, their wet bodies glistening in the early sunshine. Redshanks chimed and a curlew flew overhead and sang its fluty tune. When I returned to my car, a large bee had claimed it as part of his territory (I suspect he was a species of carder bee). He flew over the bonnet and chased off rivals, while I slipped past and got into the car without a fight.

Opposite Strangford Holiday Park, the shoreline held approximately fifty Sandwich terns (I didn't count them all). The flock included fledglings, as big as the adults but without black feathers on their crowns, which made them resemble monks. Dozens of ringed plovers scampered across the mudflats, joined by oystercatchers and curlews. The oystercatchers kicked off and began a loud piercing chatter, causing some of the ringed plovers to change direction, perhaps disgruntled by the noise.

At Killard I found another fifty or so Sandwich terns (I didn't count those either), and beyond Ardglass the Mourne Mountains loomed above the sea – an impressive sight.

After Newcastle was Tollymore Forest, its entrance lined with rugged old firs and signs promoting the resident red squirrels. The car park was already busy with visitors. In the natural woodland, I tried to use the reserve's free map, but it created confusion. I often use the sun's position in the sky to get my bearings and the map contradicted my natural instincts. I soon realised the map's north was at the bottom and south was at the top. Who conjured up that madness!?! I've owned some rubbish maps during my travels, but this upside-down chart beat them all. I stuffed it into my pocket and instead followed markers for the River Trail.

Underneath a beech tree, patches of grass were lifted and one contained beech mast. This could have been a nut cached by a squirrel (both squirrel species eat beech mast, but only greys have acorns regularly in their diet). Other patches of disturbed turf were empty; maybe some of the squirrel stores had been discovered by a thieving crow.

In my futile attempt to spot a squirrel, I gazed upwards while a family walked past. 'Are you looking for anything in particular?' a lady asked.

'Squirrels,' I replied.

Her friend bemoaned. 'Bloody grey squirrels.'

The lady quickly interjected, 'No, we have red ones here.'

It does amuse me that most people cherish red squirrels but have a deep loathing for greys. I personally don't dislike greys – they've simply been successful in a foreign country and they never chose to come here in the first place.

Plant spotting included tutsan (the closed flower heads resemble red berries) and ragwort (a yellow flowering plant which is toxic to mammals). A fritillary butterfly fluttered above the path and stopped to take nectar from the ragwort. There are many species of fritillaries and most have chequered wing patterns. This species was a dark green fritillary because of the green (which isn't particularly dark) on its underwings. One patch of ragwort was infested with cinnabar moth caterpillars, black and yellow striped – perfect camouflage against the flowers. Even if a predator discovers the caterpillars, they are unpalatable because they absorb toxins through their diet. When the caterpillars metamorphosise into moths, they are bright red and fly during the daytime: the things you get away with when you taste awful. Why don't other species do the same thing? If dodos made a bad meal, we might still have them.

The Shimna River ran red with peaty water and stepping stones were constructed for agile people to negotiate. Midday was far too early for me to fall in a river, so I waited until a sturdy stone bridge came into view before crossing into a larch and spruce woodland. This habitat had potential for red squirrels, which are better adapted to feeding on pine cones than the greys so reds prevail in coniferous plantations, such as those in Kielder Forest and the Scottish Highlands. At the end of the woodland hike I hadn't seen any squirrels or dreys, and my neck hurt from gazing up at the trees, but I enjoyed the challenge.

On the track ahead, a large group of tourists appeared, some dressed in robes and waving fake swords. It came as no surprise that they were on a *Game of Thrones* tour. Northern Ireland tourism has benefitted greatly from promoting itself as the outdoor setting for this blockbuster series. I'm a fan of the programme too, so I followed behind the crowd. They gathered around one location where the Starks discovered direwolf pups. Several tourists took photos. I would have too, had there been direwolves about.

The final area to explore was the arboretum. As I admired the various ornamental trees, a little brown job flitted between the branches. Something about its light fluttery movement suggested it wasn't a sparrow. This bird danced in the air, pirouetted and glided effortlessly back onto a branch. A sparrow performing the same manoeuvre would fly like a wet rag in a storm and rebound with all the elegance of a falling conker. Binoculars revealed the bird was a spotted flycatcher – the spots are on the bird's chest and crown. It flew upwards again and snaffled a fly. It was a good find; they aren't common birds.

Afterwards, I entered the warden's office and asked where all the squirrels were hiding. Apparently, the squirrels scarper during peak visitor times, particularly when people bring their dogs. I mentioned the presence of the flycatcher and the warden's face lit up, so I led him to the arboretum. There's always a risk when going back to somewhere you've previously seen wildlife. Animals have a habit of disappearing and making you look daft. Back home on several occasions I've told people about a basking shark offshore, pointed to where it was, only for it to vanish. Thankfully the flycatcher was still there and the warden added it to Tollymore's bird list as a new species. It was a great moment and he was a nice chap – so I didn't ruin it by remonstrating about the reserve's upside-down map.

On the return journey there were no signs for Bohill Nature Reserve, but Quoile was easily located. The reserve consisted of a footpath stretching along the Quoile river's southern edge. The bankside willows contained tweeting goldcrests and the river held mute swans, mallards and little grebes (a.k.a. dab chicks).

At the most easterly point of the reserve, a raised area presented views across a wide bend in the river. Half a dozen tufted ducks dived for subaquatic insects and plants (they aren't fans of bread). To the right, three little grebes bolted out of the reeds and joined the tufted ducks. All the waterfowl stared suspiciously back at the reed bed. Maybe they'd been flushed out by a predator, such as an otter, but nothing came into sight. The wildfowl moved from the danger zone and resumed diving for food elsewhere.

On the way back I was stricken by a painful jab on my wrist and looked to see what bit me. The culprit was nowhere to be seen. Strangford must have horseflies with great concealment skills.

A couple of weeks before the holiday I'd been on a guided wild flower walk. I was bitten then too, and the botanist guide climbed into the undergrowth and reappeared with woundwort leaves. I scrunched the leaves up and smeared the pulp onto the tender area, which successfully soothed the pain and reduced the swelling. Armed with this knowledge I explored Strangford's vegetation for the same plant. I knew it had toothed leaves, small purple flowers and a hairy stalk, similar to nettles (you don't want to put nettles on an insect bite).

I soon identified a plant which matched woundwort's description, scrunched up the leaf and was about to apply it, but was halted by the aroma. I sniffed the leaf – it was minty. I threw away the water mint. Soon afterwards I came across another plant which resembled woundwort and wasn't minty. I rubbed the leaf onto the bite but it provided little relief and left a tanned stain on my wrist – something which didn't occur when administering woundwort. I thought the plant might have been betony, but betony is rarely found in Northern Ireland. Therefore I'd probably wiped myself with a dead nettle (dead, because it lacks a sting, not because I'd trodden on it).

My throbbing wrist failed to hold me back and I continued to Castle Ward, another *Game of Thrones* location, the original Winterfell. Visitors were dressed as characters from the Kingdom of the North and a group of teenagers threw axes at large targets. I fancied throwing an axe, but axe-chucking wasn't extended to curious onlookers. Instead I entertained myself with a coastal amble through patches of purple petalled sea aster and paused to listen to a noisy shrew hiding in the undergrowth.

Back in Strangford the summer festival was still going strong with family fun runs and a raft race. Children flung themselves off the jetty into the sea, as parents stood nearby and kept a watchful eye.

One dad shouted to his son, 'Callum, Callum!'

The small boy paused before leaping off the harbour wall. 'What?' he replied.

'Get onto the boat Callum, you'll get more height.'

'Okay,' said the boy. He obligingly hauled himself onto a docked yacht and once higher, plunged into the sea with a splash. He emerged a moment later and spat out seawater.

'That's better son,' shouted his dad encouragingly.

The complete lack of Health and Safety was highly refreshing, it was like travelling back to the 1970s.

****

212

The next morning I parked at Strangford harbour where the sea was pristine and bladderwrack gently swayed against the dock. Today's excursion would start with a crossing to Portaferry; from there I would make an anti-clockwise drive around Strangford Lough. The ferry journey was calm and quick, and after a short picturesque drive up the northern coastline, I stopped beside Ballyhenry Island. Bally in a name means 'place of' – so in short, this was Henry's Island. I didn't see Henry, but there were wheatears, curlews, redshanks and another fiftyish Sandwich terns. Either it was a good breeding year for Sandwich terns, or the same flock of fiftyish birds were following me around.

The serenity allowed sound to travel far. The centre of the wide lough was a safe haven for guillemot families, revealed by the high-pitched chirping of their youngsters. A plunge-diving tern hit the Lough's surface and the smack was loud and prominent.

On the eastern coast, Kearney Point had a footpath of low mown grass, soft and bouncy underfoot. I'd done a lot of walking already and my feet welcomed the luxury of a cushioned path. The route was bordered by sea mayweed and wild roses; but the coastline was dramatic. Waves broke on jagged reefs which extended offshore and created a surf of churning water. This coastline has a history of shipwrecks and would be dangerous for marine mammals such as dolphins (which made sea-watching futile).

In Kircubbin I pulled into a car park and scanned the nearby rocky beach for new species. Instead, a common one was performing interesting behaviour: a hooded crow foraged on the strandline and plucked out a small mollusc. The crow flew up with the winkle in its beak, circled and dropped the shell over the shore. I've seen crows perform this trick before; it's a way to break the shells, like thrushes smashing snails against rocks. The falling winkle missed the rocks and landed with a splat on the sand. Using tools is a sign of animal intelligence – I would have considered the crow smarter if it'd chosen to drop the winkle over the car park, which guaranteed a hard landing. The crow checked the sandy winkle, gave it a disappointed peck and flew off hungry.

Mount Stewart was further up the lough and it was already busy with picnicking families and dog walkers. Beyond the bustling parkland was native woodland and signs advertising a red squirrel hide. Sadly, the squirrels were hiding. The afternoon was hot and a red-haired couple were dousing themselves with sun-cream. Perhaps red-haired squirrels avoid the midday sun for the same reason. The one token bit of wildlife was once again provided by a wood pigeon: maybe they get a call when everything else fails to show up. Then in the surrounding woodland I spotted a round bundle of leaves and twigs high up in the canopy. It was potentially a squirrel's drey – or a crow's nest – I'll never know, as neither crows nor squirrels visited.

A local man stopped for a chat and I mentioned my unsuccessful search for red squirrels. He said a pair lived in his garden. I dropped some subtle hints about me going to his house and seeing them for myself, but no invitation was forthcoming.

A raven flew above and made a loud deep 'Carr!'. It headed across the lough and I followed in a similar direction to Castle Espie; a Wildfowl and Wetland Trust reserve. A wildfowl enclosure housed captive birds, including red breasted geese – the same species I had spotted at Ynys Hir. Captive species are always more interesting after they've escaped and gone wild.

I left the enclosure and entered the first bird hide. It offered great views of a large expanse of mud. The tide was out and the birdlife had departed with it. The next hide was significantly better and rewarded me with sightings of little egrets and black-tailed godwits (I could see their long legs – I'm now a godwit expert).

The site of an old lime kiln provided alkaline conditions favoured by knapweed and field scabious. Another clump of flowers needed more time for identification. Large yellow flowers resembling the discs of butter you get in posh restaurants, coloured like dandelions but shaped like large daisies. This required a process of elimination. Coltsfoot could be ruled out as it flowers earlier in April and corn marigolds prefer slightly acidic soil (this ground was alkaline), so this plant was common fleabane. Most people would just dismiss the flowers as dandelions and miss out on the fun detective work.

I passed a shallow pool crammed with hundreds of juvenile fish with silvery bodies and red-tipped fins; they were rudd. When I cast my shadow across the pond the fish dashed to the surface, causing it to fizz like boiling water.

The drive back was enlivened by cricket commentary on the car radio, as Ben Stokes and Jack Leach attempted to save the third Ashes test match. By the time I returned to Strangford the batsmen only needed two runs to win a tense finale. It was bad timing – cars were leaving the ferry and the festival's fancy dress parade commenced. I listened to the climax of the victorious cricket sat in gridlock, surrounded by a family dressed as dinosaurs.

That evening I sat in the sun and read the local weekend newspaper – half of the pages were dedicated to farming. Adverts covered a wide range of topics: udder ointments, tupping preparations, fat/thin cows and coloured hens. Sadly, I had no spare luggage capacity for any purchases. The fancy dress competition had been deservedly won by the dinosaur family and I chatted with a local man called Michael. Our conversation moved onto the subject of *Game of Thrones* and Michael interjected, 'A chap up the road owns two direwolves.'

'Are they the size of horses in real life?'

'No, I think that's camera trickery.'

'Oh,' I sighed, disappointed.

Michael tried to cheer me up. 'Sometimes he brings the wolves into the village.'

'Does he let the kids play with them?'

'No.'

I decided not to ask Michael any more *Game of Thrones* questions, even though I was desperate to know if anybody had a pet dragon.

Later, while sat on a peaceful corner of Strangford harbour I watched the black-headed gulls, who were more prolific here than the larger herring gulls. The coast contained no cliffs for herring gulls to nest, whereas black-headed gulls use low-lying secluded sites and they were well serviced by the surrounding islets. The agility of the smaller gulls was also beneficial when dodging tombstoning children. A big splash was followed by the sound of squawking gulls.

I felt my wrist. In the absence of any treatment the horsefly bite was still hot and angry. Wild plants dotted the harbour and perhaps one of them might cure the pain. I searched online for herbal treatments which performed the same job as woundwort. When I was bitten, I had immediately dismissed the nearby mint – it was therefore rather annoying to read that mint would've actually helped. Sadly none of the surrounding harbour plants featured as potential remedies, but another suggestion was to cool the area with an ice cube. For medicinal purposes only, I went to the Cuan pub and bought a G&T with ice – and rubbed one cube onto the inflamed skin. The pain diminished noticeably after the third G&T.

****

The next day I departed the lovely village of Strangford. It had been a charming place to stay, predominantly because of the friendly locals. I headed towards Enniskillen and checked-in at the Killyhevlin Hotel on the banks of the River Erne. I ventured out soon after arriving and explored the surrounding countryside. The first stop was at Gortmaconnell's moorland. A track led through coppiced hazel trees and rough pastures, which resounded with the vibrating calls of grasshoppers. There were lots of sheep (the air was filled with their 'scent'). The route terminated at the top of a steep hill with expansive views across green fields, rolling hummocks and loughs. In addition, it was a great place to watch a farmer as he yelled and swore at his badly trained collie, while it scattered sheep across the opposite hillside.

At Killykeegan, overgrown verges swayed with the perfumed frothy flowers of meadowsweet. A sign said, 'You may be lucky and spot an Irish hare'. It was probably the same level of luck required to win the Irish Lottery.

After Belcoo I accidentally visited the Republic of Ireland (only revealed when the road-signs changed to dual languages and kilometres). Once back in Northern Ireland, I drove further inland and up a steep track which snaked high into the hills. Fortunately the hire car was more powerful than the Welsh one, so I successfully reached the lofty heights of the Cuilcagh Mountain. I scanned the landscape for hares, but like my Irish friend Brendan's head, they were both hairless. On the drive down, two buzzards stood in a freshly cut hay meadow. Grounded buzzards are chunky-looking birds, resembling sturdy little Russians in bearskin coats.

That evening back at the hotel, I sat on the banks of the River Erne and watched small pleasure cruisers chugging past. It was a relaxing location, particularly in comparison to the hotel's interior, which was hosting a wedding reception. At dusk, a loud piping noise could be heard from the opposite bank. After studying the overhanging trees for twenty minutes, a kingfisher eventually flew out. It skimmed the river in a fast flight and landed further away in a thick patch of shrubs. A beaming smile was on my face as a local man walked past and I excitedly told him about the kingfisher.

He replied, 'You see all sorts round here,' and strutted off without stopping. I was surprised a kingfisher was of little interest to him – because it'd made my day.

Before turning in for the night I checked tomorrow's weather forecast. It wasn't good, and in the morning I was awoken by the sound of rain belting the patio window. I decided to have another hour in bed and rose at 9am for breakfast. I was still up earlier than most of the wedding guests.

****

Crom Estate National Trust was the first destination of the day and the rain had slackened on arrival. The grounds contained farmland, wetland, woodland and some of Upper Lough Erne. Ancient yew trees were entwined and a dozen goldfinches chattered from a surrounding thicket. During summer the name goldfinch seems an odd name, due to the bird's more obvious red face, but the autumnal moult fades the red feathers and their gold wing bands become the most prominent plumage. A greater spotted woodpecker landed at the top of an ash tree and called loudly 'chip, chip, chip', while on the lough a great crested grebe youngster made a squeaky toy noise.

A bridge led to a small island and on the far side was a jetty. I always feel nervous on jetties, I expect my clumsiness to take over and send me into the depths with a splash. I timidly stopped at the edge and gazed over the wide waterscape. A minute later a bird flew over the lough and headed directly towards me. It was silhouetted by the low morning sun and resembled a starling. Once the bird saw me it diverted its course and showed me its back lit up by a bright strip of electric-blue. The kingfisher banked and gave me a fantastic flyby view. It was a guilty pleasure, because the kingfisher had presumably planned to perch on my jetty and abandoned the idea because of me.

I hoped my luck with kingfishers might transfer to red squirrels (which were advertised as being here), so I left the island and explored the surrounding woodland. Ideally I wanted to tread quietly along the track but the gravel path did its utmost to foil that with every footstep crackling and popping.

A bird hide overlooked Upper Lough Erne and bench seats inside provided a welcome opportunity to sit. The lough contained goldeneyes (identified by their white cheek patches) and a male goosander (black and white plumage). A book on the shelf recorded visitors' sightings and I added the wildfowl I'd seen, before reading some earlier entries. Alisha aged 10 noted 'ducks and a wasp', while an anonymous contributor gave credit to 'a spider in the corner'. The spider was still in the corner, and I hoped she'd appreciate the reference. Female spiders are usually the web builders, so I was basing the spider's gender on that rather than any other distinguishing features (my thirst for knowledge doesn't extend to inspecting arachnid genitalia).

On the return to the car park a heavy shower tumbled down, resulting in a soggy buzzard, two damp jays and a drenched visitor.

I left Upper Loch Erne and drove north to Lower Lough Erne. It seemed an odd arrangement for a map to display lower above upper – I suspect it was because the southern upper watercourse fed into the lower north, or the designer responsible also produced Tollymore's reserve map.

The long drive north was made difficult by heavy rain, and it was still pelting down when I arrived at Castle Caldwell's woodland. After travelling so far I was determined to get out and explore. A forestry ranger's jeep was nearby and I skipped over puddles to reach the driver's window. The ranger seemed reluctant to open his window and let rain in; eventually he couldn't ignore me any longer and tentatively lowered the glass.

I greeted him with a wet smile and asked about red squirrels.

His expression implied that it was 'odd' that a grown man was looking for squirrels during a monsoon. He humoured me and pointed in the direction of some tall pine trees, before hastily raising his window again.

I didn't think it was possible, but the weather became even more ferocious. I took shelter beneath a tree and waited for the shower to pass – five minutes later I had to concede it wasn't a passing shower and continued down the track. The squirrel hunt ended abruptly afterwards, when I gazed up at a tree and a large raindrop hit me slap-bang in the eye. Half blinded, I staggered back along the lough and stopped when my blurred eyesight spotted a flock of distant wildfowl. I rummaged in my rucksack for binoculars and the fleece on top was pulled out first. This action dragged out the rest of the bag's contents and my binoculars fell heavily on the hard track. The knock caused the binocular lenses to become uncollimated (unaligned) which resulted in double vision – in short, my binoculars were now wrecked. I tried to use them as monoculars with my one good eye, but the results were inferior and failed to help me identify the wildfowl which had caused the incident (I blamed the birds, rather than my clumsiness). I departed shortly afterwards, feeling wet and miserable. I'd driven a very long way to get soaked, hit in the eye and break my binoculars.

The return route skipped over small islands which dotted the northern edge of Lower Lough Erne. It was a bit like I imagine the Florida Keys – during hurricane season. With this amount of rain, no wonder there were so many bloody loughs.

The deluge lessened during the evening which allowed me to venture out once again to the hotel's riverbank. A troop of swallows were dancing above the river's surface. They occasionally leapt upwards in pursuit of an insect, like water-skiers hitting jumps. The frivolity abruptly finished and the swallows dispersed. I realised why, two minutes later, when it chucked it down. How did the swallows know in advance that rain was on its way? Perhaps they could sense the air getting heavier? It was something I failed to perceive and I belatedly scrambled for cover.

The eaves of the hotel provided enough shelter for wildlife watching to resume. Rooks landed in an old tatty conifer which had all the elegance of a Christmas tree dumped in someone's backyard in February. One rook worked rainwater from the top of its body down to its tail – first a head waggle, then a flap of wings and a shake of the tail, which finally dispersed the water.

Respite from the rain arrived a few minutes later and once again the swallows returned to skim the river. No idea where they'd been in the meantime, perhaps one had an umbrella.

****

The following day I travelled to Armagh and began a new quest – wood ants. I resumed an old one too – red squirrels. Peatlands Park was the destination, a place mentioned online as being home for wood ants and apparently red squirrels (although I'd fallen for that ruse before). I went into the warden's office and asked where I might see the ants and received a blank look. Clearly they weren't that well-known – or the online information was fake news. Eventually, at the far end of the reserve, I discovered a sign which noted the existence of wood ants. It explained they made huge mounds over a metre tall and were in the older part of the woodland. I went into the older part of the woodland and spotted a large mound of earth – it was a badger sett. I continued exploring the undergrowth before sensing something in the beech canopy above. Small pieces of nut casing tumbled down and pattered on the leaf litter. Could this be one of those elusive red squirrels? I couldn't see anything above, so edged closer as bits of beech mast continued to drop.

I then stepped on a twig with a loud CRACK and immediately knew I'd blown my cover. The beech mast ceased falling – whatever was above had either flown off or gone into hiding. I waited ten minutes before accepting failure and pressed on with my quest for wood ants; you'd expect their large mounds to be quite noticeable. They weren't.

Beyond the woodland was a bog garden dotted with pitcher plants. This plant and grey squirrels have one thing in common, they've both been introduced from America. Insects are drawn in by the pitcher plant's nectar, which lures them into a trap. If the visiting insect misplaces its footing, it'll fall into the hollow stem, shaped like a test tube with liquid at the bottom. The insect will drown and become digested for extra nutrients. And I thought I'd had a bad day yesterday.

The wetland area was good for dragonflies, including our largest, the emperor. In addition to size, the emperor can be identified by its black and blue chequered abdomen – plus, when it flies close to you it resonates like a little WW1 biplane.

After Peatlands there was another location of interest; Portmore RSPB (which didn't claim to have red squirrels – I appreciated their honesty). Portmore was remote and reached by narrow lanes through pretty villages. Why is it that, when you're at the tightest point of a road with no passing places, you meet an oncoming tractor?

Portmore was worth the journey as I saw common terns, a species I may have seen previously, but could now identify with certainty (with one eye using my monoculars). Common terns are similar looking to Arctic terns, but with shorter tail streamers and they're not as elegant (in my opinion). These common terns were benefitting from human intervention, using manmade rafts constructed for their nesting. The rafts were detached from land and out of reach from land predators plus little boxes were scattered about for the chicks to hide inside.

I was surprised that some young terns remained on the raft; August was late in their nesting season. The youngsters were as big as their parents, but with greyer plumage. All the young were on the cusp of fledging and they occasionally burst into frantic wing exercises. A parent flew above and dangled a fish to tempt its youngster into the air, like a human parent offering ice-cream to their child if they tidied their room. The young tern decided it couldn't be bothered, so the parent flew off with its fish. No dinner for you then!

Out on the water there were gadwall; the females are similar to mallards but fortunately males aid identification. The males have a white patch on their grey sides – dull ducks – but the male gadwall was a first recording for me (although I'd probably seen them before without realising). Something then crossed my path, a very large brown caterpillar with eye markings on its body and a tail spike. This caterpillar would metamorphose into a beautiful pink and green elephant hawk moth... a significant change from something currently resembling a long cat turd.

My final wildlife destination of the holiday was a quick visit to Oxford Island. This seemed like a place for people to enjoy the boat trips and play areas, rather than a haven for nature. It was therefore a pleasant discovery to hear a kingfisher piping beyond the woodland. The sound chimed between the trees and became louder beside Closet Bay where I found the Croaghan Hide. Once inside the hide, two people acknowledged me and I mentioned I'd heard a kingfisher outside. They confirmed I was correct, because they'd been watching the kingfisher calling for ten minutes; before I walked in and scared it off.

Two thoughts came to mind – 'oops' and 'dammit!'

I waited twenty minutes for it to return.

It didn't.

I left and continued through the neighbouring woodland. A minute later something moved above which caused me to freeze on the spot. A branch swayed, the foliage swung and an animal scrambled between the canopy. My heart raced, finally on my last day the red squirrel quest would be successful. I stared intently with mouth agape as a squirrel dangled upside down and foraged on the branch below. It was a grey squirrel, a real kick to the nuts.

I'd failed with red squirrels, wood ants, otters and Irish hares. Someone assured me that Irish hares were always seen on the grassy strips beside Belfast International Airport's runway. After more than an hour staring from a departure lounge window, I can say with complete confidence – they were wrong.

As I boarded the plane, I helped an Irish lady with her luggage and she replied, 'Oh, you are an angel.' That interaction summed up all the locals I met, they had incredible warmth.

I was unsuccessful with all the items on my wish list, and the ruddy tree rodent failure left a bitter taste in my mouth. However, it was nothing in comparison to the ultimate bitter experience after arriving home, when I harvested a fine lettuce from my allotment, made a salad and bit into a concealed slug.

Risso's Dolphin

Chapter 16

Isle of Man (2020)

In 2020, Mother Nature reminded us once again who was boss. The consequences of Covid-19 were dreadful for many. I was grateful to personally avoid the virus (as at the time of writing), and my wellbeing and mental health could be maintained with access to my allotment. The permitted time outdoors was spent basking in the unusually warm spring weather while observing nature (and occasionally doing some gardening). Great tits and robins successfully nested at opposite ends of my plot, and winter moth caterpillars flourished on my cherry tree (and stripped it bare of leaves).

The pandemic scuppered my scheduled holiday to Norway, but I was blessed to have an alternative – exploring the Isle of Man. At the beginning of June, after lockdown rules were relaxed, I planned three days out. I was eager to escape the confines of home and my neighbourhood, and immerse myself in wilderness.

Before the first outing, I posted the below announcement on my Wild Enthusiasm Facebook page:

On Monday 8th June I am going to explore the north of the Isle of Man. I'll film what I see and post the footage the following day. I'll take an anti-clockwise route from Douglas and visit Ballaglass Glen, Maughold, The Ayres and Ballaugh Curraghs (plus some other places along the way). My challenge for just one day is to see hen harriers, two different species of terns, plunge-diving gannets, common lizards, six-spot burnet moths, hundreds of orchids and a wild wallaby (happy to add other local species if anyone has sensible suggestions). You'll find out if I'm successful on Tuesday!

One of my Facebook followers suggested a cuckoo, so that was added.

I awoke at 7am for an early start and within seconds of leaving the house I saw a female peregrine falcon (they are bigger than the males). She was perched on the radio mast behind the police station, staring down from her lofty viewpoint at the passing pigeons, but she didn't seem too bothered about catching breakfast. Beside my car, two sparrows were having sex in an ivy-covered wall. It seemed a bit early for all that, so I looked away.

Thick clouds were cast across an iron-coloured sky as a cool breeze pushed down from the north, causing a choppy sea state. The recent spell of good weather seemed absent this morning. I headed north to Laxey, an old Norse name for salmon river; 'lax' relates to salmon, the same as in *gravlax* (buried salmon). Lady Isabella, the largest working water wheel in the world, peeked from the hillside woodland.

The first stop of the morning was above Bulgham Bay, a great viewpoint for sea-watching. As a result of the Manx population being trapped in their homes during lockdown, the Island's footpaths were overgrown and untrodden, and the route to the cliff edge was woven with nettles and brambles. Bulgham Bay is always worth visiting during autumn to scan the eastern coast for minke whales. Vast shoals of herring and other fish species congregate here to spawn and the minke whales turn up to spoil their fun. Alas, today there were no whales in sight (but it was summer, not autumn).

A sound resembling somebody bouncing on a rusty trampoline made me turn. Closer inspection of the surrounding undergrowth revealed a whitethroat balancing on a swaying bramble with a beakful of juicy green caterpillars. The 'burring' call was saying to its youngsters that breakfast would be late due to an interloper. I moved along so they could be fed and passed a roadside dotted with blue flowering sheep's-bit scabious.

Dhoon Glen is situated in the valley below; a woodland shrouding a deep ravine, with a cascading stream sporadically tumbling into waterfalls. A path weaves down to a secluded beach; the descent is always pleasant, the return route an uphill test of endurance. With that in mind, I passed Dhoon Glen without stopping and continued to the less rigorous Ballaglass Glen. 'Glass' in Manx means green; therefore, this was 'the place of green' – a deserved title. A local resident was noisily warming up his power tools for some early morning DIY, so I moved deeper into the glen before stopping for the birdsong. The loudest singers were blackcaps and wrens, with backing vocalists including blackbirds, robins and chaffinches. A blackcap stopped to catch its breath and a chaffinch chipped in with its call.

A fast-running shallow river runs through the southern edge of the glen, water spilling over rocky steps. The river's activity has carved shapes into the bedrock, creating circular bowls; a result of being scoured by spinning small stones over thousands of years.

After a refreshing walk, I returned to the car and continued north following verges dotted with yellow poppies. Then something appeared from a field and trotted in my direction – a brown hare. We both stopped and faced each other like gunslingers at dawn.

The hare realised it was a shoot-out it wouldn't win, turned tail and scampered back into the field. The next thing to make an appearance was the sun. Maughold was warm enough for me to strip off my coat, which was put back on immediately as a cool sea breeze hit me on Maughold Head.

As I looked at the impressive lighthouse there was the sound of a commotion breaking out behind. I turned to investigate the source of the 'zick zick zick' calls above the steep headland. An aggrieved peregrine falcon was being mobbed by three jackdaws. Birds of prey rarely retaliate against their attackers, although you occasionally see a buzzard flashing its talons at a pestering crow – a show of defiance rather than a determined attack. Birds of prey are normally chased off, with crows left behind celebrating. However, today was different; it was nesting season and the peregrine was protecting its territory and fighting back. It flew towards the jackdaws, they parted and the birds appeared to ricochet off each other before reforming. The peregrine swooped, twisted in the air and revealed its pale underside; like a white knight battling darker cloaked adversaries. One jackdaw decided this had escalated into something too risky and bolted off. The peregrine dipped again, looped the loop, tucked in its wings and raced into the remaining pair of jackdaws and they plummeted from its path.

During autumn you often see jackdaws performing acrobatics in strong winds, with barrel-roll stunts and frenetic swoops. It always looks like fun, but the real purpose was now illustrated; they were developing lifesaving skills.

The peregrine and remaining jackdaws lifted higher, each trying to gain a height advantage. When above, it's a safer defensive position and also a point from which you can attack. The peregrine called 'zick zick' as all the birds came level and it drove into the jackdaws again; just as a great black-backed gull passed alongside. For some reason the gull upset the peregrine so much it broke away from the jackdaws, tucked in its wings tightly and formed the shape of a spearhead. This diving movement is called a 'stoop'. The stoop accelerated the peregrine's speed, and the gap between it and gull closed in a split second. Just before impact, the gull banked upwards, screeched and diverted its path. The peregrine narrowly missed the gull. If it had struck, it would have been a fascinating sight (the gull would undoubtedly disagree). Surely a gull of that size would have been too big for a peregrine to take as prey?

The gull fled and by the time the peregrine returned to the cliffs, the distraction had enabled the pair of jackdaws to safely depart.

Around Maughold Head lighthouse, razorbills fired themselves from the cliffs as if jet propelled, while a pair of choughs swooped and glided in synchronised movements. Gannets, fulmars and a kestrel also commuted past. It was a fantastic place to watch nature.

A quick visit to Port Lewaigue presented a song thrush performance, calling in whoops and cheers as if celebrating true love. A juvenile robin was identified by its speckled brown plumage; after the first moult its chest feathers would become orange (they don't have red feathers, but I appreciate that robin orange-breast doesn't sound as good as robin red-breast).

North of Ramsey the road passed through Bride village, in its centre the pretty St Bridget's Church. The churchyard contains interesting headstones, including one for the famous British comedian Sir Norman Wisdom.

To celebrate the millennium in London they constructed the Millennium Bridge, Millennium Wheel and Millennium Fountain. In Bride they recognised the beginning of the 21st century by building a new toilet block. At that particular moment, the Millennium Toilets were more useful than any wheel, fountain or bridge.

Pink and red valerian flowers stood tall from the stone walls and provided a beautiful processional way to the Point of Ayre, the most northerly landmark on the Isle of Man. Swarms of sand martins commuted between feeding zones above the gravel pits and their nesting sites on the coastal sandy cliffs.

At the tip of the Point there's a triangular bank of shingle with the Irish Sea surrounding it on two sides. The deep bank has undulating ridges which are reshaped and heaved during fierce storms. They are getting bigger. Material from coastal erosion in the south is transported by sea currents and deposited here, causing the Point of Ayre to gradually grow outwards. The lighthouse was built in 1818 and has slowly distanced itself from the expanding shoreline, so an additional smaller lighthouse called a 'winkie' has been built on the area in between. Either side of the 'winkie' is where Arctic terns nest. They don't put much effort into constructing their nests, just a few twigs and scattered bits of vegetation. The lack of materials means their pebble-shaped eggs are camouflaged against the surrounding shingle.

There are two things guaranteed to wake me up in the morning; a cold shower or an Arctic tern flying at my face. I cowered as a tern screeched and swooped at my head. I hadn't even considered myself close to their nesting area and I moved away until the harassment ceased.

I had a quick chat with the warden who explained there were twenty-five pairs of nesting Arctic terns and their eggs were scheduled to hatch soon. Ringed plovers were also within the cordoned-off nesting area, benefiting from the extra security provided by their bolshy neighbours.

Gannets were on regular passage around the Point, with their singular habit of circumnavigating the entire triangular coast, rather than cutting across land and shortening their journey. Do they have an aversion to travelling above anything which doesn't contain fish?

Above the heathland, a pipit flew high, cupped its wings and performed a parachuting territorial display; spiralling down as if riding an invisible helter-skelter. I returned to my car and drove along the west coast, with the next stop at Ballaghennie signposted as the Ayres NNR (National Nature Reserve). Beside the single-track road, a sign said to beware of ducks (no ducks seen) then another warned of horses (no horses seen) and finally a third sign advised people to look out for wildlife (which was my intention).

Near the first car park, a pair of six-spot burnet moths rested on the sun-facing side of a wooden post. Like cinnabar moths, these are diurnal insects and brightly coloured to deter the interest of predators. Their black wings are decorated with six bright red spots; fair warning because they contain hydrogen cyanide. Beside them was a small yellow tube, split open at the top; a cocoon from which one of the splendid moths recently emerged. It was a pleasure to see the moths, but as I moved for a closer look, I inadvertently knelt on a stunted gorse bush and I spent the next minutes plucking thorns out of my leg.

I'd finally ticked off one of today's target species and I began searching for my second; common lizards. Lizards regularly use the same posts as the moths in order to soak up the sun's heat and raise their metabolism. However, on this overcast morning, the lizards decided it was too cool to venture out. It was several degrees chillier on the viewing platform behind the visitor's centre. From this lofty viewpoint in summer it is customary to see gannets plunge-diving. Today they were far offshore, but on other days they will come close and plummet into the sea with loud audible smacks. They withstand these impacts due to various adaptations: they tuck their wings tightly against their bodies, internal airbags act as shock absorbers and they can close their nostrils (rather than have their beaks fill with seawater).

From Ballaghennie you can look back inland to the old cliff line, called the Bride Moraine. This range of undulating hills was created during the end of the Ice Age when the last glacier pushed south, stopped and retreated. The land between the Bride Moraine and my viewpoint emerged in the intervening 23,000 years. This newest part of the island has been mostly cultivated, but it still contains dunes and swathes of maritime heathland. The habitat of lichens, heather and burnet roses provides home for rare insects, including heath bee-flies, dark green fritillaries and scarce crimson and gold moths (all were scarce today). Plenty of other insects were about, such as grasshoppers, which provided food for resident birds. Pipits scampered over the heathland, stonechats dipped between the gorse bushes and skylarks rose upwards and trilled. Circling curlews patrolled their territories with haunting melodies.

The sun eventually broke through the clouds and lit up the Ayres; surely it was now warm enough to tempt out the common lizards.

Nope.

A couple of walkers stopped to spectate my futile reptile search.

The lady asked, 'How big are the lizards?'

Before I had a chance to reply, the man answered, 'Tiny.'

I added, 'Yes, they are smaller than crocodiles.'

The lady seemed pleased to know that.

The sun continued to beam down as I sat in my car and ate a packet of crisps. I hoped it would bring out the lizards ('it' being the sun, rather than the smell of cheese and onion). Neither worked, so I drove further south to Smeale Beach at Rue Point where the marram dunes contained sea holly and sprawling sea bindweed (similar to hedge bindweed, but with pink flowers). A section of the upper beach was cordoned off for nesting terns. It was a large area for a modest number of birds – I saw three little terns. The delicate birds bounced in the air and chirped. Little terns are not aggressive like Arctic terns, so I was able to circumnavigate their nesting area unmolested. It was comforting to know they weren't going to fly into my face and become part of my beard.

Atlantic grey seals bobbed on the surf and stared back. Their quizzical expressions suggested they were thinking, 'What's he up to?' I walked off before they found out, while being pattered by a windswept swarm of sandflies. It was like being caught in a shower of black hail. A sanderling scampered over the tideline, a small wader with white underparts and a brown mottled back. It shouldn't go hungry with all these sandflies about.

The footpath curled back and led through marram grass, where I spotted a green beer bottle. It was tilted on its side, with the open end slightly upwards. A rubbish bin was a short distance away (presumably the litter lout failed to spot it), so I picked up the empty bottle to complete their failed task. As I reached down, I realised the bottle wasn't empty after all. Lying inside was a common lizard – trapped because it wasn't able to grip the sloping glass and reach the opening. As I held the sun warmed bottle, the lizard scurried about inside. I gently placed the bottle back down and titled it so the bottle's opening hole was lower. The lizard sprinted out and immediately vanished into the grass; the heat within the bottle had possibly supercharged its energy, or it was simply glad to escape.

A little further away was another common lizard, its lower flank tinged lime green and a spotted pattern covering its back; this suggested it was a male. Behind his front legs, his flanks pulsated – this is where his lungs are located and showed him breathing.

****

It was time to move inland to Ballaugh, a Manx name for 'the place with the lake (or lough)'. After the Ice Age this low-lying area filled with meltwater, but over recent centuries it has been drained by people to support agriculture (so it's no longer a place with a lake). Photographs from the early 1900s show the woodland cleared and the open pastures grazed by sheep. Since then the local farmers have given up on the lowest area most susceptible to flooding and it has been reclaimed by nature. This wilderness is called The Curraghs. As you walk between the gnarly, twisted willows and deep undergrowth, it's surprising to think this habitat is only a century old.

My first stop in the Ballaugh Curraghs was Close Sartfield, a reserve managed by the Manx Wildlife Trust. June is the perfect time to explore its traditionally farmed meadows, while the orchids are in bloom. One field held hundreds of displaying flowers, mostly heath and common spotted orchids (the spots in the name relate to the leaves, rather than the flowers). There were also common twayblades; a completely green plant and difficult to notice among the grass. A raised platform provides panoramic views above the willow and birch woodland, constructed for visitors to see hen harriers roosting in the surrounding wetland. I stood on the top and remembered being here twenty years ago at dusk, when several harriers came in to roost. Within a few years the harriers had decided to roost elsewhere (typical). I left the hen harrier hide, not having seen any harriers.

I met with a family at the end of my walk and we discussed wallabies. A bizarre fact about Manx fauna is that we have one of the largest populations of wild wallabies in Europe, probably in excess of two hundred of them (on a few evenings I've seen more than twenty, some with pouches bulging with joeys). Wallabies thrive in the Ballaugh Curraghs because the wetland habitat resembles their native swampy homeland in southern Australia and Tasmania. The Isle of Man's climate rarely reaches freezing due to the surrounding sea temperature, and there's plenty of lush vegetation, no natural predators and it's not far from where they originally escaped.

The Curraghs Wildlife Park opened in July 1965 and it only took five months before the first escape was documented – Wanda the wallaby had hopped off. Since then the park has had more absent wallabies, particularly when storm-felled trees have flattened enclosure fences. There's also been the occasional fugitive Canadian otter, red panda and ring-tailed lemur. The local community are undoubtedly relieved that the park doesn't exhibit man-eaters. 'Gloria, don't go into the garden, between the water feature and rose bush, there's a tiger'.

Wallabies can sometime be seen at Close Sartfield, but they are more often spotted at the nearby Ramsar site. Myself, one family, and a cyclist travelled there for a wallaby hunt.

I took a different route to them and disappeared into the undergrowth, trekking along an undulating path overgrown by royal ferns. Speckled wood butterflies and willow warblers were conspicuous, but after thirty minutes of exploring, still no wallabies. The wallabies are crepuscular, meaning they are mostly active at dusk or dawn. It was midday. Signs of their presence were about, their distinctive footprints identified by a prominent long front toe and droppings which look like Maltesers (I haven't eaten one, so I can't confirm if they taste the same).

Eventually I spotted a wallaby, far away in a patch of deep grass with only its head visible. This species are red-necked wallabies, so-named because of the rusty colouration on their shoulders. I couldn't see its shoulders. A short time later I met the family again and asked if they'd had more success. They'd seen three. So much for my experience and tracking knowledge.

Back at my car, I jumped inside and looked out of the side window. Four metres away, beside the road, a wallaby was eating the grassy verge. Why did I bother tracking through deep undergrowth when I could have just sat in my car?

I left the wetland and navigated narrow lanes as a large bird of prey flew above so I pulled into a gateway. Could I now tick off a hen harrier? Using binoculars, I had a good view... of a buzzard. The island currently has more hen harriers than buzzards but it was disappointing to see the more rare local bird.

The return journey cut through the central uplands, taking a single-track road from the back of Ballaugh over to Brandywell. I was still aiming to get the two remaining species on today's wish list – hen harriers and cuckoo; and I was travelling into harrier territory (with a slim chance of a cuckoo).

I stopped several times to scan the moorland, but only witnessed several pipits and a raven which yelled at me. All were places I'd seen harriers before – it was therefore disappointing not to find any. It was like knowing my friends were going on a pub crawl, heading into town and not discovering any of them in their favourite bars. As I drove alongside Snaefell, the island's only mountain, a large white bird cruised over the heather. A male hen harrier? Nope, a herring gull. What on earth was a gull doing out here? It was the furthest place on the island from the coast!

****

The following day I began my second outing, taking a route along the south-west coast, visiting Peel, Niarbyl and The Sound. I was going out on consecutive days because this was the only one nearby with little wind forecast – important conditions for today's main objective: sea-watching. I set myself two challenges; to spot a basking shark or a dolphin; or as a last resort a harbour porpoise (they'd need to put on a performance to improve their future ranking). I'd kicked the cuckoo into the long grass, but still hoped to see a hen harrier.

Fifteen years ago, basking sharks were regularly spotted in Manx waters, but sightings of them have dwindled recently. The sharks haven't all perished (I hope), they are probably just dwelling elsewhere. Warming sea temperatures have probably meant their zooplankton food is further north around Scotland, where sharks are now spotted frequently.

The dolphins we see in the Manx spring and summer are usually Rissos and I'd already enjoyed watching eight Rissos the previous month. Hopefully I hadn't already used up all my good luck.

Harbour porpoises are the most regularly-seen cetaceans around our Manx coast; they're always a potential fallback if the sharks and dolphins let you down.

My first stop was Peel harbour, a place recently visited by a pair of bottlenose dolphins (rather than Rissos). For several months, a mother and her calf had provided great joy to many local sea-watchers who have seen them – me excluded.

In the marina between the boats, black guillemots bobbed about; they have black plumage with white wing patches like wing-mirrors. They nest within the harbour walls and remain in Peel throughout the year. During winter their black feathers turn mostly white. Winter plumages are often scruffy, but black guillemots look great whatever the season.

A public footpath leads around the perimeter of Peel Castle and on the southern edge it overlooks Fenella Beach (named after a character in Sir Walter Scott's book *Peveril of the Peak*, which is partially based in Peel). The beach is a result of the causeway's construction, which traps sand and scallop shells. The shells are another man-made feature, as scallops are processed in a nearby factory, before the shells and other innards are discarded over the back of Peel Hill. The organic waste is churned up by the waves and becomes gradually deposited on Fenella Beach. The other by-product of all this activity is that the back of Peel Hill stinks of putrefying scallop guts.

Auks and gulls were prolific on the sea; they nest around Peel Hill (despite the smell). Guillemots formed rafts on the water, occasionally diving for fish or darting back to the cliffs with their catch.

I scanned the horizon for the tell-tale dorsal fins of basking sharks. My hopes were raised, and subsequently crushed once I realised I was being deceived. Two different things were masquerading as shark fins; first the offshore cormorants drying their outstretched black wings, and secondly, lobster pot buoys with black flags on top. Do local fishermen deliberately put out black flags to confuse sea-watchers?

Peel was very pleasant, but sadly lacking any marine mega-fauna. I travelled south and stopped briefly at Glen Maye to gaze at the waterfall, before going to Niarbyl. Beautiful coastline, blue seas and little fishing cottages, but sadly again no notable wildlife.

I drove up through Dalby searching for hen harriers and saw none. The greatest negative of being a wildlife enthusiast is if you don't see a local species for a while, you start to think the worst has happened. Have we lost all our hen harriers to human persecution or disturbance? Have they been out-competed by the new influx of buzzards? Or have they simply found somewhere else to live, like the sharks?

At Ronague I stopped in a layby and looked across the south of the island. A feral chicken approached and gave me a 'cluck'; they are relatively common here due to the absence of foxes. To recap my success at that point, that day I'd seen lots of beautiful scenery, a few guillemots, and a chicken. Fair dues, the chicken was good value as it pecked around my feet, but my expectations had been set higher. Surely things would improve at my last stop at the south-westerly point of the island.

On the approach to The Sound the most noticeable sight is the Calf of Man, a detached small island of quiet wilderness, separated from the mainland by a narrow channel of rushing water. I parked by the cafe and walked past families viewing the Atlantic grey seals (you'd be very unlucky to not spot a seal here). A couple of Dolphineers (members of the Manx Whale and Dolphin Watch) were looking beyond the seals at the eastern seascape. I headed in their direction – I needed help.

I soon learnt I should have been ten miles east at Langness, as somebody just sent them a text from there saying they were watching Rissos dolphins. Experience has taught me it would have been a fool's errand to drive across the island in the expectation of the dolphins lingering in the same spot. Rissos are very mobile and often travel the length of the Manx coast, so at this moment in time they were probably leaving Langness and heading north or south-west (towards us). Rissos travel at approximately ten miles an hour, so I estimated if they were coming in our direction, it'd be an hour before they arrived. I went for a wander in the meantime.

I left the Dolphineers to keep watch on the east while I rambled along the west. As I walked, baby bunnies dived under the gorse and twenty choughs circled above. We are spoilt by the abundance of choughs here, it's easy to get blasé about their appearance. I discovered a suitable ledge for parking my backside and settled down for a little sea-watching.

With no wind, the sea state was calm and lanes of slick sea water wove between wider rippled areas. A marine biologist once explained these flat slicks were tidal currents, created by colliding warm and cold waters, and this nutritious mixture was attractive to tiny marine creatures which are collectively called zooplankton. Where there's zooplankton, there are fish, and where there's fish there might be dolphins. Since taking his advice, I've focused my search around these tidal currents and it's proved successful. It only took ten minutes before I was rewarded again – two harbour porpoises swam around the fringe of the tidal current, but disappeared shortly afterwards, a successful sighting.

Afterwards I went back to the Dolphineers to report the porpoises. In the meantime, they'd trumped me by seeing Rissos. The dolphins must have been going faster than 10mph. Infuriatingly they'd already vanished out of sight around the Calf of Man. I don't personally know the Dolphineers, so I restrained myself from blurting out a stream of profanities.

However, something rather special then happened which made up for any disappointment. Another harbour porpoise came into view; it moved rapidly and suddenly leapt clear of the water with another porpoise following its tail. I've never seen them do that before! I even managed to film the event; I might not have believed it otherwise. That'll teach me for thinking porpoises were the dull relatives of dolphins. I am a keen amateur ethologist (someone who studies animal behaviour) and even with decades of experience, wildlife always has the capacity to surprise and teach you something new.

There was an interesting footnote to this event. I submitted my porpoise breaching footage to the Dolphineers, and they passed it to a scientist in America. Apparently, I'd captured courtship or mating behaviour and the scientist happened to be writing about the sex life of harbour porpoises (what some people do as a career!).

****

For the third and final outing of the week I decided to visit another location in the south of the island. I had a free morning to explore either Langness (where the Rissos dolphins dwelt) or Sugarloaf (for nesting seabirds). I decided to go to Sugarloaf – and it turned out to be a great decision.

Sugarloaf is located near The Sound, and as I drove south a gentle breeze blew over the flat sea while the sun shone. The calm conditions filled me with optimism, until I approached the southern peninsular and it became less promising: a deep bank of sea mist rolled over the western coast. Port Erin appeared to have been hit by a fallen cloud. We have a local name for this sea mist, it's called Manannan's Cloak. Manannan is an ancient sea god who protects his Manx people from offshore invaders by using mist to shroud the coastline.

Thankfully, Manannan stayed on the west, while the east remained clear. I walked between traditional thatched cottages at Cregneash, then walked the track over a hill and steeply down towards the Chasms; aptly named because of the deep narrow ravines, some stretching fifty metres down. The bedrock is slowly progressing towards the sea and splintering due to this movement. Every time I'm here I have the same concern, 'Will this visit coincide with a significant shift and I'll end up tumbling into the sea, joined by thousands of tons of rocks?' Thankfully the ground remained firm.

The path descended further towards the sea and provided my first views of Sugarloaf, a tower of offshore rock, our own little version of the Old Man of Hoy. It makes up for its shorter stature by being an excellent nesting site for guillemots and kittiwakes. The ledges were packed with birds, while others swirled around the base.

At the lowest corner of the field, brave visitors can stand above the cliff and see (and smell) hundreds of seabirds. As I gingerly inched towards the cliff edge, I noticed a small boat below; the skipper saw me and called up through his loud speaker, "Don't jump, it's not worth it!'

I acknowledged his joke with a friendly wave then glimpsed down at the birds. Guillemots and razorbills were making strange sounds; a mixture of guffawing laughter and gargling. I moved along to the field's corner and viewed the eastern coast, when suddenly something stopped me in my tracks. The flat sea in the distance was being disturbed. Dolphins were out there!

I'd brought binoculars for the day out; sadly, they were a twenty-minute walk away, still in my car. My eyesight is good, but inadequate when trying to distinguish a species from a couple of miles away. Distant shapes of large marine mammals continued to splash about for ten minutes before the sea calmed. Whatever they were, they'd gone.

I walked back to the cliff and looked down at Sugarloaf while Manannan's Cloak encroached. The mist slowly crept over the cliffs and the air became noticeably cooler as it blew through. Visibility returned ten minutes later, revealing a little sailboat passing underneath and I exchanged waves with the crew. After thirty minutes of seabird watching I decided to head home for lunch, and while walking up the hill, I stopped for one final look out to sea.

There was a deep splash between myself and Port St Mary. The dolphins were coming to entertain me! I later learned from the Manx Whale and Dolphin Watch these dolphins were the same ones I'd seen earlier – they'd just popped into Port St Mary for thirty minutes (without patronising any of the high street shops).

I quickly strode to the cliff edge. I didn't run; I wanted to avoid joining the dolphins in the sea and secondly, running was not favoured by my knees. I pressed record on my camera as six Rissos dolphins approached. It was a joyful moment, even though a herring gull strafe bombed me with crap (it must have been nesting nearby).

The lead dolphin was a bit of a show-off; leaping clear of the water and landing with a big splash. It did this three times; whenever I've seen this happen previously it's often performed in threes. I suspect it's a form of communication, rather than mere fun. It was fun for a boat packed with people; their cheers were clearly audible as they viewed the action. Rafts of guillemots were less impressed as they scattered from the path of the breaching dolphin, dashing across the surface like handfuls of skimmed stones.

Another behaviour I've noticed with Rissos is tail-slapping. Once performed, the dolphins usually gather closer. A rallying call, perhaps as a response to the proximity of the boat. The boat thankfully gave them space and the dolphins continued their southerly route. Three of the six dolphins were white, and once submerged, their bodies moved underwater like shimmering ghosts.

Two adults moved side-by-side, perhaps a couple, while another aimed towards the boat. The boat passengers all watched the approaching dolphin from their starboard, before it submerged beside them. Everyone waited for it to reappear. It did a minute later, on their port side. One person realised and they all shifted their attention – fortunately the boat was well balanced and didn't tip over as everybody turned from starboard to port.

The dolphins eventually departed south to hopefully share their joy with people at The Sound. I headed back up the hill and was in such good spirits I never even noticed the climb.

******

Over three separate days I'd seen a diverse range of wildlife: wallabies, peregrine falcons, gannets, terns, porpoises, seals, and I possibly saved the life of a trapped common lizard. All the birdsong, insects and wild flowers made the experience more special. Seeing Rissos was a wonderful and perfect way to conclude the day, and it marked the first fourteen years of my British Wildlife Safari adventures. It also shows you don't have to travel continents to see wildlife.

It would have been a great moment to celebrate with a pint – unfortunately all the pubs remained closed because of lockdown.

Mayfly

Summary

I truly enjoyed all the places I've explored – the fun was amplified and given a focus by the search for nature. Being a wildlife enthusiast in the countryside is equivalent to being an artist in a gallery, or a historian visiting a museum – the experience is more thrilling the more knowledge and interest you have in the subject.

I'd recommend all the regions I've visited. However, some were extraordinary.

Overleaf I've created a list of my favourites based on different categories.

Friendliest places I stayed

Holidays are an opportunity to escape the daily routine and explore new places. These places were elevated by their terrific locals:
Blakeney (Norfolk)
Newport and Tenby (Wales)
St Margaret's Hope (Orkney)
Strangford (Northern Ireland)
Tobermory (Mull)

Best nature reserves

Every nature reserve is important and worth seeking, but my most memorable times were spent at:
Arne RSPB
Ayres NNR
Farne Islands National Trust
Hermaness National Nature Reserve
New Forest National Park
Noss National Nature Reserve (by boat)
Radipole RSPB
Titchwell Marsh RSPB
Ynys-hir RSPB

Best animals spotted

Most of these sightings were exceptional because they were first discoveries:
Great Skuas
Bottlenose Dolphins
Minke Whales
Orkney Vole (which Joe still claims he spotted first)
Ospreys
Otters
Pied Flycatchers
Pilot Whales
Sand Lizards
White-tailed Sea Eagles

Best wildlife experiences

These were personal moments and intimate encounters. For me, sharing my allotment with a nesting blackbird was just as important as seeing my first otter, therefore this list includes common species:

Arctic Terns (Farnes)
Blackbirds and Rissos Dolphins (Isle of Man)
Cetti's Warblers (Norfolk)
Cetaceans (Tiumpan Head)
Gannets and Puffins (Shetland)
Kestrels and Sand Lizards (Dorset)
Otters (Mull) / Snipes (Orkney)

Best scenery

I love natural landscapes and these places are stunning:

Bosta Beach (Lewis)
Calgary Bay (Mull)
Esha Ness and Hermaness (Shetland)
Glen Coe (Scottish Highlands)
Mull Head (Orkney)
Luskentyre Beach (Harris)
The Sound (Isle of Man)
The Storr (Skye)

Best times for wildlife

If you are a football fan, think of it as either a match on a cold November day or a sunny May final – the spring event is usually the most fun. Spectacular events do happen in the winter, but to see wildlife in its full splendour you cannot beat April, May and June. However, if you're looking for reptiles and insects, the south of England during the summer months is also great.

Best coastal walks

To me it's important that coastal walks are a stroll rather than a hike, ideally with great scenery and wildlife spotting opportunities:

The Chasms (Isle of Man)

Esha Ness, St Ninian's Isle, Hermaness and Sumburgh Head (Shetland)

Mull Head (Orkney)

Stackpole (Pembrokeshire)

Best pubs

Last, but not least...

Golden Lion (Newport)

Kings Arms (Blakeney)

Murray Arms (St Margaret's Hope)

Red Lion and Queen's Head (Hawkshead)

Ship Inn (Lindisfarne)

Sumburgh Hotel (Shetland)

Glossary

arthropods   Invertebrates such as insects, spiders and crustaceans.

auks   Family of seabirds which includes puffins, razorbills and guillemots.

bat detectors A machine which enables the ultrasonic sounds of bats to become audible to humans.

bonxie   Great skua.

buzzard   A bird occasionally mistaken for an eagle by holidaymakers.

capercaillie   A very large grouse which can get bolshy during the breeding seasons.

ceilidh   A Scottish or Irish social event which often includes dancing where newcomers are spun around until nauseous.

cetaceans   Whales, dolphins and porpoises – British dolphin species include Rissos, bottlenose and common dolphins. The most frequently-seen whale species in Britain are minkes. There are also harbour porpoises – but they aren't normally as entertaining as the others.

Chanonry   A difficult-to-pronounce place, allegedly visited by bottlenose dolphins.

cloaca   A bird's bottom – it comes from the Latin word for 'sewer'. Lovely.

clootie   Scots word for a piece of cloth or rag.

corvidae   Family of birds which includes carrion crows, rooks, ravens and magpies.

crustacean   Family of arthropods which includes crabs, lobsters and shrimps.

dipped out   Birding term for missing out on seeing a particular bird.

dipper   A British aquatic songbird.

divers   Large water birds which family in the UK includes red-throated, great northern and black-throated divers. Like seals, they are graceful on the water, but on land have the dexterity of a sandbag.

ethology	The science of animal behaviour.
fledgling	A young bird which has developed flight feathers and has recently flown the nest.
flycatcher	Britain has two main flycatcher bird species: pied and spotted; both are summer migrants.
granite	A type of igneous rock.
gulls	Family of seabirds which includes herring, black-headed, greater black-backed and common. Some people just call them all seagulls.
Jorvik	Old Norse name for York.
LBJ	Little Brown Job – a small brown bird which departs before a formal identification. Usually a pipit.
lichen	A symbiosis of algae (or cyanobacteria) and fungi.
machair	A coastal grassy field improved by shell sand.
Mavis Grind	Old Norse name for 'gate of the narrow isthmus' (nothing to do with prostitution).
midges	A swarming mass of violence – attracted to wildlife enthusiasts.
mollusc	Soft-bodied creatures which are food for many wonderful animals; snails are enjoyed by song thrushes, mussels are eaten by oystercatchers, while squid are consumed by Rissos dolphins.
Munro	A mountain in Scotland higher than 3,000 feet.
murmurations	Large numbers of swirling starlings – sometimes performed as a defence mechanism against birds of prey.
mustelid	Family of mammals which includes weasels, otters, badgers and stoats.
Neolithic	'Neo' means new and 'lithics' are stones – so the Neolithic is the new stone age.
orca	Also known as killer whales (even though they are dolphins).
Pant	Welsh for 'hollow' or 'valley'.

phenology The study of seasonal changes in plants and animals from year to year.

phrenology Feeling the bumps on a patient's head to diagnose character (not to be mistaken for phenology).

ptarmigan A mountain-dwelling grouse which in winter changes its plumage to white, as camouflage against snow.

raptor A bird of prey. In Latin it means, 'robber or plunderer'.

RSPB Royal Society for the Protection of Birds.

seal Britain has two main types: Atlantic grey and harbour (previously called common).

Sound A channel of water running between two bodies of land.

tern Family of seabirds which includes Arctic, Sandwich, little and common.

troglodyte From the Greek word 'trogle'; a cave dweller.

UNESCO United Nations Educational, Scientific and Cultural Organization.

unicorn An animal which appears in written fiction. Other examples of animal fiction are the information boards in Northern Ireland which claim the existence of resident red squirrels.

waders Family of long-legged water birds which includes turnstones, curlews, oystercatchers and most importantly snipes.

Buzzard

Acknowledgements

Thank you in particular to those who directly helped with the book, David & Moi Ashworth. And importantly, the other support provided by John Quirk and Joe.

The following people have either joined me on this journey, given their friendship and support, or simply shared my enthusiasm for wildlife: Jen Adams, David Allwood, David Anderson, Ian Anderson, Louise Angus, Dave Armstrong, Beth Atkinson, Adrian & Jennifer Bailey, Martin, Rhoyda, Mark & Sarah Bell, Alan Blears, John Bolton, Sam Bowers, Neil & Fiona Brew, Duncan Bridges, Jean Buck, Patrick & Tina Burden, Felicity Cain, Colin Caley, Kirsty Caley, John 'Dog' Callister, Tom & Linda Clucas, Lauren Collister, Peter Compton, Phoebe Convery, Rob & Pam Cope, Jo Corkish, Ian Costain, Gilli Cowley, Steve Crellin, Garry Curtis, Dylan Cuthbert, Bill Dale, Perry Davenport, Dr Peter Davey, Cathy Dawson, Stephen Dawson, Mike Dilger, Geoff Dobbin, John & Lorraine Donnelly, Marj Donoghue, Andree Dubbledam, Chloe Duke, Paul Ellison, Tom Felce, Andrew Foxon, Richard Fryer, Andy Garrett, Dr Fiona Gell, Colin Gibson, Dr Mauvis Gore, Graham & Jackie Hall, Laura Hanley, Brendan & Emma Harper, James, Sarah, Cloud & Alex Harris-Burland, Rachel Hartnoll, Bill Henderson, Nicola Holt, Michael Howland, Dr Mike Hoy, Colin & Linda Jones, Malcolm Kelly, Jacqui Kelly, Quentin & Hazel Kelly, Tim Kenyon, Kim Kneen, Joanne Lowe,

Inger Johanne Lunde, Catriona Mackie, Donald MacLeod, Jan Maddrell-Staines, Jane Mayhew, Anna McCanney, Bob & Sue Moon, Dan Newport, Patricia Newton, Emma Morter, Helen Peet, Tony & Pauline Quaye, John Quayle, Kelvin & Sophie Revere, Martin Rigg, Mark Salisbury, Louise Samson, Wendy Sayer, Richard Sayle, Dr Richard Selman, Elli Sewell, Chris Sharpe, Kath Smith, Erica Spencer, Nigel Sperring, Jan Staines, Shane Stigant, Eleanor Stone, Graham & Helen Sydney, Danny & Michelle Teare, Karen Tomlinson, Phillipa Tomlinson, Louise Trimble, Rodney Trimble, Martin Vaughan, Brett Venables, Sheila Waiting, Suzanne Watson, Craig Whalley, June Whiteman, David Wigg, Pixie Wilde, Andrew Willoughby, Karen Wilson, Helen Withers and Dave & Natalie Wiseman... a long list of people.... and I've probably still missed somebody.

The following people have made the holidays more memorable; Denise Campbell, Katherine Shaw and David Loutit. Although I don't know their surnames, I'd also like to thank Alan, Arthur, Dougie, Jan, Pam, Michael, Will and of course Jess.

Staff of the Clerk of Tynwald Office & Members of Tynwald.

All the Wildlife Trusts and the RSPB – without their reserves I'd have missed seeing and enjoying so many species.

With special mentions to Sir David Attenborough, Chris Packham, Mike Dilger, Miranda Krestovnikoff, Iolo Williams, Bill Oddie, Simon King, Michaela Strachan and the legendary Gordon Buchanan. In addition, all the natural history teams behind *Springwatch* and *The One Show*.

All my local conservation charities, in particular Manx Wildlife Trust, Manx Whale & Dolphin Watch, Manx Basking Shark Watch, Manx Bat Group, Manx National Heritage, Wildflowers of Mann, Wildflowers of the Isle of Man, Manx BirdLife and The Calf of Man Bird Observatory.

Wildfowl & Wetlands Trust, The National Trust, Cadw and Scottish National Heritage.

In memory of Mum & Dad, William Cain, Billy Condon, John Galpin, Anne Marie Kilgallon, Diane Oxbury and Brian Waiting.

Further reading from Merlin Unwin Books

The Countryman's Bedside Book BB

Wild Flowers of Britain Margaret Erskine Wilson

Woodland Wild Flowers Alan Waterman

My Wood Stephen Dalton

Wildlife of the Pennine Hills Doug Kennedy

Wild World Richard Barrett

The Hare Jill Mason

The Rabbit Jill Mason

The Otter James Williams

The Black Grouse Patrick Laurie

The Scottish Wildcat Christopher Clegg

For full details of these books
www.merlinunwin.co.uk